Leadership in Post-Compuls

Also available from Bloomsbury

Perspectives on Educational Management and Leadership, Les Bell
Perspectives of Quality in Adult Learning, Peter Boshier
Dimensions of Expertise, Christopher Winch

Leadership in Post-Compulsory Education

Marian Iszatt-White, David Randall, Mark Rouncefield and Connor Graham

BLOOMSBURY

LONDON · NEW DELHI · NEW YORK · SYDNEY

Bloomsbury Academic
An imprint of Bloomsbury Publishing Plc

50 Bedford Square	175 Fifth Avenue
London	New York
WC1B 3DP	NY 10010
UK	USA

www.bloomsbury.com

First published by Continuum International Publishing Group 2011
Paperback edition first published 2012

British Library Cataloguing-in-Publication Data
A catalogue record for this book is available from the British Library.

ISBN: HB: 978-1-4411-5699-0
PB: 978-1-4411-5618-1

Library of Congress Cataloging-in-Publication Data
Leadership in post-compulsory education / Marian Iszatt-White . . . [et al.].
p. cm.
Includes bibliographical references.
ISBN 978-1-4411-5699-0 – ISBN 978-1-4411-3259-8 – ISBN 978-1-4411-0438-0
1. Educational leadership. 2. Post-compulsory education.
I. Iszatt-White, Marian. II. Title.
LB2805.L3444 2011
371.2'011–dc22
2010052174

Typeset by Fakenham Prepress Solutions, Fakenham, Norfolk NR21 8NN

Contents

Foreword by Lynne Sedgmore CBE

This illuminating and exciting book draws on findings of a major research study into leadership in the post-16 education sector commissioned by the Centre for Excellence in Leadership (CEL). CEL played a crucial role in improving the calibre and diversity of the leadership talent pool of over 40,000 managers in the learning and skills sector. A well-funded research programme spearheaded a new and exciting body of research highlighting the need for a radical change in perception of what it takes to create new generations of leaders capable of both transforming organisations and fostering successful learning and student success.

The 'Explicating Leadership' project was one of my favourite projects as it pushed the boundaries of how we thought about leadership. The research team engaged powerfully with leaders working on the front line and opened new discourses on the very nature of leadership in the reality of everyday working life. The project examined the nature of leadership and leadership challenges specific to the learning and skills sector and involved detailed ethnographic case studies. The project was led by the simple research question: 'how do we train leaders if we don't know what leadership is?' The study developed an understanding of the everyday, practical accomplishment of leadership, and provided a more sophisticated, empirically based, understanding of everyday leadership work. A critical intention for this research included creating a central resource for the development of bespoke teaching materials for use by CEL programmes.

The results of the project informed and radically expanded our understanding of the nature of leadership and leader-led relations; enterprise and entrepreneurship; risk and risk-taking; the role of the leadership in the knowledge economy and learning society; the nature of skill and the communities of practice within the sector. Overall, the project provided a more nuanced understanding of leadership and leadership issues through detailed descriptions of leadership work in practice. I believe a key contribution lay in demystifying leadership and leadership work in a way that makes leadership more accessible to both managers in the field and to leadership developers.

I acknowledge and commend not only the academic rigour of Mark, Marian, Dave and Connor but also the significant impact of their work and their commitment and dedication to the hardworking managers they researched.

Lynne Sedgmore CBE

Founding Chief Executive of the Centre for Excellence in Leadership (CEL)
Director of The Higher Education Leadership Foundation
Advisor to Cabinet Office on Public Sector Leadership
Senior Fellow of Surrey University

Acknowledgements

There is an irony in the fact that, immediately prior to declaring this book (or more specifically, any errors and omissions) to be all our own work, we begin by thanking all the people without whom it would never have been written, but such is the way of things. And the errors and omissions are, indeed ours! For the rest, thanks must go to the DfES for their funding of the Centre for Excellence in Leadership, and specifically to the 'Explicating Leadership' project under the auspices of which much of the research contained in this volume was conducted. Thanks, in particular, goes to our 'Explicating Leadership' project colleague, Dr Simon Kelly, some of whose data appears in Chapters 5 and 8.

Marian Iszatt-White

I am deeply grateful to everyone at 'Lambton' Sixth-Form College, and the other fieldwork locations I visited, for their kindness and hospitality in welcoming me into their respective colleges, their patience and good humour in explaining themselves and their work to me, and their unfailing dedication and commitment to education, which was a constant source of inspiration. I wish I could thank you by name, but you know who you are.

Special thanks must go to two people without whom this book really wouldn't have been possible. Firstly, to my co-author, Mark Rouncefield, who was also my PhD supervisor for much of the research's gestation period. I am deeply grateful for the robust intellectual challenge and generous sharing of time and ideas which he provided in equal measure, together with the odd Salsa lesson and numerous cups of tea. Secondly, to my husband, Simon, who despite the fact that he clearly thinks I'm barking mad, has been a constant source of support and encouragement for all my academic and literary exploits. Much love, and, as promised, I didn't ask you to proof-read this one!

Finally, my father, who died a number of years ago, spent most of his working life in the printing industry and would have been immensely proud to see his daughter's name on the cover of a book. This one is for him.

Mark Rouncefield

I would like to thank my fellow researchers on the CEL funded 'Explicating Leadership' project and friends and colleagues at The Centre for Excellence in Leadership. As a former college lecturer I traded on various friendships to obtain fieldwork access and am particularly grateful for the graceful acceptance of the 'professional strangers' in their midst by the principals and members of staff of the colleges that participated in our study; their continued cooperation and patience was greatly appreciated. I am also appreciative of the support provided by a Microsoft European Research Fellowship 'Social Interaction and Mundane Technologies' and a Xerox Research University Affairs funded project on 'Technologies of Leadership'. Finally, I would like to thank my research colleagues and friends, Marian, Simon and Connor for their hard work and continued tolerance of my untidiness, unpunctuality and, frankly, weirdness. On a better day I might also thank Dave but, as he would probably admit, that would just spoil things.

Connor Graham

I would like to thank the research projects which have provided me with the opportunity to investigate the theme of 'technologies of leadership' and technology work more generally, in particular Microsoft European Research Fellowship 'Social Interaction and Mundane Technologies' project and Xerox Research University Affairs funded project on 'Technologies of Leadership' project. In addition, I would like to acknowledge the support that the managing partner of a medium-sized law firm (who happens to be my brother!) gave me in allowing access to his organization and observation of his leadership work and to the research participants there for their ongoing cooperation and patience. The ethnographic work there provided further insights into technologies of leadership. Finally, as a relative late-comer to this project, I would like to thank Marian, Mark and Dave for inviting me to work with them as a co-author.

About the Authors

Dr Marian Iszatt-White

After a successful career in financial risk management, latterly as Group Treasurer of Top 100 plc Enterprise Oil, Marian moved to Cumbria and built a business as a freelance training consultant. During this time she gained an MSc in Organizational Behaviour at Birkbeck, including a dissertation on 'what makes employees feel valued at work'. Still with more questions than answers, she undertook her PhD research at Lancaster University, within the Centre for Excellence in Leadership. She is now a Teaching Fellow at Lancaster University Management School, specializing in leadership and organizational behaviour. She is Programme Director for the School's Master's in Coaching in Organisations, and the Diploma in Public Service Leadership, and teaches on the MSc in Management and the Executive MBA. Her research interests include leadership as emotional labour and the practice turn in leadership.

Dr Mark Rouncefield

Mark Rouncefield is a Senior Research Fellow in the Department of Computing, Lancaster University and former Microsoft European Research Fellowship for his work on social interaction and mundane technologies. His research interests are in Computer Supported Cooperative Work and involve the study of various aspects of the empirical study of work, organisation, human factors and interactive computer systems design. His empirical work has included the study of financial services, information giving services, hotels, steelworks, hospitals and libraries. Recent work has focused on socio-technical aspects of the design and deployment of technologies in domestic settings. He is particularly associated with the development of ethnography as a method for informing design and evaluation.

Dr David Randall

Dave Randall is a Principal Lecturer in Sociology at Manchester Metropolitan University working primarily in the interdisciplinary research area called Computer Supported Cooperative Work (CSCW). He is particularly interested in the application of the ethnomethodological 'studies of work' programme to problems of new technology and organizational change, and in the conduct of ethnographic enquiry in relation to these issues. He has conducted a number of ethnographic studies of 'work in organizations' in his career, including Air Traffic Control, retail financial services, museum work, classroom interaction with new technology, ontology-based design, mobile phone use, and 'smart home' technology. He has undertaken consultancy and other work with organizations such as the Riso national laboratory, Denmark; Xerox plc; the Children's Society; Orange plc; Vodaphone plc; Microsoft plc and the national Centre for E-Social Science (NCess).

Dr Connor Graham

Connor Graham is a Research Fellow in the Science, Technology and Society Research Cluster at Asian Research Institute at the National University of Singapore and an Honorary Fellow in the Department of Information Systems at the University of Melbourne, Australia. His interest in Leadership arises from research on a Xerox Research Centre Europe funded project through Lancaster University on 'Technologies of Leadership'.

Chapter 1

Introduction: The Practice of Leadership

Leadership is like the Abominable Snowman, whose footprints are everywhere but who is nowhere to be seen. (Bennis and Nanus, 1985:19)

We all think we know what education is about: after all, we all went to school and many of us went on to further education in some form or another. But the 'misrememberings' of long ago – be they idealized, demonized or totally apocryphal – are actually a far cry from the complexities of modern education, and still further from modern educational leadership. Over recent decades, the study of leadership has produced a swathe of theories, models and prescriptions for would-be leaders. Many of these have been taken up by educational leaders, with some sector-specific models also emerging, primarily in compulsory education. The notion of distributed leadership (Bennett et al., 2003) resides mainly in the field of education, for example. There is little leadership wisdom, either original or adaptive, aimed at the post-compulsory learning and skills sector, however. Unfortunately, too, current research in the field of leadership, educational or otherwise, does less than it might to supply the nuanced understanding of educational leadership work from which both practitioners and a wider readership could draw benefit. In the process of theorizing and model construction, much is lost in the abstraction and generalization, which are an inherent part of those processes. While models and theories undoubtedly offer a useful simplification of the complexities of leadership, discussed later in this book in terms of the sensemaking role ascribed to them by practitioners, such simplification becomes ineffective if it occurs at the expense of recognizability. The grounding of theories in the day-to-day activities of leaders as they undertake the practical doing of leadership is a vital, though often neglected, aspect of leadership research. It is a function of just how neglected this 'studies of work' approach to leadership has been that the methodology and conclusions of this book may appear radical and, at times, even dismissive of what has gone before. Radical it certainly is, but in taking an approach to the study of leadership which is incommensurate with much mainstream research, we are not seeking to undermine or dismiss what has gone before, merely to ask different questions concerning the phenomenon of study, and to couch our findings in different terms. Our research seeks to explore the nature and accomplishment of everyday leadership in the learning and skills sector, in recognition both of past neglect of the field by the research community and of the abstracted, decontextualized nature of what little research does exist. This is not to dismiss the work of leadership researchers which has gone before, but to conceptualize how we might understand leadership through research studies in a different way: a way which can exist alongside the other and add the richness of situated detail to its prescriptions.

The aim of the research, then, is to provide more situated, empirically-based understandings of everyday leadership work and to explore the conditions, processes and outcomes of leadership practices in this important sector. This is accomplished through taking an ethnomethodologically-informed approach to the ethnography of educational leadership. Based on extended shadowing of college principals and their senior management teams, this approach seeks to develop a more detailed understanding of the practical accomplishment of leadership work through the provision of 'thick descriptions' (Geertz, 1973) of what practitioners actually do. Ethnomethodology's contribution to the study is its focus on the situated accounting practices through which members of a setting make sense of, and make recognizable to others, the events and activities in which they are engaged. That is, it pays attention to, and seeks to make visible, the 'ethno-methods' through which the social order of the setting is intersubjectively constructed as the everyday, mundane matter it is for most of us, most of the time.

As such, the findings of the study may appear unfamiliar to those more used to the models and theories of mainstream leadership research. In describing, in rich detail, the mundane work of leadership – the listening, talking, running meetings, sending emails, making presentations, etc. through which college principals accomplish their work – the focus may appear to be on something too ordinary to constitute 'leadership'. But it is in precisely these ordinary, mundane, everyday activities that leadership is seen and understood to reside by those people doing it or on the receiving end of it. It is these 'vulgar competences' (Garfinkel, 1967) – available to us all but exercised by particular people in particular settings – which constitute leadership in all its nitty-gritty detail, and with which we must get to grips if we are to fully understand the 'Leadership with a capital L' of mainstream theory.

In this book, we thus seek to get away from some of the more theoretical approaches to leadership (and management, for the two are obviously related in some way) and instead ground our approach in evidence taken from those who do the job. That is, from interviews, observations, diaries, etc. produced with leaders, and specifically with leaders in further education. This does not mean that we are unacademic in our view. The authors of the book are academic sociologists and management theorists with a significant background in the study of organizational life, the changes that organizations undergo, and the various factors that impact on organizations, such as new technology, new rules and procedures, instructions or guidance from 'above' and so on. It is our academic grounding which leads us to suggest the limitations of theoretical approaches and to offer this book as a radical alternative.

Leadership: the 'Missing What'

The primary emphasis in this book is on understanding the everyday, practical accomplishment of leadership, rather than on 'theorizing' such work as exemplars or indicators of more general social processes. It seeks to *understand* leadership through the provision of 'thick descriptions' (Geetz, 1973) of the practical, everyday, accomplishment of leadership work, and to develop a nuanced understanding of the 'skills' of leadership in educational settings. This aim recognizes that, despite the proliferation of academic approaches to understanding 'skill' (Braverman, 1974; Penn, 1990), there remains a general tendency to ignore the complex interweaving of skills in everyday work as it is accomplished (Darrah, 1994). Thus even distributed leadership, the current darling of educational leadership writers, remains largely theoretical in the coverage it has received, with little exploration of how it is actually accomplished on the ground.

More generally, what has been described as the loss of the phenomenon under study as a result of the abstraction and decontextualization which theorizing necessarily entails is a common failing in what purport to be 'studies of work'. For example, Button (1993) draws attention to the 'missing what' in research claiming to focus on the content of technology, and calls for attention to be paid to the situated practices of technology that make it recognizable for what it is. The same could be said of leadership work: while research has produced many leadership theories, it has yet to produce an account of leadership practices which would be recognizable to those who fulfil the role of leader. It is this 'just whatness' (Heritage, 1987), this 'quiddity' (Garfinkel, 1967), of leadership practices as they occur, that we aim to lay open for inspection in the chapters which follow.

If leadership research in general is lacking in recognizable specificity, then this is doubly true of leadership research in the learning and skills sector, what little there is of it. Once described as the 'Cinderella sector' (Kerfoot and Whitehead, 1998) FE (Further Education) differs from its primary and secondary counterparts in having been largely ignored by the research community. Where research in the sector does exist, the importation of leadership models from the management and other public sector literatures, and their application to topical educational issues (e.g. raising standards and remodelling practice) at a policy or 'big picture' level, do little to further an understanding of how such initiatives are actually accomplished on the ground. The emphasis is on generalized, normative prescription in preference to situated, contextualized explication. It is easy to see why this has been the favoured approach to making up some of the deficit in FE leadership research: selecting likely theories of leadership from the commercial and/or not-for-profit sectors (and, indeed, from the primary and secondary education sectors) and exploring their applicability here has a lot to offer. As a 'top down' approach, it has the advantage of being structured, and circumscribed, by the chosen theory and of offering potentially appealing 'sound bites' of explanation in respect of educational leadership.

At the same time, however, there must be a very real danger that such an approach either misses or indeed obscures that which is unique about FE-sector educational leadership in favour of that which is common to leadership *per se*. It further elaborates the 'leadership theory' edifice without addressing the need for a firmer footing in terms of recognizable, detailed description of how the work actually gets done. As such – and despite the fact that this persists as the 'mainstream' way to conduct research in the field – this seems to us to be unhelpful and precipitate. Better to open up the field with 'bottom up' exploration of what leadership work for college principals actually looks like, than to ask the more limited question, 'does it look the same as for leaders elsewhere?' Better to identify what is going on here and then compare it with what is happening elsewhere, than to ask merely 'does this – insert the components of any given theory of leadership – happen here?' This being the case, the ethnomethodologically-informed approach adopted by this book, with its focus on the detailed description of everyday practice, is ideally suited to the task of providing this corpus of data and understanding. Its emphasis on explication rather than explanation is highly appropriate to the development of a body of evidence concerning what educational leadership work practically consists in, on the basis of which it might then be appropriate to draw out similarities and differences, construct theories or develop normative models.

Ethnomethodology: Making the Ordinary Visible

The 'analytic purchase' (Rouncefield, 2002:79) which we believe ethnomethodology offers to the study and understanding of day-to-day educational leadership is a direct consequence of its radical approach to the conducting of studies and to what it considers to be the task of sociological research. Its creator, Harold Garfinkel, coined the term ethnomethodology – that is, the study of 'ethno-methods' – to denote the study of those methods by which members of a group or organization make sense of the everyday world around them, and make their actions in response to the world accountable to others. It 'literally means the methods people use on a daily basis to accomplish their everyday lives' (Ritzer, cited in Edles, 2002:166). As such, ethnomethodology is:

> ... concerned with the ordinary, day-to-day activities, in all their lived *in vivo* details, which are neglected or idealized by other approaches. (Travers, 2001:64)

In the context of work studies – a strong theme within the ethnomethodological program of research – this translates into the study of the day-to-day practices through which members of a setting (that is, the organization's staff) collaboratively produce and organize the work of the setting. As such, it focuses on the embodied skills and material competencies through which formal plans and policies are accomplished on a routine, day-to-day basis. Thus organizations are seen as self-organizing social settings, in which social order is locally produced by members and work is accomplished as a collaborative achievement of those members.

The motivation for Garfinkel's radical endeavour stemmed from his observation that in the formation of sociological theories about ordinary, everyday things the recognizable features of those things seemed to disappear: they were lost in the abstract constructs which were overlaid upon them by way of 'explanation'. At the same time, the under-determination of theory – the impossibility of constructing a theory that detailed what would happen in every possible circumstance – resulted in the theorist having to step outside the theory's pre-defined terms of reference in order to derive the explanation the theory itself purported to offer. Garfinkel's response to these perceived failings was to attempt to devise a way of 'doing sociology', of investigating sociological topics, such that the phenomena to be studied did not disappear from the final analysis.

Central to this approach is a focus on the real-time, processual character of action. By this, we mean that actors in a setting make sense of what is going on *as it happens*: they don't have the benefit of knowing in advance how their actions will turn out. This is contrary to much sociological and management theorizing, where researchers are able to look at the whole course of events in a given situation before deciding what was significant or successful about – or in the current case, what constituted – acts of leadership. As they respond to the situation in which they find themselves, real-time actors may not even have a definite outcome in mind. They may have a desired outcome but be uncertain as to the reliability of their chosen course of action to produce it. It is this relationship between ends and means, and the extent to which they relate to each other in the understanding and practices of society members themselves, which is the subject of empirical study for ethnomethodology. In solving problems, making decisions, providing direction and so on, leaders are constantly 'making it up as they go along': dealing with events and situations as they arise, without knowing in advance how things will turn out. They don't have the luxury of hindsight, nor of resting on purely theoretical outcomes. In understanding both the practical work that they do and the methods they use to make sense of the setting in which they are called upon to lead, a focus on these features is surely essential. If theory tells us that leaders are required to be 'transformational' (for example), it doesn't tell us what this looks like, sounds like, even feels like, from day to day and minute to minute. In the abstraction of analysis, the situated, real-time practices which constitute 'doing transformational leadership' have been lost. In the case of leadership in further education, they are, perhaps, yet to be sought – a clear remit thus exists for this study's use of an ethnomethodologically-informed approach in an attempt to document the real-time, real-world practices of educational leaders.

In eschewing a more theoretical approach, we are strongly suggesting that our ethnomethodologically-informed alternative can do something immensely useful by simply giving detailed and thorough descriptions of what people do in whatever context they find themselves. Since the time of Garfinkel, there have been a number of studies which have done exactly that. They include studies of the working lives of air traffic controllers, of bank and other office workers, of scientists, of workers in a steel mill, of radiographers, and so on. In taking this approach, we are uniquely focused on activities within a specific context. Indeed, it is inherent in our approach to see actions as only having the meaning they do in the context they occur, and as a result of the way in which members of the setting intersubjectively agree on the meaning they have. So, for example in the current case, leadership is only leadership because the members of a particular setting have the shared understanding that *this* act by *this* person in *this* setting constitutes leadership, and the social context of the actions are an intrinsically inseparable part of the actions themselves. The act of picking up litter in a school playground will rightly be seen as a mundane act when undertaken by the janitor, but if the school principal performs the same act, in the context of a school policy which prescribes certain standards of behaviour (including, say, respect for the environment), it will be interpreted as an act of leadership, and oriented to as such. In this specific context, it will have a symbolic significance in terms of 'setting an example' or 'walking the talk' which is inseparable from its situated occurrence, rather than being a property of the act itself.

In taking this very context-specific approach we are trying to draw attention, not to the individuals who inhabit the setting under study but to their skills and competences: precisely what it is that enables them to be good at what they do. Relatively few studies have been conducted in this fashion in the realm of management and leadership. That we were able to undertake the research we did is thanks to the support of the Centre for Excellence in Leadership, whose aims relate specifically to the study of leadership in further education. Under their auspices, we were able to spend significant amounts of time in FE colleges shadowing, talking to, and otherwise engaging with the work that the leaders of these institutions do. The result, we hope, is a detailed description of what leadership work looks like in the sector and how individual leaders go about accomplishing it on a day-to-day basis. This, we believe, makes a significant contribution to our understanding of leadership practice, in the education sector and beyond, and offers a rich resource for the future development of better leadership theory.

A rejoinder to our research policy might be, 'but what is the point of it?' After all, presumably leaders already know how to 'do leadership', and if one's research policy is to tell leaders what they already know, one can argue that such a policy is of limited value. However, it is a commonplace in organizational life (and this is true wherever one looks) that a person busy doing one kind of job is unlikely to pay an awful lot of attention to a person doing another, unless the two roles have a direct and immediate impact on each other in a moment by moment way. This is the sort of impact that relates to the interdependency of work roles in an 'oh, she's doing that, so I need to do this now' kind of way. It is a feature of leadership that, although it has an obvious impact (for what would be the point if it did not?), the impact is often amorphous and relatively long term – it takes place in the background; has to do with policy or strategy; does not require action right here, right now and hence is a somewhat unknown quantity for everyone else. It is not unusual in organizational life to hear working people complain of their leaders, 'but what is it that they actually do?' Moreover, there is a case to be made for the idea that even leaders themselves do not always know what they are doing, in the sense that much of what they do may be instinctive, unreflective and so on. Garfinkel talked about this as a 'seen but unnoticed' aspect of working life. People can be too busy doing what they are doing to give precise and careful accounts of exactly what is entailed in what they are up to. In contrast, organizational ethnographers – those of us who conduct our research by making detailed observations of others while they work – do not have work of their own to attend to in the organization, and so can pay particular attention to the minute-by-minute activities of those they are there to observe. Within the limitations of the situation, such researchers have a relatively free rein to wander about and see what it is that different people are doing and how their work relates to other features of the organization – a luxury that few people within the organization have the opportunity to indulge in. We are also able to interview those we observe, to ask them in detail about what we have seen. In sum, the ethnographer is able to pay attention to matters that leaders and others could pay attention to if they only had the time.

Further, although it may seem something of an arcane distinction, as ethnomethodologists we insist that we are 'understanding' and not 'interpreting'. What we mean by this is that, if the people we are interested in are competent, skilled members of their environment then they are bringing quite ordinary, common-sense reasoning processes to what they do: processes which make perfect sense to them in that context. In other words, members of the setting will not waste any time trying to work out why they did what they did, for they will know. They do not, in other words, normally have to do any interpretive work. Most of the time, 'what on earth is going on here?' is not a question that skilled and competent practitioners need to ask (although there will, of course, be occasions when they do ask precisely that question). If our job as researchers is to understand how skill and competence in work are manifested then we do not normally need to ask such questions either. We merely need to hang about long enough that what we see 'makes sense' to us, in the same way that it does to those we are observing.

The contrast with other approaches to management and leadership should be obvious. There is an extensive literature, dating back fifty years and more, which deals with management and the organization, and a more recent, but burgeoning literature dealing with the specific issue of leadership. In the way of academic material, the first step with all of this research is, of course, to define one's terms and then engage in discussion about defining the terms this way rather than that, and justifying one's decisions in terms of the theoretical consequences they might have. We do none of this. For us, 'leadership' consists of whatever it is that people think they are doing when they think of themselves as 'leading'. This is the essence of ethnomethodology – a reliance on members of a setting to know what they are doing, to make it accountable to others, and to have arrived at a shared understanding of what constitutes – in this case – leadership in that particular setting.

With regard to ethnomethodology as a radical approach to sociology, there is always more to be said and more to be argued. It presents a challenge to mainstream research methods which is not always popular and not always understood. Hopefully, however, enough has been said of this unique approach to the conducting of studies, and the resultant 'reclaiming' of the phenomenon of study, to explain the 'analytical purchase' we expect it to provide in the current instance. Garfinkel described the work of astronomers (in discovering a pulsar in the midst of a series of astronomical observations) as that of 'abstracting an animal from the foliage' (Garfinkel, et al., 1981:132): thus:

> Their discovery and their science consists of astronomically "extracting an animal from the foliage". The "foliage" is the local historicity of their embodied shop practices. The "animal" is that local historicity done, recognized and understood as a competent methodic procedure. The "animal" formulates their embodiedly witnessable astronomical competent practices as the transcendental properties of the independent Galilean pulsar. (Garfinkel, et al., 1981:132)

In the same way, the aim of the present book – and the ethnomethodologically-informed ethnography upon which it draws – may be said to be that of finding the 'animal' of leadership in the 'foliage' of the everyday practices of leadership work.

Laying the Foundations

Chapter 2 – 'The Trouble with Leadership' – sets the current study in context by reviewing the leadership literature and establishing what it contributes to our knowledge and understanding of leadership generally and in the education sector in particular. The chapter begins with a brief overview of the main strands of research in this voluminous and diverse collection, charting its progress from early trait theories (reviewed by Stogdill in 1948), through various models of contingent and situational leadership (e.g. Blake and Mouton, 1964; Hersey and Blanchard, 1984), to more recent trends towards transformational (Bass, 1985) and charismatic (Bryman, 1992) notions of leadership. With most of these approaches still in use, and numerous alternative typologies on offer, the essence of leadership remains unclear. The chapter seconds the proposal made by Grint (2005, after Gallie, 1955–56) that leadership may, in fact, be an 'essentially contested concept'.

The chapter moves on to consider leadership in education, in particular discussing the transition away from the notion of 'college principal as lead professional' which underpinned instructional leadership (e.g. Hallinger, 2000). This has been replaced by a view of college principals as business managers, and stems largely from the adoption of leadership models from outside the sector on the back of incorporation.[1] The complexity of the resultant educational context, and the consequent impossibility of the entire task of leadership residing in one individual (i.e. the principal), has been one of the sources of distributed leadership as a normative model for education.[2]

Inherent in all of the literature discussed is what may be described as a 'loss of phenomenon' (Garfinkel, 1967): that is, the abstraction and generalization of research findings such that they cease to be recognizable as the underlying phenomenon of study. Common to much mainstream sociological research, this conclusion concerning current research paves the way for the radical approach of ethnomethodologically-informed ethnography in returning the researcher's focus to the 'missing what' (Button, 1993) of the phenomenon itself. In the case of leadership work, this means paying attention to the day-to-day, mundane practices through which leadership work gets done, and which make it recognizable *as* leadership work to those in the setting concerned. Building on the philosophical groundwork laid down in this Introduction, Chapter 3 – 'The Art of Purposeful Hanging Around: A Study in Ethnomethodologically-informed Ethnography' – says more about the 'analytic purchase' (Rouncefield, 2002) afforded by the practices of ethnomethodology, and the mechanics of conducting an ethnographic study with this mindset. This is approached through a discussion of ethnomethodology's 'requirements of method' (Garfinkel, 1967) – specifically the notions of unique adequacy, perspicuous settings, and the documentary method of interpretation – and their implications for the collection of data. The requirement of unique adequacy – that is, for the researcher to acquire a 'vulgar competence' (Garfinkel, 1967) in the practices and activities of the setting under study – is at the heart of ethnomethodology's non-ironic, egocentric stance, while the requirements to seek settings which make perspicuous the phenomenon of interest, and to view situated actions as 'documents' or evidence of the practices of which they are an example, are key policies in ethnomethodology's approach to data collection. This methodological underpinning is accompanied by an outline of the background to the study setting and the data gathered within it.

The Heart of the Matter

The next four chapters discuss a number of themes drawn from the data. Chapter 4 – 'Leadership as Mundane Work' – draws attention to the day-to-day detail of leadership work in a number of 'perspicuous' (Wittgenstein, 1958) settings. As such, it draws on the rich observational data provided by the study fieldwork to detail the 'real-time, real-world' (Rouncefield, 2002) activities through which leadership work is accomplished in all its mundane familiarity. In so doing, it explodes the idea of leaders as exceptional people or the possessors of exceptional skills by drawing attention to the 'ordinary' skills of talking, writing, listening, planning, etc. that we can all call upon to organize and make sense of our everyday lives. The quality of 'leadership', it is argued, is often attributed to these skills and activities on the basis of who performs them and with what intention (Alvesson and Sveningsson, 2003a).

The centrality of meetings – planning them, conducting them, disseminating and implementing the outcomes of them – to the accomplishment of leadership work provides a fertile strand within this theme, as does the burden of bureaucracy in 'getting the job done'. This provides an interesting contrast with theories of charismatic (Conger and Kanungo, 1987; Weber, 1948) and transformational (Burns, 1978; Bass, 1985) leadership, where the focus is all on 'big picture' visions and motivational work, to the exclusion of the more managerial 'grunt work' required to underpin them. This juxtaposition takes on particular significance in the widespread 'audit culture' (Strathern, 2000) acknowledged to exist in today's education sector, and is discussed in more detail in the chapter which follows. The chapter concludes with a discussion, which arises out of the notion of leadership as mundane work, of the supposed distinction between leadership and management and questions whether it is a useful distinction to make.

Chapter 5 – 'Leadership as Presentation, Production and Performance' – considers the work undertaken in accounting for educational outcomes in an 'audit culture' (Strathern, 2000) environment, and the production and performance which this entails. Inherent in this chapter is the notion that there are no 'right answers' that can simply be lifted from the data (student numbers, funding requirements, progress against targets, etc.) by the principal: instead it is a work of selection and interpretation to make the numbers tell the required story to achieve the desired goals and objectives. The ideas of 'calculation work' (Anderson et al., 1989) and 'gambits of compliance' (Bittner, 1965) are discussed and their application to educational leadership work is illustrated from the study data. Also explored is the idea of strategy as a 'perennially unfinished project' (Knights and Mueller, 2004) and the consequent need for improvisation and adjustment in order to successfully implement, not the letter of a strategic plan, but its intent. The link is made to Suchman's (1987) groundbreaking work on plans and situated actions, and the error of concluding the latter to be causally determined by the former.

Another area of interest for the authors of this book is what might be characterized as 'technologies of leadership' – the use of information and communication technologies to support leadership work. This is the subject matter of Chapter 6 – 'Technologies of Leadership – The Medium and the Message'. The enormous growth in the deployment of information and communication technologies in modern organizations, including those in the education sector, and its application in data analysis and processing, communication and decision support (Zuboff, 1988; Scott Morton, 1991), has been reflected in the growth of research in this field. The chapter thus begins with a review of the technology literature. It moves on to discuss the range of issues faced by educational leaders in their everyday use of information systems, including the collection, selection and interpretation of data – in effect, the requirement to turn data into information. The role of technology in the dissemination of such data to staff, higher level management and external, regulatory bodies is also discussed, in the context of making leadership and educational work accountable. Finally, the chapter picks up on Yates's (1989) thesis of 'control through communication' by exploring what gets communicated, to whom, and with what 'spin'.

Chapter 7 – 'Leadership: Success and Failure' – explores how practitioners in the learning and skills sector construct notions of success and failure. It does this through explicating a situation of 'failed' leadership through the accounts of a self-confessed 'failing' Principal and her Assistant Principal in the context of the inspection success achieved by the College of which the former was head. The different versions of events are used to illustrate the application of Wittgenstein's (1958) idea of 'language games' and how language is used to make ideas of success and failure in leadership accountable/observable. The chapter goes on to consider the ways in which success and failure in leadership are 'grossly observable' (Rouncefield, 2002) through a comparison of leadership practices in two contrasting Colleges, one with two failed Ofsted inspections behind it and the other with a recent Ofsted grade 1 for leadership and management. The chapter concludes by discussing the implications for attempts to theorize the constituents of 'effective' leadership.

Pulling It All Together

In the final chapter – 'Conclusions – Reflections and Cautionary Tales' – an attempt is made to pull together the various strands of the book and draw some tentative conclusions about how this study contributes to our understanding of leadership in the learning and skills sector. The contribution, we believe, takes the form of rich, detailed explication of the situated practices of educational leadership, centred around a number of themes which emerged from a consideration of the data. Not unsurprisingly, these themes are discernable in the titles of the preceding chapters and relate to such topics as leadership as mundane work, and leadership as presentation, production and performance. They include the extension of the emotional labour construct into the realms of white collar, professional work and look at the role of technology in supporting the work of leadership. Finally, they consider how practitioners use theory as an 'ethno-method' in the accomplishment of that work.

While one book can barely scratch the surface of any perceived 'gap in the literature', we believe that the ethnomethodological focus on real-time, real-world situated action which underpins this volume begins to establish a previously unavailable resource in support of future research. Stealing a metaphor from Bennis and Nanus (1985), we have sought to use an ethnomethodological approach to determining what kind of animal the 'Abominable Snowman' of leadership might be: if we have failed in that, we may, at least, have provided some evidence of what size shoes it wears.

Chapter 2

The Trouble with Leadership

If, as we have admitted, there is no shortage of books around the topic of leadership on the market, then our justification for this one lies both in its radical approach and in its focus on the previously neglected Further Education sector. There is no mystery to our approach, nor are we trying to create (or perpetuate) one around leadership: there are no magic theoretical or conceptual devices which enable leaders to assert unequivocally that right now, at this minute, they are engaged in the business of leadership but at other times they are not; and there is no reason for leaders to believe that, simply because academics argue that 'leadership' means this set of activities but not those, that they should be required to think the same way. Indeed, what we hope to show in the chapters that follow is that leadership is a very personal, situated phenomenon and that the abstraction and generalization which is a necessary part of the theorizing process doesn't always help us to understand leadership as much as we would hope it would. It is on this perceived limitation of the literature that we base our claims for our fundamentally data driven alternative.

The existing literature tends to divide into two broad ways of looking at leadership. The first tends to have the flavour of self-help books and 'how to do it' manuals. More politely, we can say that they orient to leadership in terms of policy and practice, or what 'good' leadership should look like. The second consists in theoretical texts which typically examine the various competing approaches to understanding the generic features of leadership. This book will be different in that its aims and approach are descriptive and analytic rather than theoretical, and it does not seek to prescribe 'how to do it' for others. Instead, it will seek to examine, through presenting the empirical results of a two-year ethnographic, observational study of leaders in Further Education in the UK, how leaders actually conduct the business of 'leading'. Each chapter devotes itself to one of the observed themes of everyday leadership work: its 'mundane' character; the idea of 'performing' leadership; the technologies involved in leadership work; the idea of emotional labour as a characteristic of everyday leadership work; the different perceptions of success and failure by leaders themselves and some 'cautionary tales' for readers. It will be aimed at academics and practitioners. For academics, in both the field of leadership studies and in the field of education, it will provide some rich empirical detail with which to compare and contrast theoretical positions. For practitioners, it will provide a series of real-world examples of policy and practice that, at a minimum, inform as 'cautionary tales' or resources for reflection.

Having made much of the distinction between 'theoretically-driven' and 'data-driven' enquiry, we do need to at least make more detailed reference to the existing literature. Academic views concerning what leadership is and is not, whether it is 'good' or not, and so on *do* have an impact on both policy and practice. It is as well to understand what those views are, if nothing else to show where the gaps and omissions are and to provide for the contrast – if there is one – between theory and experience. It is also a necessary precursor to our endeavour to locate ourselves within the existing literature on leadership in order to justify our claims concerning the radical nature of our approach. We will go about this through a discussion of some of the key themes which emerge from a review of the leadership literature. These include the issues of whether leadership is actually different from management and if so how; the debate as to whether successful leadership rests on innate traits with which one is born, or on a range of learnable skills and behaviours; the suggestion that the significant emphasis placed on the study of high-profile senior leaders is, in fact, misdirected and that researchers should instead be focusing their attention on acts of leadership at all organizational levels; and the belief that leadership rests not in the intentions of the leader but in the perceptions of potential followers. We will also be considering critical approaches to leadership which would have us do away with the whole idea.

These key themes have considerable resonance with the four basic 'problems' of leadership as identified by Grint (2004), namely:

- The process problem: is leadership derived from the personal qualities or traits of the leader or is followership induced through some social process in which leaders and followers are engaged?
- The position problem: does leadership stem from formal authority – what Grint calls 'being in charge' – or from informal influence, described as 'being in front'?

- The philosophy problem: is leadership an intentional, causal effort on the part of the leaders, or are followers' actions determined by the situation or context? Alternatively, is 'leadership' attributed by followers after the event?
- The purity problem: is leadership embodied in individuals or can groups be leaders?

In these problems can be seen the classic concerns of the social scientist: the relationship between 'structure' and 'agency'; the Weberian concern for the sources of authority; the distinction between the 'formal' and the 'informal'; the nature of 'rules'; the degree to which leadership can be understood as an 'individual' as against a 'cooperative' business, and so on. We will return to some of these issues later but first we want to address the fundamental question raised above, namely the putative difference between 'leadership' and 'management'.

Management or Leadership? And Does it Matter?

Despite much debate and disagreement concerning how 'leadership' should be defined, we would suggest that there is an uneasy agreement among writers and researchers that, at its core, leadership has something to do with influencing others. So for example, Yukl (2002), an often cited writer in the field of organization studies, concludes that:

Most definitions of leadership reflect the assumption that it involves a process whereby intentional influence is exerted by one person over other people to guide, structure, and facilitate activities and relationships in a group or organization. (Yukl, 2002:2)

One cannot be said to lead if others do not follow, and effective leadership policy must by definition have to do with strategies for securing the chosen path through persuading others to contribute their time and skills. This is by no means straightforward. Bryman (1992) has shown how even this loose notion of a 'social influence process' is not without its problems, since it is unclear how one is able to differentiate leadership from other social influence processes in group and organizational contexts. Likewise, how one distinguishes the concept of leadership from such concepts as power and authority is fraught with difficulty. Bryman and others have also raised methodological concerns such as how the researcher is able to identify and distinguish groups of followers from those who lead them, and whether leadership necessarily implies the setting and achievement of goals and objectives laid down by the leader.

Grint (2005) makes a case for the distinction between leadership and management, and the situations in which one rather than the other might be in play, by drawing on Rittel and Webber's (1973) distinction between 'wicked' and 'tame' problems. He asserts that inherently intractable 'wicked' problems are amenable only to leadership, whereas 'tame' problems, though often complex, can be subdued through management. Our stance on this ought now to be obvious. If leaders and managers draw such distinctions themselves, then they are worth attending to. We suspect that, for the most part, they would not make such a distinction, nor would they make any radical distinctions between 'wicked' and 'tame' problems (though no doubt they would think that some matters are harder to deal with than others) but that they nonetheless do recognise different 'things that need to be done' and will readily distinguish between, for instance, acts of persuasion on the one hand and process management on the other.

Implicit in Grint's distinction is the notion that leadership is somehow more exciting than management: that most of us could deal with 'tame' problems but that is takes someone special to take on the 'wicked' ones. This idea of the superiority of leadership is common to much of the literature and, we suspect, to general perception. This said, 'leadership studies' as a discipline sometimes closely aligns itself with business and management theories and models. This has led some to question the supposed difference between 'leadership' and 'management' (e.g. Bennis and Nanus, 1985; Kotter, 1990) and the usefulness (both practically and academically) of perpetuating the divide. Of course, that problematizes the whole notion of 'leadership studies' as a distinctive endeavour, and so a common rebuttal is that leadership transcends the bureaucracy of management and is about 'doing the right things' rather than just 'doing things right' (Bennis and Nanus, 1985:21). Similarly in his book *The New Meaning of Educational Change,* Michael Fullan (1991) makes the distinction between leadership as relating to such things as mission, direction and inspiration, and management as involving designing and implementing plans, working effectively with people and getting things done. As early as 1977 – well before leadership became the buzzword it is today – Zaleznik was associating leadership with the dynamic acts of developing a vision and driving change, whereas management was seen as the more mundane acts of monitoring progress and solving problems. Central to most attempts to distinguish between leadership and management has been the issue of orientation to change. For example, Kotter (1990:104) defines management as 'coping with complexity' and leadership as 'coping with change'. This dichotomy is echoed by, for example, Barker (1997) and Buchanan and Huczynski (2004), the former claiming that 'the function of leadership is to create change while the function of management is to create stability' (Barker, 1997:349). Certainly, most organizational members in the context of education would recognize that their work increasingly involves an 'outward-facing' regard: that some aspect of 'leadership' involves the practical business of translating policy as determined by other agencies into practical relevance for the organization seems beyond question. This does not mean that the two concepts are fundamentally distinct however: the need for consistency, predictability (Rost, 1991) and a sense of continuity (Gosling and Murphy, 2004) – things historically associated with management – suggest a considerable overlap between the two. On this basis one can argue that it makes no sense to distinguish between 'managers' and leaders'; rather, at various points any given individual may recognize that there may be a number of roles entailed in, for instance, 'deciding what needs to be done', 'persuading other people that it needs to be done', 'finding ways of doing it' and 'persuading people to adopt those ways'. These roles, as Mintzberg (1975) suggests, overlap but contain different elements. For Mintzberg, leadership is just one role amongst many for the effective manager, who has informational and decisional roles as well as those interpersonal roles of which leadership is but one. This more moderate, modest view of leadership is seldom heard today, however, in the face of the 'romanticization' (Meindl, Ehrlich and Dukerich, 1985) which currently surrounds both leadership and leaders.

In the way of academics, this kind of conceptual hair splitting provides an opportunity for more theorizing, because it suggests that leadership is, in fact, an 'essentially contested concept' (Gallie, 1955–56, cited in Grint, 2005) and thus one for which a 'definitive' definition is impossible. The contestation (or confusion) is increased when other forms of social influence – power and coercion being the most frequently cited – are distinguished from leadership at the same time as 'leaders' exhibiting these tendencies – again, Hitler and Saddam Hussein appear with monotonous regularity – are put forward as archetypal examples in leadership texts. Those wishing to dissociate such tyrants from the notion of 'true' leadership should, perhaps, recall the following reminder from Kellerman (2004):

Scholars should remind us that leadership is not a moral concept. Leaders are like the rest of us: trustworthy and deceitful, cowardly and brave, greedy and generous. To assume that all leaders are good people is to be wilfully blind to the reality of the human condition, and it severely limits our scope for becoming more effective at leadership. (Kellerman, 2004:45)

This opens up one of the salient issues in leadership theory – the notion that such theories can tell us what a 'good' leader looks like. Kellerman is trying to remind us here that they cannot. A similar reminder might also be aimed at many of the leadership writers currently in circulation. Regardless of this, considerable effort has been expended on trying to identify those personal or behavioural characteristics which might explain why some leaders are better than others. Early studies rehearsed the various factors that might be relevant to this in a number of ways. One very relevant approach is trait theory or the so-called 'great man' approach, with its more modern variants. As the name suggests, such theories emanate from psychology and suggest that 'good' leadership is associated with various personality traits or, more latterly, certain competencies. This leads us to the second of the key debates in leadership theory we mentioned earlier, that of whether leaders are born or made: does leadership rest on the possession of innate traits, or does it arise from the application of a range of learnable skills and behaviours? This debate also echoes Grint's 'process problem', discussed above.

Born or Made? Leadership Traits and Leader Behaviours.

In its earliest form, 'trait theory' attempted to define and delineate the concept of leadership in terms of innate ability, and specifically, to identify the traits required for leadership effectiveness through empirical research. Studies of traits sought to establish taxonomies of the personal features of 'born leaders', which distinguished them from others. These early studies of traits tended to focus on three main areas:

* Physical characteristics such as height, physique, appearance, and age,
* Aptitudes, such as general intelligence, verbal fluency, and creativity,
* Personality characteristics such as those later to be designated 'The Big Five' (e.g. Fiske, 1949; McCrae and Costa, 1989) namely conscientiousness, introversion –extroversion, emotional stability, agreeableness, and openness to experience.

The debt to psychology is obvious. The biggest problem with these early studies was that the various 'traits' identified did not appear to correlate in any meaningful way with 'effectiveness'. Stogdill (1948), for instance, reviewed 124 trait studies conducted between 1904 and 1948, and cast doubt on the credibility of the evidence that could be gleaned from the ever-growing number of seemingly unrelated traits that were put forward as contributing to leadership effectiveness, although in a later work (Stogdill, 1974) he did conclude that some qualities appeared to be associated with leadership more often than others. It is probably fair to say that, at best, only weak generalizations concerning leadership traits could be made (see e.g. Shaw, 1976; Fraser, 1978) and that none of the traits identified, such as intelligence and sociability, were sufficient in themselves for the recruitment of successful leaders. More tellingly, this kind of approach does not provide for the possibility that there are elements of leadership that can be trained or learned through experience; that leaders can, in effect, be developed. Despite these drawbacks, the trait approach continued with, for example, McClelland's (1965, 1985) work on managerial motivation, Boyatzis' (1982) managerial competencies (which included personal traits as well as motives, skills, knowledge and specific behaviours) and McCall and Lombardo's (1983) study of 'derailed' leadership, which focused on what distinguished managers who went all the way to the top from those who advanced to middle management but then subsequently failed to perform successfully (i.e. they were dismissed or transferred, 'plateau-ed' or took early retirement).

The approach also experienced something of a renaissance in the late 1980s with Lord and Maher's (1991) argument in favour of traits' importance as 'perceived constructs', whereby followers are influenced in their perceptions of someone as a leader based on the traits they are seen as exhibiting. This approach has been criticized, particularly in respect of the psychological tests designed to identify leadership traits, on the basis that they have a tendency to construct rather than discover personality types (e.g. Carless and Allwood, 1997). The resurgence of the trait-related approach can also be seen in the recent research on charismatic leadership, discussed below, and in some aspects of competency frameworks.

Debates surrounding the innate abilities and qualities of individual leaders in the guise of charismatic (Conger and Kanungo, 1987; Weber, 1948) and transformational (Bass, 1985) leadership models became common in the 1980s. The argument for reviving this approach, under the loose heading of 'New Leadership', was that while there are many behaviours, skills and styles that can be learned and adopted by leaders, there remains something unexplained about how certain kinds of people seem to naturally emerge as effective leaders. The emphasis of both transformational and charismatic leadership on the articulation of a vision, and the values which support it, reflected a new conception of leaders as 'managers of meaning' (Smircich and Morgan, 1982).

Burns (1978), for instance, put forward the idea of 'transforming leadership' as a relationship which bound both leaders and followers 'in a mutual and continuing pursuit of a higher purpose' (Burns, 1978:20) and converted leaders into 'moral agents'. At the same time, he highlighted the contrast between the aspirational and empowering nature of transformational leadership, compared with the 'rewards for compliance' exchange, which underpins transactional leadership. The link between transforming leadership and vision – a ubiquitous buzzword of modern leadership – was made explicit by those who built on Burns' theme (e.g. Bass, 1985; Bennis and Nanus, 1985; Tichy and Devanna, 1986).

Vision was also central to the notion of charismatic leadership, which was presented as an antidote to widespread organizational downsizing and the climate of demoralization and demotivation to which it gave rise. Max Weber had previously described the charismatic leader as 'one who enjoys loyalty and authority by virtue of a mission believed to be embodied in him' (Weber, 1968:1117). In similar vein, Conger (1989) broke down charismatic leadership into a four-stage process aimed at instigating organizational change. Key to the process was a perceived need for change – and a solution to that need – articulated and role-modelled by the leader. Unsurprisingly, this approach has been extensively criticised for, amongst other things, focussing exclusively on senior leaders, for telling us nothing about the situations in which leaders exercise leadership, for not noticing that strong, charismatic leaders can lead organisations into disaster (see, for example, Tourish and Vatcha, 2005, on events at Enron), and so on. For example, Bryman's (1992) text, *Charisma and Leadership in Organizations*, points out that most studies of charisma tend to involve historical analyses of prominent political and military leaders already famous for their supposed charisma. There is something of the self-fulfilling prophecy about this. We call upon examples of charismatic leaders who were by some measure successful, and we discover that charismatic leaders can be successful. Others are critical of the assumption that charisma necessarily resides within the leader figure, arguing that it may be attributed by followers, or produced through the relationship between social actors.

The criticisms that can be levelled at the various forms of 'trait theory' do not mean that it goes away. No theory in the social sciences ever does. Bolden (2004) observes, and we can only agree, that the renaissance of trait theory in the form of 'competence frameworks' has led to an almost super-human list of competencies being required of anyone deserving of the title 'leader', and a return to notions of 'heroic' leadership embodied by the 'great man'.[1] As Bolden goes on to state (2004:16):

> This almost iconographic notion of the leader, as a multi-talented individual with diverse skills, personal qualities and a large social conscience, posses a number of difficulties. (Bolden, 2004:16)

Quite apart from the fact that the list of desired qualities is so extensive that no individual could possibly match it, there are two significant difficulties with trait or competence theory. First, it fails to distinguish the different situations in which some traits might be more desirable than others: too often, every possible leadership competency is lumped together in one unwieldy mass which it would be both impossible and unnecessary for one individual to embody (a contextual failure). Secondly, this rather 'heroic' approach to leadership excludes the possibility of leadership by teams or groups. Even when we can point to qualities held by individuals, it has been pointed out both in the past and more recently that this is of questionable efficacy in terms of performance (Gronn, 1995).

On the other side of the 'born versus made' debate, leadership researchers dissatisfied with the idea that leaders are characterised by what they *are*, have contended instead that leaders are better defined according to what they *do*. The notion that leadership is an innate ability, in other words, is challenged by the prospect that we might more fruitfully look at leadership behaviours. The importance of this shift historically was that it suggested that understanding and describing the behaviour of 'effective' leaders meant that such behaviours, and their associated skills, could not only be documented and measured, they could also be *learned* through leadership training.

Early examples of the shift of research attention to leadership behaviours was the work of the Ohio State University (e.g. Fleishman, 1953; Halpin and Winer, 1957; Hemphill and Coons, 1957) and University of Michigan (e.g. Katz, Maccoby and Morse, 1950; Katz and Kahn, 1952; Likert, 1961), whose studies were characterized by an attempt to categorize leadership behaviours across a wide range of contexts, including business, the military and education, and to develop questionnaires testing for the relevant behaviours. Based on the results of these studies, Ohio State produced a framework that suggested subordinates saw leader behaviour in terms of two broad categories, one concerned with relationship behaviour (designated Consideration) and the other (designated Initiating Structure) concerned with task objectives. The University of Michigan identified three types of leadership behaviour which differentiated between effective and ineffective leaders, which they termed respectively Task-Oriented Behaviour, Relations-Oriented Behaviour and Participative Leadership (Likert, 1967). The Managerial Grid (Blake and Mouton, 1964) also built on the idea of different orientations producing different styles, this time with combinations of 'concern for task' and 'concern for people' producing one of five management styles. 'Team Management' – the name given to the style likely to be adopted by someone with a high concern for both task and people – was proposed as the most effective leadership style, irrespective of the situation to be managed.

Later, and more sophisticated, behavioural approaches argued that these early models tended to emphasize 'types' of leader at the expense of the specific situational factors that might affect leadership style, and paid little attention to the complex and often changing relationship between leaders and followers. In a bid to overcome the limits of the behavioural approach, many researchers began to explore the situational factors that influence leader–follower relations and group performance. Such approaches, called collectively 'situational' or 'contingent' leadership approaches, began from the position that the effectiveness of any leadership style is contingent, and hence that a range of styles will need to be employed in order to be effective across a range of situations. Best known amongst these more sophisticated frameworks were Hersey and Blanchard's Situational Leadership model (1984) and John Adair's *Action Centred Leadership* (1973). The former relies on an assessment of subordinates' 'readiness' in terms of ability and motivation (termed Skill and Will) in order to determine the appropriate leadership style to adopt, with the effective style being both person and task specific. This framework was similar to an earlier model developed by Tannenbaum and Schmidt (1958), who presented a continuum of leadership styles from autocratic to laissez-faire, designed to be applied after consideration of the developmental level of subordinates. Adair's framework called for a leader to focus on the completion of the task, the well-being of the team and the development of the individual, with the degree of attention being given to each varying with the situation.

What is entirely evident from the above review of these classic approaches to leadership studies is that they universally orient to a problem–solution model. The point of the research, that is, is to find ways of either choosing better leaders or making leaders better at what they do. The supposed relationship between 'good' leadership – however defined or operationalized – and organizational effectiveness remains a vibrant and topical issue, as does the process through which effective leadership is arrived at. The whole leader-centric nature of these classic approaches has, however, itself been challenged, bringing us to another key theme within the literature. Closely aligned to Grint's 'philosophical problem' of leadership is the question of whether we should be defining leadership in terms of the intentions of leaders or the perceptions of followers. This suggests a 'socially constructed' view of the phenomenon whereby leadership can be understood as being 'in the eye of the beholder'.

In the Eye of the Beholder? Socially Constructed Views of Leadership

The vast majority of leadership literature is written from the perspective of the leader – leadership as the intentions of the leader, related to their traits or behaviours, etc. Even situational and contingency models, which recognize that the leader may need to change their leadership style for different people and different situations, still tend to see the follower as a largely passive recipient of what the leader does or is. There is, however, a significant strand within the literature which challenges this viewpoint, and suggests that leadership is 'in the eye of the beholder'. That is, what constitutes leadership and who is considered to be a leader is determined by the perceptions of potential followers rather than the intentions of would-be leaders.

The broad heading of 'socially constructed leadership' refers to a collection of follower-centred rather than leader-centred approaches to understanding leadership as a phenomenon. Shamir, Pillai, Bligh and Uhl-Bien (2007) set out a summary of the five roles attributed to followers within the literature. The first two are what we would recognise from the traditional, mainstream leadership literature. 'Followers as recipients of leader influence' equates neatly to early trait theories and charismatic/ transformational leadership, in which the follower is seen as a passive recipient of whatever the leader is or does. 'Followers as moderators of leader impact' aligns with situational and contingent approaches whereby the leader is required to adjust their behaviours to suit different individuals or situations, but the followers are still largely passive. 'Followers as substitutes for leadership' was a theory originated by Steven Kerr and John Jermier (1978) which argued that under certain conditions, the influence of a leader over a follower may be neutralized or even substituted. For example, where the task in hand is routine or straightforward and there is thus little need for leadership or where the task is intrinsically satisfying such that workers don't need to be motivated into doing it or praised afterwards (for example, a paramedic may fit into this latter category). Virtual working – where leadership is effectively absent most of the time – could also be seen as a situation where followership and/or the work itself are substitutes for leadership. 'Followers as leaders' attempts to do away entirely with the distinction between the two, and is thus neither leader nor follower centred; distributed leadership, which we will look at later, may arguably be seen as falling into this category.

It is with the final role – 'Followers as constructors of leadership' – that we move into the truly follower-centred approaches where 'leadership' is attributed and defined by the follower in an ongoing process of social construction. Here, the focus is on how followers construct and represent leaders in their thought systems, and collectively, how they inter-subjectively agree what we mean by 'leadership', the underlying premise being that unless followers recognise and orient to particular behaviours as leadership, then they aren't leadership whatever the intentions of the person doing them. You really can't be a leader unless people are prepared to follow you!

The main area of theory here is around Meindl's (1995) notion of the 'romance of leadership', which is an exploration of the tendency (both within the literature and in organizational settings) to overestimate the significance of leadership and its impact on organizational success. A strong emphasis on leadership in the research literature has both mirrored and perpetuated the 'hype' and often unrealistic expectations that are routinely placed on real leaders, most particularly in the arenas of business and politics. According to Meindl this romanticizing of leadership denotes 'a strong belief – a faith – in the importance of leadership factors to the functioning and dysfunctioning of organised systems' (Meindl and Ehrlich, 1987:91). In effect, their research suggests that leadership acts as a simplified, biased and attractive way to make sense of organizational performance, and that this 'romantic tendency' seems to have the greatest sway in times of extreme success or extreme failure. Meindl also suggested that superior organizational performance arose through the attribution of leadership rather than as a result of leadership *per se*: that is 'leaders keep on winning because their followers perceive them to be winners' rather than the other way around. Finally, Meindl coined the phrase 'social contagion' to denote the way in which the understanding of what was leadership and who was a leader was socially constructed through the 'spontaneous spread of affective and/or behavioural reactions among members of a group' (Meindl, 1995:192). Obviously, media accounts of high-profile political, organizational and social leaders can be very significant in spreading this contagion.

Less well recognized is the psychoanalytic strand of research, which builds on the importance of our early years in shaping and defining our individual philosophies of leadership. Derived from the work of Sigmund Freud and Carl Jung, and highlighting the centrality of our family origins and upbringing in understanding our behaviour as a leader or a follower, this approach suggests that the models of leadership we have from our parents, teachers and the like during our youth are likely to influence our understanding of what leadership is as well as our choice of whether to lead or to follow. Psychodynamically, then, we might react to a leader in a dependent, counter-dependent or an independent manner (Stech, 2004), thus looking to them for emotional and practical guidance in everything, rebelliously rejecting their directives, or objectively assessing their directives in order to decide if they are ethical and reasonable before choosing how to act. In explaining why followers construct leaders in a dependent way, Shamir (2007) points to the psychodynamic processes of projection and transference, and notes that these processes can be particularly salient during periods of crisis or threat, when people feel confused, helpless or insecure. Their idealization of the leader is in no way related to the leader's actual abilities or any special characteristics.

These psychological processes, which cast leaders as a means by which followers can reduce their level of anxiety and obtain a measure of psychological safety, can also result in followers allowing or tolerating the creation of 'toxic leaders' – leaders who manipulate their followers' ordinary human needs and exploit their natural fears for their own advancement. Cult leaders such as Charles Manson are an obvious example here, but there is a large and worrying grey area around media figures – such as pop stars and fashion models – and even possibly around 'management gurus'. The commercial success of some well-published management authors – we hesitate to name names – might arguably be on the wrong side of the line here!

Social identity theory has also been utilized to suggest that the extent to which a leader is either selected or accepted by a particular group will depend on how 'prototypical' (i.e. representative) they are to that group (Van Knippenberg and Hogg, 2003). Hogg defines proto-typicality as 'a fuzzy set of features that captures in-group similarities and intergroup differences regarding beliefs, behaviours and feelings' (Hogg, 2005:56) and uses this idea to suggest that 'like attracts like' in the field of leader and follower. Contrary to the popular idea that, as managers, we 'recruit in our own image' however, the suggestion here is that the followers choose the leader rather than the reverse. Ironically, having appointed or accepted a leader on the basis of their proto-.typicality, over time, group members are said to begin attributing the success of their leader to that person's special personality rather than because of their proto-typicality. According to Shamir (2007) it is through this process that the charismatic personality of a leader is constructed. Social identity theory can be helpful in making sense of a number of contemporary issues in leadership. For example, research has shown that in Western societies, demographic minorities (e.g. women and ethnic minorities) find it difficult to attain top leadership positions. If organizational (or wider cultural) prototypes (e.g. of speech, dress, attitude, and interactional style) are socially cast so that minorities do not match them, then this theory would explain why they are unlikely to be endorsed as leaders, particularly under conditions when organizational proto-typicality is important (i.e. when organizational identification and cohesion are high, such as in times of uncertainty or crisis). By way of example, we would recommend Puwar (2001) for a fascinating exploration of the 'idealized somatic norm' of the white, middle-class male in the British Civil Service.

Critical Approaches to Leadership

So far, we have tried to draw a picture of the way in which leadership studies have oriented to a number of themes, themes which derive both from a 'market' concern with what it might take to produce 'good' leaders and an academic concern with re-inventing disciplinary foci through new topics. Crucially important here, in trying to understand why 'leadership studies' is able to continually re-invent itself – without ever, seemingly, resolving any of the questions it sets itself – is the fact that ongoing disagreement is fuelled by fault lines in the social and human sciences. There is no room to discuss these in any detail, but where disciplines such as psychology retain some commitment to the 'scientific' – the idea that there is an objective, measurable way in which 'leadership' can be assessed – sociology and its cognates have progressively rejected what they see as 'scientism'. As a result, the disciplinary interest of the social scientist has come to emphasise the 'critical'. 'Critical' here does not refer to criticism but to the examination of basic assumptions. As we have seen above, terms such as 'good', 'effective', 'efficient' and so on, have not always been critically examined: recent writing in relation to leadership is attempting to remedy this deficit.

More explicitly, a range of critical approaches in recent years has sought to characterize leadership itself as an 'alienating social myth' (Gemmill & Oakley, 1992). There is also a growing body of work that suggests the study of leadership might be fundamentally problematic in that such studies merely serve to bolster the dominant belief in patriarchal social structures that serve to oppress under the guise of empowerment (Sievers, 1993). That is, 'leadership' is just an idea that those who want to exercise power over others have dreamed up to make it sound like a good thing! On this view, and according to Gemmill and Oakley, we do not need leadership and it does more harm than good when we have it, because it oppresses those who are destined to be followers and, based on existing class structures – which it perpetuates – prevents them from breaking out of their subordinate roles. Going even further, Gemmill and Oakley suggest that the continuation of this myth of leadership results in emotional and intellectual deskilling of subordinates, such that they cease to be capable of leading themselves. At the same time, they actually come to like being subordinates because it reminds them of the feelings of security associated with the symbiotic environment of the womb and the dependence of childhood. As a result of this feeling of dependence, they then look for so-called 'heroic' leaders or leadership to 'rescue' them from their sense of individual helplessness, again perpetuating the social divisions between leader and led.

While this view seems, to most of us at least, somewhat extreme, there is no doubt that the exercise of leadership has created as many problems as it has solutions. As already discussed, it is easy to cite national, political and organizational leaders who have brought ruin to those over whom they exercised influence. Perhaps this explains – continuing with the theme of a turn towards the critical, albeit in a more moderate fashion – the recent emphasis in leadership writing on the moral or ethical aspects of leadership, and their impact on followers. This focus has spawned a swathe of publications on ethical leadership (e.g. Ciulla, 2004), spiritual leadership (e.g. Fry, 2005; Reave, 2005), servant leadership, (e.g. Spears and Lawrence, 2004) and authentic leadership (e.g. Avolio and Gardner, 2005). In addition to significant overlap between the various constructs,[2] there can also be seen a number of similarities between these supposedly 'new' constructs and the transformational and charismatic varieties they purport to supersede. While these, largely philosophical writings have yet to be operationalized in practical, implementable approaches for everyday leaders, they are emblematic of a key issue exercising leadership thinkers at the present time.

Leaders or Leadership? The Chosen Few or Something for Everyone?

In tracing the themes we have considered so far through the history of leadership thinking, we can see the developing emphasis on 'social relations' (Bolden, 2004) and a recurrent suggestion that leadership has little to do with the individual at all. At the very least, the early emphasis on leaders as 'great men' – and the more recent popularity of books by or about high-profile senior leaders – seems to be misdirected and to ignore the potential for acts of leadership at any level within an organization. On this broader reading, leadership becomes something of a distributed (Gronn, 2003) phenomenon: we are reminded again of Grint's 'purity problem' concerning the embodiment of leadership in individuals versus the potential for groups to be leaders. Referred to also as informal, emergent or dispersed leadership, these largely philosophical models emphasize the importance of follower participation, democratic leadership and organizational citizenship, and argue for a less formalized, hierarchical model of what leadership is and where it resides. Gronn (2003), for instance, suggests that a number of conceptual problems serve to make the concept of 'leadership' redundant when applied to individuals, but that we can fruitfully see it as dispersed across the organization. As already discussed, this represents a marked contrast to the focus on senior figures within the organization we have largely seen so far.

Various strands exist within this approach. A number of them – Sims and Lorenzi's (1992) 'Super Leadership', Katzenbach and Smith's (1993) 'real teams', and Kouzes and Posner's (1993) 'credible leaders' – focus on the ability of leaders to develop leadership capacity in others, and so become less dependent on formal leadership. Sims and Lorenzi refer to this as (1992:295) 'leading others to lead themselves', while Katzenbach and Smith suggest that this is done by building commitment and confidence, creating opportunities and removing obstacles and by operating as one of the team. For Kouzes and Posner, credible leaders are ones who are able to (1993:156) 'turn their constituents into leaders', rather than handing down leadership from above. Another expression of the turn towards distributed leadership is an increased focus on leadership skills and processes, and a recognition that these do not necessarily reside in those who hold formally designated leadership positions. This leads, for example, Knights and Willmott (1992), to suggest that more attention should be paid to leadership 'practices', by which they mean to the way in which leadership is constituted in organizational life.

Educational Leadership: From Lead Professional to Business Manager

As already noted at the start of this chapter, most studies of educational leadership have tended to focus on primary, secondary, or higher education, to the neglect of FE, which some have described as the 'Cinderella Sector' (Kerfoot and Whitehead, 1998). Yet FE is the largest education sector in the United Kingdom and, through the diversity of both its student base and curriculum offering, arguably presents some unique leadership issues for potential study. Since its incorporation in April 1993, Further Education in England and Wales has undergone a profound transformation, in which the old culture of benign, liberal paternalism (Kerfoot and Whitehead, 1998) has, according to some, been replaced by a 'quasi-market' economy (Goddard-Patel and Whitehead, 2000), with the consequent emergence of a more entrepreneurial and managerial style of leadership than is usually found in the rest of the education sector. Research into the FE sector has lagged behind, however, with studies of educational leadership tending to draw heavily on the compulsory education sector and on commercial or business oriented models rather than developing sector-specific ones.

While education generally has adopted some of the generic leadership models outlined in the above literature, it has also developed some specific versions. Dominant amongst these, particularly in North America but also in the UK, has been the notion of instructional leadership. Beginning in the late 1980's, studies of instructional leadership drew heavily on the 'effective schools' literature (Hallinger, 2003), and emphasized the role of the principal (headteacher) in school improvement (e.g. Edmonds, 1979). In this way, although there is a specific theme – instruction – embedded in the model, it nevertheless relies heavily on conceptions of leadership outlined above: conceptions which see leadership as involving individual properties. The instructional model casts the leader in the role of 'lead professional', with the primary focus of leadership work being the development of behaviours in teachers that directly influence their relationships with students through the planning and delivery of teaching and learning (Sawbridge, 2000). Although there were several conceptualizations of the model, the most frequently discussed features included the direct involvement of the principal in developing, co-ordinating and controlling the curriculum (e.g. Hallinger and Murphy, 1985); leadership as the unitary role of the principal (e.g. Leithwood and Montgomery,

1982); leadership as a combination of expertise and charisma (e.g. Cuban, 1984); and leaders as 'culture builders' (e.g. Mortimer, 1993) for both staff and students. Hallinger's (2000) operationalization of instructional leadership – perhaps the most widely referenced – proposes three elements to the construct, namely defining the school's mission, managing the instructional programme, and promoting a positive learning climate. Implicit in this – and indeed most – conceptualizations of instructional leadership, which is a largely schools-based model, is the presumption that most headteachers are ex-teachers themselves and so their own teaching experience and expertise is drawn upon in supporting staff in improving their teaching practices, and in monitoring the quality and effectiveness of the learning delivery.

With regard to the Further Education sector, Sawbridge (2000) suggests that the size, complexity and more commercial context of general FE colleges in the UK has tended to result in a move away from this kind of direct involvement in the curriculum in favour of greater attention being given to managerial and business issues. That said, instructional leadership may exist at other levels within these colleges where, arguably, it overlaps with the notion of distributed leadership, discussed below. The instructional model is still arguably found in some sixth-form colleges, however, where the smaller size and more focused mission lends itself to this approach and where college principals may even retain a direct teaching commitment.[3]

While models of 'transformational' leadership originated outside the education sector, as we have already seen, this has not prevented their deployment within it. In this context, the idea sits well with the emphasis on developing capacity which is prevalent in primary and secondary education, particularly in the leadership training aimed at this audience (e.g. in the National College for School Leadership's Leadership Programme for Serving Headteachers, 2001). Transformational leadership found a receptive audience in the sector as part of a wider reaction to the directive imagery of the instructional model and to policy initiatives imposed from outside (Hallinger, 2003). In the most comprehensive reworking of transformational leadership for use in an educational setting, Leithwood, Jantzi and Steinbach (1999) translate the four central tenets of the model (idealized influence, inspirational motivation, intellectual stimulation and individualized consideration – Bass and Avolio, 1994) into the school context by suggesting that transformational leaders should focus on: building the vision and setting the goals of the school; providing individualized support and intellectual challenge for teachers and other staff;

modelling best practice and organizational values; creating a productive school culture; and developing participative structures and systems for decision-making within the school. Unlike the instructional leader, who supports staff in their teaching relationships with students, the aim of the transformational leader is less direct, emphasizing empowerment and building a supportive environment rather than developing specific skills. The aligning of the staff's values and beliefs with those of the school, and the consequent development of organizational commitment, creativity and motivation, is the primary goal of the transformational school leader. As such, the emphasis is on motivating rather than controlling, on bottom-up school improvement rather than top-down, and on second-order targets for change rather than first-order, i.e. on creating the conditions in which people can generate change rather than on attempting to change specific instructional practices (e.g. Mulford and Bishop, 1997). In this sense, transformational leadership may also be said to be distributed in nature (Jackson, 2000) rather than centred on the person of the principal. The model has also found favour in FE, where a more hands-off approach has been suited to both the size and the culture of the larger, more commercial, general FE college.

In contrast, the idea of moral or spiritual (Leithwood et al., 1999; Reave, 2005) leadership deemed appropriate to some denominational schools, has never gained wide credence in FE. This may be because it is associated with religious commitments (although there is no particular reason why it should be – it is, after all, only a variety of value-consensus sociology). Similarly, formulations of authentic (Avolio and Gardner, 2005) and ethical (Ciulla, 2004) leadership seem to have found little purchase in post-compulsory education.

Also not widely adopted are the contingent and situational models described above. More successful imports, although still not prevalent across the sector, have been John Adair's (1973) *Action Centred Leadership* – usually referred to as managerial leadership, e.g. FENTO (2000), and Senge's (1992) organizational learning model, adapted for the educational context by Michael Fullan (1993). Of these, the managerial model has been most widely applied in Further Education, with the Further Education National Training Organisation's draft management standards (FENTO, 2000) advocating the skills-based approach inherent in Adair's 'task, team and individual' framework, in preference to a more behaviour-based view of leadership. Silins and Mulford (2004) have suggested that the leadership practices required to foster the learning organization result in a combination of transformational and distributed leadership:

... schools that operate as learning organisations are led by principals whose practices reflect the six dimensions defining transformational leadership. Leaders of learning organisations involve all the staff in setting school priorities so that staff build a shared sense of purpose. The principal promotes a culture of caring, trust and respect among staff and students, modelling reflective practice. The principal establishes school structures that support shared decision-making and distributed leadership and provides individualised support to enable staff to learn and lead. (Silins and Mulford, 2004:459)

The notion of distributed leadership, advocated by Gronn (2003) and referred to variously as participative (e.g. Abzug and Phelps, 1998), democratic (e.g. Mahony and Moos, 1998), dispersed (Bennett et al., 2003) or teacher leadership (e.g. Frost and Harris, 2003) is a strongly emergent theme in the educational leadership literature, as well as in the 'official' discourse of the sector, as represented by the National College for School Leadership (NCSL) (e.g. Southworth, 2002). It is underpinned by a widespread sense of shared ownership of decisions, based on the exercise of leadership at all levels within the organization, and is reflected in an increasing number of co-ordinator, lead practitioner and school improvement group roles within the teaching staff of UK schools. Its normative impact is embodied in the NCSL's 'Leading from the Middle' training programme (see National College for School Leadership website) aimed at bringing teachers and middle managers into the framework of school leadership. It is also being applied to or assessed in relation to the pressing educational issues (such as failing schools, e.g. Nicolaidou and Ainscow, 2005) and latest government initiatives (such as 'remodelling practice', e.g. Rayner and Gunter, 2005) of the day. These initiatives share a commonality – that of 'capacity building' (Earl and Lee, 2000) – with the standard assumptions of transformational leadership in that both can be seen as taking a participatory approach to school leadership and culture rather than a controlling or directing one.

A recent review of the distributed leadership literature offered by Bennett et al. (2003) offered what it called an 'interpretive construction' of its main features in the following terms: leadership is an emergent property of a group or network of interacting individuals; in turn that suggests an openness of the boundaries of leadership, and entails the view that varieties of expertise are distributed across the many, and not limited to the few. They failed to find a consensus within the sector, however – or even within the literature – as to how distributed leadership should be defined or how it could be practiced. Indeed, Bush and Glover (2003) in another review of educational leadership conducted for the same organization (i.e. the National College for School Leadership) at roughly the same time, in listing eight leadership models to be used for the normative assessment of school leadership, did not even mention distributed leadership – though they do make reference to 'postmodern' leadership, which appears to contain some features of the distributed model. While distributed leadership is clearly being driven forward as part of a schools-based leadership agenda, it is also finding applicability – though without much of the rhetoric – in FE, and the learning and skills sector generally.

We should also note that not all authors are equally enthusiastic about its merits. For example, Timperley (2005) draws attention to the lack of empirical work to support the operationalization of distributed leadership in (both successful and unsuccessful) schools and, in seeking to remedy this omission, highlights some risks and challenges associated with it. The lack of empirical evidence supporting the use or efficacy of distributed leadership is echoed by Lashway (2003):

> [the] research base for distributed leadership is still embryonic. While there is considerable theory, we have relatively little empirical knowledge about how, or to what extent, principals actually use distributed leadership. And evidence that firmly links distributed leadership to student achievement is still far in the future. (Lashway, 2003:3)

Harris (2005) suggests that distributed leadership in schools is evolving, but is by no means the dominant institutional structure. Indeed, she maintains that the success – and even the existence – of distributed leadership is dependent on the sponsorship of more formal leadership structures. Reporting on a rare empirical study of school leadership, she concludes that:

> This study found that distributed leadership is unlikely to flourish unless those in formal leadership positions positively promote and support it. (Harris, 2005:261)

Hatcher (2005:253), echoing the 'critical' turn we mention above, takes a somewhat stronger and less charitable view, seeing fundamental contradictions between the prominence of distributed leadership discourses as 'a means to achieve participation and empowerment of teachers and to create democratic schools' and the 'hierarchical power structure of schools.' In such a view, the increasing complexity of the school context by definition makes principals dependent upon their staff for the implementation of mandated reform, but at exactly the same time the authority vested in the principal as the agent of such government-driven agendas circumscribes the possibility of any genuinely distributed leadership. Thus Hatcher (2005:256) sees distributed leadership as not only requiring an 'official sanction', but also to be 'always delegated, licensed, exercised on behalf of and revocable by authority – the headteacher.' He draws on Wright (2001) in highlighting how what he calls 'distributed and pseudo-democratic leadership' can be seen as 'the translation into school management discourse of the idea ... that some concessions to participatory processes at lower levels of a managerialist power structure represent popular democracy' (Hatcher, 2005:259) In a similar vein, Wright contends that:

> Leadership as the moral and value underpinning for the direction of schools is being removed from those who work there. It is now very substantially located at the political level where it is not available for contestation, modification or adjustment to local variations. (Wright, 2001:280)

Such critiques draw heavily on Gramscian notions of hegemony and contestation, and hence on disciplinary notions of a critical sociology. As Wainwright (2003) so succinctly puts it:

> I participate, we participate, but they decide over what kind of issue we can decide. (Wainwright, 2003:193)

Thus in the context of educational leadership, as elsewhere, we see debates are largely constructed out of positions in relation to the market and in relation to disciplinary discourse. This will be our starting point – regardless of the conceptual difficulties various theorists try to deal with, and the refinements they propose, all are concerned with the same business overall, and that is the business of positioning themselves within an academic and disciplinary tradition and in a market for their work (though the two may overlap). At exactly the same time, organizational members engaged in various matters which pertain to management and leadership, regularly and routinely go about their business with a degree of indifference to these academic and market-led matters. Whatever decisions they make about leadership style and policy (if, indeed, they make such decisions at all), they will distinguish the things they have to do in quite practical ways. They will do this minute-by-minute, day-by-day, and they will do so without any systematic recourse to the kind of academic knowledge we have so far rehearsed. There ought to be a puzzle in this. If the market for 'leadership studies' is so obviously predicated on theoretical stances on the relation between problems and their solutions, then there is something of a mystery in the fact that educational leaders in their practices seem to get along perfectly well without them.

Chapter 3

The Art of Purposeful Hanging Around: An Ethnomethodologically-Informed Ethnography

Ethnography – 'Hanging Around' Leadership

We have already alluded to the fact that we have an analytic scepticism about the interests and approaches of the social sciences in studying leadership, and in this chapter we spend some time outlining our own academic and disciplinary concerns; concerns, methods and approaches that are very different from those conventionally associated with the study of leadership. Despite the fact that leadership research in the last twenty years or so has seen more acceptance of qualitative approaches in principle, largely as a result of the 'New Leadership' approach of the 1980's – in which the emphasis is on the leader as a 'manager of meaning' (Smircich and Morgan, 1982) – it remains the case that there is a paucity of data relating to what leaders and the people they interact with on a daily basis are actually engaged in doing. There are a few case studies in existence (e.g. Alvesson, 1992; Smircich and Morgan, 1982) or semi-structured interviews with leaders (e.g. Bennis and Nanus, 1985; Tierney, 1989; Bryman et al, 1996), but by and large little has been done which approximates to our interest in the accomplishment of activities which pertain to 'leading'. If leading can be understood as a 'defeasible achievement verb' – which means simply that occasions can be seen where 'leadership' is achieved and occasions can equally be seen where it is not – then it is rather surprising to see that for the most part the existing literature does not tell us how this 'leading' is being done. Indeed, the standard ways in which 'leadership' is understood almost explicitly leave out detailed examination of the sequential ordering of activities that must by definition be involved. As Grint (2005) argues, existing literature focuses in a number of ways on how we might categorise the 'leader' and spends no time at all on what is being done when we 'lead'. It is in an attempt to rectify this omission that we rely on something which is conventionally termed an 'ethnographic' stance.

Our research involved an 'ethnography' and was based primarily on extended fieldwork in a sixth-form college in England (hereafter: Lambton[1] Sixth-Form College) and a number of FE Colleges around the country. At the same time, we gathered data by conducting interviews – or, as we prefer, talking to people and focus groups, or talking to groups of people. We did so in a number of institutions, including Lambton. The data gathered here is supplemented by similar data from other sixth-form and general FE colleges that formed part of the study. This serves both to add richness to the choice of data included and to further preserve the anonymity of data sources referred to. The main ethnographic location is described in some detail below. While the other locations differed in a variety of respects, the method of approach (i.e. through personal contact) and the openness of access provided were similar in all locations. FE colleges tended to be larger, with leadership being exercised at more levels within the staff. Principals, not surprisingly, tended to be more distant from hands-on teaching issues and to have a greater element of commercial management within their roles. These differences in scale and commerciality between sixth-form and general FE colleges resulted in some differences in structure and style of leadership, but at the level of day-to-day leadership practices the commonalities were far greater than the differences. Hence no distinction is made in what follows between the two types of location.

Lambton Sixth-Form College consists of approximately 1,800 students, aged 16 to 19, and 230 staff. Courses are mostly academic and most students who come to the college go on to university. There is also a more vocationally oriented college in the town, with the result that the sixth form takes on a somewhat 'elitist' status for both staff and students. In line with the local community, the student population is culturally diverse, and the college prides itself on its inclusivity and safe working environment. It sets high academic standards and has recently received an excellent Ofsted report, including a Grade 1 (outstanding) for leadership and management. The college mission statement, which appears on walls and posters throughout the college, states that 'The main purpose of Lambton Sixth-Form College is to be a centre of excellence for academic and general vocational education of young people.' The principal, referred to in the text as Steven, has been at the college for four years and previously held senior management positions in other colleges, in both post-16 and general FE. Although he was originally a teacher, he describes himself as a 'business manager' rather than the 'lead professional' within the college. Access was gained on the back of the ethnographer having been a student at the college some 24 years previously, and by the simple expedient of asking for it. The principal, Steven, was, we think, flattered to be asked to participate in a major research project and interested in the process itself. He was extremely open and expansive in the access he was prepared to grant us, and reflective and insightful in his awareness of what 'might be interesting for a researcher to observe'. As a result, we were in college for all the major events of the academic year, from enrolment and induction through to results day, as well as seeing a wide range of more day-to-day activities. Our work involved shadowing the principal, as well as repeatedly interviewing him and members of his senior management team, shadowing curriculum managers, conducting focus groups with staff, and collecting documents. The principal's activities included staff appraisals, lesson observations, governors' meetings, staff and student briefings and external meetings. We also observed him working at his desk, touring round the college, visiting the staff room and staff/student canteen and other less formal activities. At no time were we asked to leave a meeting or denied access to anything in which we expressed an interest, even when the staff involved might have viewed the meeting as potentially sensitive or private (for example, appraisal meetings). We were freely provided with copies of reports, governors' papers, college literature, performance data, etc. and given access to the college intranet and the principal's e-mails. Over the period of fieldwork, we were able to talk freely to students and staff and to move about the college as we wished. We were allowed to record meetings and interviews, as well as to take notes on whatever activities we observed, and to take photographs of settings and artefacts where these seemed relevant. Staff quickly became used to seeing the ethnographer around and, we believe, had a relaxed attitude to her presence. Field notes and interviews were subsequently transcribed to provide a rich and detailed resource in relation to the routine activities and practices of leadership work in the setting.

Our work is, then, based on a substantial piece of 'ethnography'; but while, for sociologists, ethnography becomes a complex tool, deployed by experts, in order to furnish them with 'data' that they can then use to construct and refine theories, we try to distance ourselves from such considerations of 'method'. We make no great claims for the business of doing 'ethnography' and will not engage in arguments concerning its methodological superiority to other methods (for those interested in such arguments, see Randall et al, 2007). One of the things which characterises our ethnomethodological approach is a broad indifference to method, viewed as a professional activity with special devices, tricks, strategies, technologies or expertises which in turn lead to a 'good' job of ethnographic research.

We will not spend too much time on discussions surrounding the nature of ethnographic method and the commitments entailed. It is our view that ethnography should not be understood as a 'method' at all, and that much of the debate concerning ethnography as one branch of a 'qualitative' tradition is misconceived. This literature trades on professional piety – that there are specific skills pertaining to how to conduct oneself in the field that only experienced ethnographers who have plied their trade for many years can competently perform (ignoring a staggeringly obvious feature of academic research – that it is seldom the 'experienced' academic who actually goes out into the field and does the work). It is our view that, apart from some obvious practical, technical and ethical considerations, the skill involved in the ethnographic trade is *analytic*. To the extent that it is learned, it is learned through a developing sensitivity to a variety of issues. The basic characteristics of this type of research have been summarized by Atkinson and Hammersley (1998), as follows:

In practical terms, *ethnography* usually refers to forms of social research having a substantial number of the following features:

- A strong emphasis on exploring the nature of particular social phenomena, rather than setting out to test hypotheses about them
- A tendency to work primarily with 'unstructured' data, that is, data that have not been coded at the point of data collection in terms of a closed set of analytic categories
- Investigation of a small number of cases, perhaps just one case, in detail
- Analysis of data that involves explicit interpretation of the meanings and functions of human actions, the product of which mainly takes the form of verbal descriptions and explanations, with quantification and statistical analysis playing a subordinate role at most. (Atkinson and Hammersley, 1998:110–11)

Ethnography thus emphasizes the observation of people in naturally occurring settings, in order to gather qualitative data and generate descriptions of a 'culture' or cultural setting. As such, it substitutes natural settings for laboratories, non-interventionist approaches for

manipulative ones, and detailed descriptions for reductionist measure-
ments. In describing what happens in a setting, ethnography sees its
primary aim as capturing how the people involved saw and understood
what was happening, rather than imposing some externally-formulated
(i.e. researcher-formulated) theoretical explanation of events. To this
end, ethnography concerns itself with the meanings of situated actions,
observed in a specific setting, rather than with issues of generalizability
across a number of settings. In its original, anthropological setting,
ethnographic study involved the field worker in transplanting (usually)
himself to foreign climes to live amongst a strange and unknown tribe
for an extended period. With the transfer of ethnographic methods to
more familiar settings – replacing the tribal village location with that of
the factory, the hospital, the school, or the office – the need to retain the
illusion of strangeness becomes simultaneously more important and more
difficult to maintain. Hence:

> ... ethnography is a form of research in which the social settings to be
> studied, however familiar to the researcher, must be treated as anthro-
> pologically strange; and the task is to document the culture – the
> perspectives and practices – of the people in these settings. The aim is to
> "get inside" the way each group of people sees the world. (Hammersley,
> 1985:152)

Such analytic tropes are a means to avoid the accusation of subjectivism.
Over-familiarity and excessive sympathy could in principle lead to the
ethnographer 'going native' – losing critical distance, accepting accounts
at face value, being one-sided, and so on. That is, 'seeing things from
the point of view of the native' could lead to a progressive loss of other
points of view including – most critically – the disciplinary point of view we
associate with sociology and anthropology (a point of view we have already
expressed some scepticism about). It is not especially surprising that in
these disciplines a considerable amount of time has been engaged in
debates around the maintenance of critical distance, and the ways in which
it is, or is not, justified. According to Hammersley and Atkinson (1985), it
is inevitable that this should be so:

> Neither positivism nor naturalism provides an adequate framework [for
> the logic of social research and the implications for ethnography]. Both
> neglect its fundamental reflexivity: the fact that we are part of the social
> world we study, and that there is no escape from reliance on common-

sense knowledge and methods of investigation. All social research is founded on the human capacity for participant observation. We act in the social world and yet are able to reflect upon ourselves and our actions as objects in that world. (Hammersley and Atkinson, 1985:21)

The cultural baggage we necessarily bring with us is likely to involve theoretical baggage too. Here again, the possibility of a truly 'naturalistic', theory-blind ethnography is put in doubt by a whole raft of critical perspectives. As Edles (2002) says:

> Thus far we have seen that "naturalist" ethnography is pointedly "descriptive" and "atheoretical." The goal is to "abandon" preconceived ideas, simply *observe* a natural situation or environment, and "report" *whatever* is going on. However, as we have also seen, postcolonialists, postmodernists, and feminists have all challenged the *alleged* "atheoretical" attitude of the ethnographer. These analysts have all pointed out that regardless of their intent, ethnographers necessarily write from a specific subjective (and thus quasi-theoretical) position. (Edles, 2002:157, original emphasis)

This, then, delimits ethnography in terms of an attitude, if you will, but still leaves a wide range of choices open to the ethnographer – choices which in our case are defined by the ethnomethodological project. What follows is a more practically focused account of the methodological choices we made that result from those key features and commitments of ethnomethodology, and how they operate in the current context of making choices about studying leaders and leading. Ethnomethodology, often to the irritation and bemusement of sociologists-at-large, insists on taking a radical view of these problems. It does so by a resolute commitment to a particular kind of study. It too has a commitment, in a sense, to the 'point of view of the native' but the sense is very different. The sociologist or anthropologist, we suggest, sees this point of view as entailing meaning and/or morality. An ethnomethodological study is indifferent to such matters, and brackets them. It does so through the expedient of choosing not to concern itself with various problems, including not only the truth or otherwise of members' claims but also 'internal' matters such as the putative existence of systems of signs in the head, or 'meanings' which are held (apparently) in the same place. Instead, it is concerned with meaning as a visible and accountable phenomenon. It is content with a descriptive and analytic stance that details what people do and how they account for it in their talk, writing and actions. An ethnomethodological study involves the researcher understanding the setting and the actions of the people in it well enough to understand what it means to be 'good at' something. The following extract demonstrates the way in which a principal (Steven) has a view of what leadership might entail and reflections on the qualities it might take to do 'proper' leadership:

Steven: And I can think of several others, where they are driving and everything else is shaped by that, and they I'm sure will adapt and listen, whatever, but they are driving that vision. And that – what I was trying to decide is whether that is actually proper leadership or whether that is only one variant of leadership, and whether you can do it in another way. Because I, for a long time, was not convinced that I should be a principal, and served a very long time as a vice-principal because I didn't think that I could do the leadership role.

MIW (Marian Iszatt-White): Why – what did you think you couldn't do?

Steven: What I felt was, what I was really good at was implementing other people's visions, and a really – and that was back to being a good manager and good implementer, good synthesizer, good criticizer. So somebody had a vision, and (gesture indicating orderly implementation) I make it work, and very good in that secondary role. And I wasn't sure that I had the, if you like, the imagination and the single purpose – because this was following behind a … type who had a very clear view of whatever, all sorts of gaps which you then filled in and made it work. And I'm still not sure that I do have that certainty that there is only one right way. That I have a view as to what we're about, in which students are there (indicates centrality) and it's about the quality of what they get, and we are about changing their life chances. If it sounds redolent of what Blair started saying in '97, I'll deny it. (laughs)

MIW: Fair enough.

Steven: But I've come to the belief that it's actually right, and it's what I'd always thought before he appeared, that education was about the means of transforming society and undermining lots of the traditional political, traditional establishment structures and whatever – is by using education to liberate people from the places they were in. And so how did you do that? And having worked in FE, which was essentially, in the

'70s, inefficient, mildly corrupt – or seriously corrupt, depends where you worked – and certainly the outcomes for students – "oh, well, yes, we've got 50 per cent retention and, oh, 6 per cent pass rate, oh, well, never mind". And then on to the next. So the drive – I was fully part of the drive through incorporation and the FEFC that you are accountable for the outcomes and we have to try and ensure that students get on the right course, stay on it, have a good time, and pass. So students and learning are at the focus, but how you get there and how you move a group of people – the people who work in the place – to do that, is something that I don't have a definite vision that there's a right answer. And that is a continual development process, but what that doesn't provide, then, is this charismatic, "this is the way to go" ... that this is what I think education should be about and this is what I think we're here for. Now is that a vision? Then OK, yes, I'll sign up to it. But somehow, I've always associated vision with somehow being more total than that and more, more certain than that, and therefore questioned whether I actually had the vision, or the imagination, to do that. I just felt that this is what we should be there for and how do we get there?

This Principal orients to a number of recognizable features: an awareness of the personal qualities required to perform the leadership role, which – for him – entail some 'vision', which means a view of where he wants the organization to go, and is quite distinct from the managerial business of implementation; a view of the obstacles to that vision, which is construed largely in terms of the management of a 'professional' culture (one which he views as having been semi-corrupt); some assessment of the specific evidence which would constitute grounds for pursuing that vision *("oh, well, yes, we've got 50 per cent retention and, oh, 6 per cent pass rate, oh, well, never mind".)* and so on.

The ethnomethodological commitment entails rigorously sticking to descriptions of a certain kind – of the 'minute-by-minute' or 'real-time' unfolding of events and the visible and accountable way in which 'members' orient to, or construe, them. The people engaged in organizational activities in which 'leadership' is recognizably implicated – i.e. in situations where they act and talk in such a way as to make it evident – will manifest their interest in notions of 'good' or 'bad' leadership, of 'good practice' and 'mistakes', of 'things that work' and things that do not. Ethnomethodologists would see no particular reason why situations that entail some reflection on the part of members should be treated as distinct from the other quite ordinary activities that members might be engaged in. They are only what Garfinkel described as 'normal, natural troubles'. Again, the business of 'bringing people with you', persuasion, 'being on board', and so on, are constantly referred to in our data and constitute the most striking example of such troubles that leaders typically contend with. The following extract provides a flavour of that:

> Steven: And most of the teachers in this place will sign up to the vision, but they will have very different views as to how you get there. And with teachers, there is a set of tensions between signing up to that commitment to students and putting a boundary around their professional commitment to do it. And it's this ... erm, 1960s trade union culture, which I think is wholly inappropriate to education. That you have a contract that says "I work 1265 hours a year, in my contract" as opposed to "I do what ... I do ... is necessary and whatever reasonable management." And in this college, that culture is strong, that they will volunteer to do things, but what they won't have is an open approach that would allow management to exploit them, which is a complete lack of trust. And it's systemic to teaching, but in FE colleges that was broken largely by force, on incorporation. And the staff there don't necessarily work any, much longer hours, but they can do as is required, and it's been quite difficult to adjust to that mindset. And so there have been a number of pointless arguments, which is that basically people want to say, "well, you can't tell us to do that because it's outside this ..."

> MIW: But they'll often do it anyway?

> Steven: As long as you don't ask them! (laughs) And when your managers are on those conditions of service, it can be quite frustrating.

For the leader, there are certainly situations where she or he may wonder what their best policy might be, or how to implement their strategies such that they are caused to reflect on the situation, but regardless those reflections will either be available in exactly the same way as other activities – through talk and action – or are not available at all and thus not part of our interest. Associated with our position, as we have already pointed out, is an anti-methodological stance: we resist the idea of methodological 'privileging' – that there is a 'one best way' of collecting data or that it involves any technical expertise. Our position is that, if we want data about the things that interest us, in the manner we have described, then we will make pragmatic decisions about where to find it. We elaborate on these themes below.

Ethnomethodologically-Informed Ethnography – Analytic Choices and Consequences

Being Data-driven

From what we have briefly laid out above, it should be obvious that there are some foundational assumptions in our work. The first of these lies in the notion of being 'data- driven'. One must be led by the phenomenon under study in determining what counts as data and how best to capture it: one must start from the situated nature of the setting and gather what is there rather than bringing themes and approaches from outside the setting in order to go looking for them. Ethnomethodology, then, stresses *the importance of the specificity and distinctiveness of settings as inherent in its focus on the situated production of social order.* Being 'data- driven' means that our analytic task is to *accept whatever data the setting offers* and to see what members can show or tell us about the setting in their talk and action. This immensely practical approach thus represents a refusal to fetishize the collection of data, or to look for a generalized 'one best way' of approaching the task of data collection. Data will arrive from whatever source we happen upon and we will use common-sense judgements to figure out where to go next in order to collect some. This said, one may enter the setting with what Randall, Harper and Rouncefield (2005) have referred to as a collection of 'tropes' – 'sensitizing' or 'illuminating' concepts which the experienced practitioner will be familiar with. The point here is not to impose analytic categories on the activities one finds in a setting, but to bring common-sense knowledge to bear. Leadership itself may be viewed as a trope: a guiding idea of what the researcher may be interested in and on the lookout for as they conduct their observations. We need not worry too much about definition or theoretical division because we will know it when we see it in our chosen setting since our members orient to it in recognisable ways, ways which we may well be familiar with.

Unique Adequacy

We have rather laboured the point that ethnomethodology has no prescribed methods and is, in fact, reluctant to think of the business of talking to people and watching them as 'method' at all. Ethnomethodologists, never-theless, have policies. The first, and most central, of these is the notion of 'unique adequacy'. Michael Lynch (1993) sets out the 'strong' version of unique adequacy but a weaker version, and one which we are more comfortable with, has been developed as a working precept for the 'jobbing ethnomethodologist'. The weak version comprises the requirement that:

> ... the analyst must be *vulgarly* competent in the local production and reflexively natural accountability of the phenomenon of order* he is 'studying' ... that the analyst be, with others, in a concerted competence of methods with which to recognize, identify, follow, display, and describe phenomena of order* in local productions of coherent detail. (Garfinkel and Wieder, 1992:182, original emphasis)[2]

Thus the essence of 'weak' unique adequacy lies in knowing how to go on in a setting; in being able to describe the practices of the setting in a manner that is recognizable and meaningful to members rather than in sharing their experience of those practices. This leaves room for the recounting of the 'field experience' in text, but leaves the setting member as the final arbiter of whether the unique adequacy requirement has been satisfied. Thus, we do not require of our researcher in the present context that she be an accomplished leader, but that she become familiar with the way in which leaders conduct their business so that they are recognizably (to themselves and others, in the course of their work) doing 'leading'. The leader of an educational institution such as Lambton, when s/he does certain kinds of work, does them in ways that participants to that work will describe as 'leadership', but is not doing something that stands as an example of the general characteristics of leadership as found in a textbook. They are doing leading in this situation, and what doing leading means is the product of what is happening in this situation, and not elsewhere. Of course, these are not any old settings, they are sixth-form and FE colleges – what Wittgenstein (1958) might term 'perspicuous settings' in which to study leadership. In ethnomethodological terms, the aim was to find settings that illuminate recurrent, routinely enacted and familiar acts in such a way that typical, organizational relevancies become clear. To put it another way, the ethnomethodologist is required to find settings which make plain the work practices of members: or rather, to pay attention, in any given setting, to the naturally occurring practices through which members locally produce and make accountable to others (researchers as well as fellow members) the sense and meaning of what they are doing. It is the 'just-thisness' of the activities, as situated practices, that mark them out as an instance of what they recognizably are: mundane and commonplace but at the same time specific and unique. This reciprocity between individual instances and that which they are representative of is reflected in what Garfinkel refers to as the 'documentary method of interpretation':

> The method consists of treating an actual appearance as "the document of", as "pointing to", as "standing on behalf of" a presupposed underlying pattern. Not only is the underlying pattern derived from its individual documentary evidences, but the individual documentary evidences, in their turn, are interpreted on the basis of "what is known" about the underlying pattern. Each is used to elaborate the other. (Garfinkel, 1967:78)

This 'documentary method of interpretation' is a key feature of common-sense reasoning. It is in constant operation as we navigate our way through daily life, with each new event or activity serving to enrich our understanding of what has gone before and to provide a basis upon which to deal with what is to come. It is the use of this method in our everyday lives as the basis of common-sense reasoning that enables us to recognize events for what they are and to respond in accordance with shared understandings of their meaning. We don't need to see a large number of instances of something to detect its status as a regular occurrence. The reactions of those who are party to the occurrence will tell us that they view it as routine, unremarkable, commonplace, and so on. The regularity of the event is not detected *post hoc,* after examining a number of comparable instances, but is available to us in real time in the way in which the individual instance is performed. Hence from an ethnomethodological point of view, 'generalizability' – or rather the location of regularity – is not to do with statistical representativeness but with demeanour, with how people comport themselves while doing something. It is this that tells us it is something they do all the time: this that gives 'generalizability' to our findings.

Postmodern moves over the past 20 years or so have led increasingly to a concern for the relationship between ethnographer, ethnographic practice and ethnographic narrative. In other words, there has been an industrial scale growth in concerns for notions of genre, poetics, narrative, and so on. This has been built on a scepticism towards epistemology; about the nature of 'facts' and 'facticity'; a more approving nod towards relativism and an emphasis on playful, clever, ironic (or pastiched) approaches to theory. In turn, this has created interest in the ways in which the ethnographic text is constructed and in the reflexive role of the ethnographer. The foundation for this is the recognition that texts, academic and otherwise, are always in the business of persuading the readers as well as informing them. In this view, if ethnography is the interpretation of cultures, whereby the 'meaningful intention' of actors is brought out, then the process by which we arrive at this patterning, or conceptual array, is vitally important and is disguised by the *apparent* neutrality of the ethnographic 'voice'. As Clifford and Marcus (1986:6) put it, 'Ethnographic truths are thus inherently partial – committed and incomplete (they may be committed in more than one sense, e.g. politically or theoretically). This point is now widely asserted – and resisted at strategic points by those who fear the collapse of clear standards of verification.' In discussing this 'reflexive' turn, Hammersley and Atkinson (1985) suggest, our choices of what to capture must have some basis and:

> Reflexivity thus implies that the orientations of researchers will be shaped by their socio-historical locations, including the values and interests that these locations confer upon them. (Hammersley and Atkinson, 1985:16)

If there is any substance to these claims, then a new standard is being imposed on the ethnographer, one that demands an explicit acknowledgement of his or her role in the construction of the account. While we believe that ethnomethodology provides us with something of a 'get-out clause' in respect of the debates between rationalists and relativists, the postmodern insistence on the reflexivity of actors and researchers should act as a reminder about certain things. Most obviously, it should remind us that it is all too easy to provide accounts of 'leadership' which support definitional claims as though leadership is 'out there', is present in *this* example but not in *that*. That leadership is an endlessly contingent matter, produced out of the reflections of both senior figures in organisations and the people who study them can be seen in the following:

> MIW: OK, erm, we've had various conversations about leadership, about your style of leadership, leadership within the college, and it just occurred to me that as a result of having been shadowed you might have contemplated that subject again, and whether you had any sort of concluding thoughts on the subject of either leadership in general or your leadership in particular.

> Steven: Erm, probably more the latter than the former. In that I think that leadership in general, erm … I don't believe there's a right way to do it. Erm, in that sense, and a lot of it is to do with the context in which you are operating, and the team that you are working with. Because I

think the leader has to adapt to that, and I think I said to you right at the beginning that what I had reflected on is the extent to which the leader adapts to that or the leader changes the environment to adapt to them. And ... whether there is a right/wrong answer to that, and that I had a feeling that at some time since I've been at Lambton, I had done more adapting to them than erm, being firm enough about adapting them to me. Erm, and I've reflected upon that element of that conversation, and I think part of my uncertainty on that was rooted in immediacy – if that's not being too elliptical – that in an institution such as this, it was not necessary or necessarily desirable to have very rapid change.

MIW: Right.

This Principal touches on a number of themes, all of which can, if one chooses, be couched in terms of various theories of leadership. From our point of view, however, what is interesting here is the fact that these musings can be both provisional and retrospective. He is quite clear here that 'leadership in particular' is his preferred topic, and this because he rejects the idea of a 'right way'. Instead, he makes explicit reference to context, and to the nature of the 'team' he works with. In doing so, he exemplifies the 'leader's problem' which has to do with, taking into account these factors, what amount of change is to be sought. In turn, this involves decisions about whether he has to adapt to the institution or it has to adapt to him.

Steven: And a number of people – having had conversations with a number of people – it's quite clear that the perception is that this place has changed quite significantly over the four years – and it would be interesting to know whether you've picked up any of that – although I feel that there's still lots of things that haven't changed that might have done. Hence my concern that perhaps I haven't been as erm, if you like ... there hadn't been as much drive as opposed to moulding and shaping, and that perhaps I had ... yes, it's looking at it from the different ends, isn't it? That others may view the level and the rate of change as much greater than I have done, and certainly in terms of outputs, then, there have been quite a lot of changes. So I've reflected in that way. Erm, in terms of activities, I'm always reflecting on what I do anyway, erm, and conscious that there are all sorts of imperfections in the way in which I operate, some of which stem from my personality and your own ability to change and adapt. Others from, I suppose, a ...

are some things that still fundamentally irritate me and I suspect they always will and that's just part (MIW laughs) ... you know, goes with it, but I don't know that's necessarily a failing. I think it's probably OK if ...

MIW: It's being human, I suspect.

In lines 3–5, the Principal touches upon the issue of 'transformation' – without ever calling it that – and recognises the different ways in which change might be viewed. He expresses the view that he, perhaps, has not driven through change at a pace that he might have chosen, but equally sees that others might view such changes differently. He refers to the need to build a 'team', something which has not yet been accomplished to his satisfaction, but reflects on the problem of doing that without destroying autonomy and authority and while faced with clear opposition.

Steven: Or being rooted in a set of views, values – don't want to [...] anything like a value and belief system, or whatever – but just how it should be, and it's still OK to be irritated when it isn't OK. What's harder is where you have differences and where you have a strong independent – we have a strong team ... no, we have a team of strong, independent individuals – in, erm, developing a cohesive way forward from those strong individuals. And to try and get the balance between getting a collective will without undermining their authority and their autonomy, but actually stopping it being silos, which is certainly what was there when I came. And that's an unanswered question ... is the extent to which we have got there – no, we haven't got there, erm – and building the new team over the next year, erm, is the crucial piece of change management for me now, which started with the session we had a couple of weeks ago. Which made only a couple of tentative steps, but everybody recognises the agenda – the issue is whether a couple of people can change their behaviour. (muttered exchange about who may not want to change) And actually, I think, it's already very obvious that the senior management team is now in two halves, that the other three members of the principalship are going to be seen as the blockers.

Subsequently, he spends time discussing what it would mean to have a team in place, rejecting the view that 'Stepford leaders' might be desirable. That is, he does not appear to think that a uniform culture is demanded. Rather, he expresses a belief in the value of 'strong, independent individuals' but the concomitant need to blend that into a 'collective will'. In other words, his 'reflexivity' is evident in his *account*. It is this 'essential' reflexivity, as Slack (2000) terms it, which concerns us. It refers to the practices of members in making their actions accountable to others in the setting. As Garfinkel (1967) suggests:

> In exactly the ways that a setting is organized, it consists of members' methods for making evident that setting's ways as clear, coherent, planful, consistent, chosen, knowable, uniform, reproducible connections – i.e. rational connections. In exactly the way that persons are members to organized affairs, they are engaged in serious and practical work of detecting, demonstrating, persuading through displays in the ordinary occasions of their interactions the appearances of consistent, clear, chosen, planful arrangements. In exactly the ways in which a setting is organized, it consists of methods whereby its members are provided with accounts of the setting as countable, storyable, proverbial, comparable, picturable, representable – i.e. accountable events. (Garfinkel, 1967:34)

Having said all this, what is less obvious in the above extracts is the fact that this account is 'recipient designed'. In other words, what is being said here is being said to the researcher and being said in relation to what the principal knows about the researcher, including the fact that they have previously conversed about these matters. In just the same way, the researcher's observations, brief as they are, are similarly constructed. In saying this, we do not seek to *problematize* the principal's account but to recognize that it is precisely an account generated in and through a specific situation – an interview with a researcher. It is a feature of 'ethnomethodo-logically informed ethnography', as with any other, that it will depend on the researcher's accumulated knowledge; their organizational position and history, and so on. Where we differ from the postmodernists is in respect of the problem this poses. We believe our analytic choices largely obviate the difficulties insofar as understanding the world in this 'common-sense' way brackets the problem of whether the world is 'really' like this. Insisting on the choices we outline above – being data-driven; the analytic interest in unique adequacy; the ambition of 'vulgar competence'; the interest in the processual character of interaction; and so on – acts as prophylaxis. If members talk and act sincerely on the basis of their accumulated organisational knowledge, then so do we.

Ethnomethodology – Understanding Mundane Work

Just as we cultivate a broad indifference to method, viewed as a professional activity, so too we have much the same attitude to academic theory. Our analytic strategy is taken from a radical alternative to the kinds of socio-logical, psychological, management theory and other interests that come together in 'leadership studies'. These disciplinary interests are always theoretical. Ours are not. The value of the theories in question relates to disciplinary approbation, not to their relevance to practitioners. This is not to say that theory is necessarily irrelevant to practitioners, but leaders show their interest in theory and its application in some demonstrable way, in their practices. We do not disapprove of theory; we are indifferent to it. Theories must be judged on the claims they make. If they claim to make a contribution to our understanding of management theory, sociology, or what have you, then they have to be judged by the standards that those disciplines apply. Whether they serve any other kind of purpose – and in the context of leadership studies and the claims made for it, we might imagine that they would help us understand what 'leaders' do when they do 'leadership'; how to do it well, and so on – is open to question. Our prefer-ences lie in a 'data-driven' stance. In studying 'leaders', we aim, as best we can, to develop a way of understanding how leaders themselves construe 'good' or 'best' practice and how they implement change by emphasizing the ordinary and practical skills exhibited when leaders are 'getting the job done'. The primary emphasis in this study, then, is on understanding the everyday, practical accomplishment of leadership, rather than on 'theorizing' such work as exemplars or indicators of more general social processes. It seeks to *understand* leadership through the provision of 'thick descriptions' (Geertz, 1973) of the practical, everyday, accomplishment of leadership work, and to develop a nuanced understanding of the 'skills' of leadership in educational settings.

New theories are seldom accompanied by descriptions of how things are actually accomplished 'on the ground'. As Hopkins and Jackson (2003) observe:

> ... despite more than two decades of writing about organizational devel-opment we are still in the position of needing to develop understandings about what leadership really involves when it is distributed, how schools might function and act differently, and what operational images of distributed leadership in action might look like. (Hopkins & Jackson, 2003:17)

This is what ethnomethodologists refer to as, 'the loss of the phenomenon' under study and typifies much of the research on leadership that, while it has produced endless leadership theories, has yet to produce an account of leadership practices that would be recognisable to those who actually fulfil the role of leader. Harold Garfinkel, largely responsible for the establishing of ethnomethodology as a serious empirical endeavour, has variously referred to 'quiddity' of 'haecceity' which roughly, if clumsily, translates as 'just-thisness' – the thing that makes whatever is going on whatever it is, rather than just another example of some more general theme (see e.g. Garfinkel, 1991:10). That is, the typical disciplinary emphasis is on generalized, normative prescription in preference to situated, contextualized explication, and in the limited context of leadership in FE, we want to correct that tendency. But of course any given individual organizational member may be too busy doing whatever it is that they are doing to pay a great deal of attention to how they are getting it done, or alternatively may be so 'practised' that they no longer pay attention to exactly how they get things done. Similarly, though we each of us work with other people in an organizational context, we seldom pay attention to the kinds of problem they might have, or indeed what their work looks like to them. For this reason, ethnomethodologists often refer to the 'member's problem' as they try to draw out exactly what it is that the person in question is trying to do. When ethnomethodologists talk about explication instead of explanation they are drawing attention precisely to the need for the production of a body of evidence that demonstrates exactly what is entailed in X, Y and Z doing the things they do in order to produce the outcomes they produce, in the context in which they find themselves. Because ethnomethodology is engaged in the business of making such ordinary, typical, ways of doing things visible to all those who might be interested in how that was done, the result is rich or 'thick' descriptions of the 'just thisness' of the subject matter we are interested in, in this case educational 'leaders' doing whatever it is that they routinely do in order to display 'leadership'. Three aspects appear especially important in this process and in our accounts: the processual character of action; knowing how 'to go on'; and the 'accountability' of practical actions.

The Processual Character of Action

The processual character of activities is arguably fundamental to the ethnomethodological endeavour. If we are interested in the ordinary and the mundane then an obvious feature of this is that much of the time mundane activity involves the sequencing of tasks. That is, the individual is concerned with how they 'order' the things they have to do and, just as importantly, how this ordering is meshed with the things that other people are manifestly engaged in doing. Furthermore, in their actions and their accounts of actions, participants provide us with the only resources we have for making sense of what they are up to. The concern with getting a better understanding of the actor's point of view thus transmutes for ethnomethodology into the examination of the organization of social action *over its course*. This transmutation is a product of a basic feature of ethnomethodological investigations, which is to conceive of the social actor as a 'practical doer'. It is an indisputable fact about members of society that they are continuously engaged in the conduct of practical affairs – crossing the road, going to the supermarket, and, as college principals making presentations to staff, students or governors, conducting staff appraisals and so on. Somehow, some way, things get done, and they do so on the basis of the understandings social actors have of the ways in which the social organization within which they work operates. Their courses of action have an essentially temporal character and in talking about the actor's empirically observable conduct we are necessarily talking about activities that are at some stage in a course of action. Ethnomethodology makes this an integral feature of that analysis, with the actor's point of view always located as some *here and now* within an ongoing course of action. The temporal structuring of the sequence is integral to the production of the course of action itself, and arises from the determinations that the actor, the college principal in our case, makes *as part of the means of carrying out the action*. It is inherent in the answers they give to such questions as, 'where am I up to now? how much have I done? is this course of action turning out as anticipated? what, exactly, do I need to do next?' and so on.

Both the processual character of action and the conception of the social actor as a practical actor are strongly resonant with the observable work of leaders and leadership (in education and elsewhere). In solving problems, making decisions, providing direction and so on, leaders are constantly 'making it up as they go along': dealing with events and situations as they arise, without knowing in advance how things will turn out. Likewise, it is in the nature of their role to be practical doers: to have practical goals and objectives to achieve, and things that need to be done in order to achieve them. They don't have the luxury of hindsight, nor of resting on purely theoretical outcomes. In understanding both the practical work that they do and the methods they use to make sense of the setting in which they are called upon to lead, a focus on these features is essential. If theory tells us that leaders are required to be 'transformational' (for example), it doesn't tell us what this looks like, sounds like, even feels like, from day to day and minute to minute. In the abstraction of analysis, the situated, real-time practices that constitute 'doing transformational leadership' have been lost. In the case of leadership in Further Education, they are, perhaps, yet to be sought – a clear remit thus exists for this study's use of an ethnomethodologically informed approach in an attempt to document the real time, real world practices of educational leaders.

Knowing How to Go On

The later philosophy of Wittgenstein, and particularly his work on rule following and 'knowing how to go on' (Wittgenstein, 1958) has been identified by a number of British ethnomethodologists (e.g. Sharrock and Anderson, 1984; Coulter, 1999; Sharrock and Button, 1999) as akin to the ethnomethodological notion of 'accountability', of accounting for one's actions in such a way as to make them recognizable to others for what they are. 'Rule following' entails an understanding of how a necessarily under-determined set of rules[3] should be applied to a specific situation. The rules can never be fully explicated, and understanding of them is demonstrated by 'knowing how to go on' rather than by an ability to list them. The classic ethnomethodological example of the under-determination of rules, and the role of 'knowing how to go on' as the test of whether a rule has been properly understood, can be found in Wieder's (1974) account of the 'convict code', as a normative set of rules, roles and prescriptions adhered to by residents in a halfway house for convicted offenders. While numerous maxims of the code – for example 'above all, do not snitch' – could be called forth by relevant situations or occasions of their being violated, the code could never be detailed in its entirety. It was not a list of rules that could be written down and, once thus detailed, would contain a rule for every eventuality. Instead it was both articulated and extended through its usage (what Wieder referred to as 'telling the code'): one's understanding of the code was demonstrated by one's appropriate behaviour in situations as they arose. Thus, while inmates could not necessarily tell in advance what the code would require of them in any given situation, they would demonstrate their understanding of it by its occasioned application to each situation as it occurred: that is by 'knowing how to go on'. There are obvious parallels between leadership work and the 'telling' of the convict code: leadership is about 'knowing how to go on' in the face of unanticipated, unpredictable events – about dealing with such events appropriately as they arise and about being seen and recognized as doing so – rather than about following a pre-determined prescription which has been laid out in advance. A leader could no more write down a comprehensive list of how to 'do leadership' than a convict could write down all the requirements and prohibitions of the convict code, yet both can show their understanding of their respective 'rules' when called upon by their circumstances to do so. Thus in performing the recognizable practices of leadership, in 'knowing how to go on', the college principals who participated in this study could arguably be said to have been 'telling the leadership code'.

Such 'knowing how to go on' is similarly linked to what Zimmerman and Pollner (1970) describe as the 'occasioned corpus':

> The features of a setting attended to by its participants include, among other things, its historical continuity, its structure of rules and the relationship of activities within it to those rules, and the ascribed (or achieved) statuses of its participants. Under the attitude of everyday life, these features are "normal, natural facts of life". Under the attitude of everyday life, these features are objective conditions of action that, although participants have had a hand in bringing about and sustaining them, are essentially independent of ... anyone's doing. When viewed as the temporally situated achievement of parties to a setting, these features will be termed the occasioned corpus of setting features. (Zimmerman and Pollner, 1970: 94)

Crabtree, in discussing this formulation, goes on to say that:

> The occasioned corpus assembles a "family" of organizational practices in and through the performance of which *this* or *that* distinct activity is accomplished, coordinated with other activities, and some aspect of organization produced and produced locally. Thus, the occasioned corpus assembles the family of organizational practices whereby organizational activities are ordered, and ordered as "routine" activities "within" the working division of labour. (Crabtree, 2000:228)

In implementation of this programme, Garfinkel began his studies with the world of our commonplace experience, the social world of everyday life. Again, and because it clears up some misconceptions about ethnomethodology, there is neither a 'realist' claim inherent in the programme nor anything approaching its opposite, an 'idealist' or 'subjectivist' claim. Rather we can start from Schutz' (1970) observation that,

> In our everyday life ... we accept as unquestionable the world of facts which surrounds us as existent out there. To be sure, we might throw doubt upon any *datum* of that world out there, we might even distrust as many of our experiences of this world as we wish; the naïve belief in the existence of *some* outer world, this "general thesis of the natural standpoint", will imperturbably subsist. But by a radical effort of our mind we can alter this attitude, not by transforming our naïve belief in the outer world into a disbelief, not by replacing our conviction in its existence by the contrary, but by suspending belief. We just make up our minds to refrain from any judgement concerning spatiotemporal existence, or in technical language, we set the existence of the world "out of action", we "bracket" our belief in it. (Schutz, 1970:58)

That is, we can resist (or bracket) any ontological or epistemological claims and limit enquiry purely and simply into the way in which members orient to their world, a world which *for them* has an objective, naturally occurring, reality.

The Accountability of Practical Actions

It is apparent from the above that enquiry into the routine activities of people at work is a typical feature of our approach. Another way of putting this is to say there is a focus on *practice*. We choose to observe how activities unfold and how reasoning will be embedded in the activities themselves and the talk around them. The things that are said while accomplishing tasks serve to make the accomplishment of the task intelligible, and what is done serves to orient us to what is said. Thus ethnomethodology is concerned to look at work activities as socially organized phenomena: to examine them in terms of the actions that make them happen and make them what they are. Hence:

> ... [to] talk of social actions as accountable is to talk of them as observable and reportable, to say that they are such that people can see them for what they are and can tell each other about them. (Sharrock and Anderson, 1986:57).

This organization of actions as recognizable and intelligible is contained in the idea of 'accountability', a term intended to convey the notion that actors design their actions such that their sense, their meaning, is immediately apparent to other social actors involved in the setting. Social actions are, then, necessarily observable and reportable. We make sense of the activities and talk of others in and through those activities and that talk. Social organization of whatever kind could not be otherwise: for social organization to 'work' it has to be accountable to the members of the setting.

In sum, our programme entails understanding the ordinary, practical ways in which 'leaders' go about their business. They will do so in settings that are available to us, and the way in which what is going on in those settings is construed is also available to us in the activity and the talk to be found there, both of which are mutually constitutive. These activities, that talk, are our data. The data does not stand proxy for something – for a theory or other set of assumptions about what is 'really' going on. It stands as a close and careful attempt to understand how these people orient to their world, how in their practices, their reasoning about their 'problem and how to solve it' is undertaken.

Chapter 4

Leadership as Mundane Work

The 'Interactional What' of Leadership

We have already suggested that it is a failing in the study of leadership that the growing profusion of theories has (to our minds, at least) seemed to obscure rather than clarify leadership's true character. In the light of this, it seems ironic that while theories of leadership continue to proliferate, drawing upon different social, political and psychological perspectives (Yukl, 2002; Grint, 1997), very few studies actually venture into the everyday *doing* of leadership. Consequently, as Lynch (1993) indicates, it is a feature of the majority of leadership theories that the phenomenon of interest, what it means to actually be doing leadership, seems to have mysteriously disappeared from the final analysis. In such accounts of leaders and leadership work, instead of examining the activities and interactions that make leadership the recognizably distinct phenomenon it is understood to be by those who work in (in this case) FE colleges, what typically happens is that some kind of theoretical analysis of the varied, abstract, forces that supposedly shape leadership work and various institutions are emphasized. In the process, the particular setting, the FE College, becomes just another incidental arena in which to observe such generalized social, economic and political forces and processes at work. Many of the problems of under-standing leadership work appear then to be an unfortunate by-product of this desire to construct theoretical, 'explanatory' accounts of aspects of social life. For us, and many practitioners, the real problem of most social scientific attempts at understanding leadership, lies in the fact that what results from the various studies is fundamentally unrecognizable to members of the setting under study, leaders and their colleagues. The description and analysis produced explains little and hence is of little value for informing policy or practice. We have pointed already to the way that such *explanations* of the 'underlying realities' miss the 'interactional what' of the occupation studied (Lynch, 1993:271) – the actual and observable business of doing leadership work.

In contrast, for the ethnomethodologist, understanding a setting is a matter of *describing* the practices whereby the members of that setting *make* it understandable to one another, rejecting the application of pre-defined and 'externally-' or 'theoretically-derived' analytic frameworks. It also rejects any claim that 'an understanding' of social organization is achieved through the construction of these kinds of explanatory theories or narratives, as Crabtree et al. (1999) make plain:

> The business of explanation – of abstracting from witnessed appearances and constructing master narratives or models according to the rules and procedures governing the production of factual knowledge of a calculable status – *trades on, offers accounts of and about,* rather than makes visible, the social practices in and through which members produce and manage the daily affairs of a setting ... ethnomethodology eschews explanation and urges the researcher to treat practice as a topic of inquiry through and through rather than a resource for building explanatory constructs. (Crabtree et al., 1999:670, original emphasis)

Following this ethnomethodological policy, this chapter aims to draw on the rich observational data of the study to provide detailed, nuanced descriptions of mundane leadership work as it occurs in daily college life.

Leadership as Mundane Work

One could select almost any extract from the mass of field notes, interview transcripts and documents gathered during the study as being illustrative of the everyday circumstances, practices and activities that constitute the 'real world', situated character of leadership work. In their character as 'mundane' work, these practices are 'an expression of shared order, articulated in generic activities, ordered by protocols, procedures, documentary genres, and other artefacts' (Davenport, 2002:1039). It is their mundaneness which makes them expressive of order: they are recognizable as things that everybody does in ordinary situations. It is through their taken-for-granted-ness that:

> ... orderly social conduct emerges from the detail of each setting in

which it is undertaken, and how orderliness is *achieved* in the face of the endless contingencies to which it is subject. (Dourish, 2001:96, cited in Davenport, 2002)

There is nothing special about the talking, listening, deciding, sending e-mails, attending meetings, etc. that apparently, observably, constitute leadership work: these activities are resources we all have at our disposal. It is their situated accomplishment – and as Alvesson and Sveningsson suggest (2003a), the fact that it is those perceived as '*leaders*' doing them – that makes them significant, that makes them leadership. What follows, then, is a brief selection of some of the skills and activities that may be said to constitute the 'mundane work' of educational leadership.

Leadership: 'Giving a Clear Message'

The notion of leadership as 'giving a clear message' – ensuring that staff, students and parents had a clear idea of what was expected of them and what they in turn might reasonably demand of the college and its staff – was a recurrent theme in both our observations and interviews. As part of their everyday leadership work 'good' leaders give clear messages. However, this was not about the transformational, inspirational communications – 'we will fight them on the beaches' – of the charismatic or visionary leader, but the straightforward communication of objectives, plans, progress and the like that members of the college needed in order to know what they were required to do next in the performance of their own roles. So, for example, references to the '3Rs' (recruitment, retention and results), 'quality' and 'excellence' were a commonplace shorthand for the aims college leaders had for their organizations, reiterated frequently in interactions with staff at all levels:

> [We had] a great inspection report ... we went up in everything, mainly by focusing in on quality. I mean, I started talking about the three Rs – recruitment, retention and results – as soon as I came ... I think most people out there would say I've always given them a clear message. (Kate – Principal)

On occasion, this communication of clarity appeared to descend to the level of prescriptive micro-management:

> Our Quality Team met in December and produced an action plan to

build upon our existing high standards. By any benchmark, our college has state of the art facilities and excellent accommodation. Its support for students is outstanding. Nevertheless, we realize we need to work hard to maintain the high standards and to respond to emerging problems and 'hotspots'. In the meantime, for immediate attention, could we all: Strictly enforce the ban on eating and drinking in class; Communicate our expectation that students should not even bring empty can or food containers into classrooms; Report immediately to line managers any cause for concern about classrooms, e.g. litter, graffiti; Put chairs on desks at the end of the last lesson of daytime classes; Challenge inappropriate student behaviour in public areas or report it.' (Staff Bulletin)

Underpinning the creation of clarity is the performance of 'articulation work', that is 'all the tasks needed to co-ordinate a particular task, including scheduling subtasks, recovering from errors, and assembling resources' (Gerson and Star, 1986:258). Rather than seeing clarity in leadership as the bland simplicity of the vision statement, or the one-off communication of a desired goal, the notion of articulation work recognizes that 'it will always be the case that in any local situation actors 'fiddle' or shift requirements in order to get their work done in the face of local contingencies' (Gerson and Star, 1986:258). Plans are, in practical effect, 'situated actions' (Suchman, 1987). The achievement of clarity requires consistency of purpose in the face of the unexpected: a transparently common thread running through every task and decision. This underlying consistency can be seen across the wide range of activities undertaken by college principals, be it interpreting the edicts of the Learning and Skills Council, monitoring staff in relation to the drawing up of lesson plans or the delivery of the curriculum, or constructing an annual budget. Thus the everyday work of negotiating compromises, devising temporary fixes, utilizing tacit knowledge within the organization, reconciling seemingly incommensurable requirements, etc. in order to get the job done are an integral part of keeping the organization on track (i.e. moving in the direction of whatever goals and objectives have previously been communicated) in the face of unanticipated contingencies. The following extract, from a transcript of a discussion between members of the Senior Management Team (SMT) of Lambton Sixth-Form College, suggests some of the aspects of articulation work as practiced by the Principal, Steven. The discussion concerns the updating of a schedule of things to be done by the team with revized completion dates for outstanding items:

Steven: Right, good. OK, so that's OK. Right, going to the grid then, the stuff in bold is question marks. That was all the stuff from the previous implementation schedule – the stuff that on the 26th of April, which is today, which is in bold – they're all the things that there doesn't appear to have been a determination on and we either have to delete them or attach them to a future date. Right. OK, admin support for ... I'm sorry, learning support is done, student management you're saying speaking next week, Paul?

Paul (Vice Principal): I don't know when it's in the diary for next week. I'll check with Jean (secretary).

Steven: Yeah, if you can – we'll check on what the date of that is. OK. Admin support for our office?

Sue (Vice Principal – Curriculum): I think is sorted. Jenny Collins is willing to do some extra time. I sent Jean to talk to her immediately after she'd come to ask you whether she had a job or not because evening classes were closing down. (laughter) I said, "Jean, now is the time to strike."

Steven: And now the evening classes aren't cancelled, she's got two jobs. OK, and summer building – when are we going to come back to that, Peter?

Peter (Director of Finance): Hum, yes.

Stuart (IT Manager): The teaching accommodation, staff work-rooms – I am now close, like he and I can talk turkey next week.

Steven: Right.

Stuart: I've launched some of these on the unsuspecting public: the more delicate ones, I haven't yet.

Steven: OK. So that could be 14th of May, we might have got those sorted out by.

Stuart: Yeah, that'll be fine.

Peter: We've gone out for quotes on that one. My problem is the one beneath, the final plan for the Registry, and I feel uncomfortable with it going out as final plan for the Registry. I'd like something vaguer for that. I'd like it to say "changes to teaching accommodation and Registry" rather than say final plan.

Steven: Yeah, OK.

Peter: And the surveyor who was coming in last week was ill, and is coming in tomorrow, so – to actually tell us whether or not it's structurally sound. I don't think it works, Stuart, the problem that we were working – the proposal that we were working on before. I don't think we can cram the people in.

Steven: Can we discuss the issue outside. This is simply the piece of communication within side. So the 14th of May is the date we're saying for the next announcement as to what we're doing on the building changes.

Peter: In that case I don't want to raise expectations, then, by saying it's going to be a final plan for Registry.

Steven: No, no, that's fine. As you just said – changes to teaching accommodation and Registry; staff work-rooms and Registry.

The discussion, which is clearly led by the Principal, involves gaining commitments from the Vice-Principal (Paul) and Finance Director (Peter) to complete various tasks by agreed dates, in the light of various contingencies and sensitivities. As the leader of the meeting, Steven sets the pace; decides when the subject is to be moved on (for example, curtailing a discussion of practicalities between Peter and his IT manager – Stuart – which he indicated should be conducted outside the meeting); sanctions proposed courses of action (such as a change in wording to the announcement to be made concerning Registry); and works around delays and uncertainties (Paul being unsure of what's in his diary and the postponement of the surveyor's visit due to illness). In addition to the verbal skills which Steven demonstrates, he also exercises control over the discussion by recording the dates agreed upon, often pausing over an entry in the grid until he is happy with what it is proposed that he should write. The result is a workable schedule of dates for members of the group to work to, which nonetheless enforces their accountability for completion of their commitments. This extended extract demonstrates the messiness of articulation work, and the 'workarounds' (Gergen and Star, 1986) which result, as being a far cry from the sterile tidiness and idealized representations of leadership work presented in most leadership theories. Also evident in this extract, are the elements of distributed coordination (whereby work tasks are performed as part of larger patterns of activity – in this case, all the regular and strategic work which the SMT currently have in hand), the plans and procedures through which such work is supported, and the practices through which an awareness of the work being done is shared with others involved in its accomplishment, which Hughes et al. (1997) propose as a 'framework for the analysis of work'. Hence the tasks being scheduled can be seen as significant elements within the division of labour, or 'steps' within protracted operations, through which ongoing work within the college gets done. By setting dates for completion and updating other members on progress, all within the setting of a regular, procedural meeting, the work is organizationally supported and made visible and intelligible to others involved. Independent of its use as an aid to systems design, for which it was intended, the application of the proposed framework to the data around leadership work serves to illustrate the commonalities between this and other socially organized forms of work: commonalities through the weaving together of which the data attests to these characteristics as a feature of leadership as mundane work.

Leadership and the Mundane Character of Meetings

... meetings remain the essential mechanism through which organizations create and maintain the practical activity of organizing. They are, in other words, the interaction order of management, the occasioned expression of management in action ... (Boden 1994:81)

In *The Business of Talk: Organizations in Action*, Boden (1994) describes meetings as 'the very stuff of management', a place 'where organizations come together' (1994:81). Through her own study of several organizational settings, Boden carefully documents and analyses both the accomplishment of meetings themselves and the role of meetings in the accomplishment of organization. Even if the claim that meetings are 'the very stuff of management' seems a trifle bold, it is difficult for anyone who has spent time in any kind of organization to argue that meetings are not an important and increasingly regular part of working life. Meetings form a central part of organizational work, whether they involve formal gatherings around a table, or more *ad hoc* occasions, in which talk, opinions, information, gossip, or jokes are exchanged. As Boden states, meetings of one kind or another, are very much a part of the *doing* of organization. And as such, the convening, attending, ordering, and following up of meetings is very much a part of *doing* leadership.

For college principals, a significant though mundane requirement of their role is that of making decisions about which meetings to attend:

> ... and the relationship thing about who matters in the county – not who invites you, but who matters. That's a different thing, particularly in B—— because there is a sort of, quite a sort of flattering network of the private schools and H—— Trust and – well, all that sort of certain type of bits of the County Council and other things, and that's all very flattering to get invitations, but actually that won't take the College anywhere. What I'm much more concerned about is school heads, and the university. (Andy – Principal)

On occasions, it is important to be seen at a particular meeting even if it is likely to be uninteresting or unproductive. Similarly, some meetings may be viewed as interesting in and of themselves, but not an effective use of the principal's time in relation to the aims of the organization.

In addition to attending meetings, there is the requirement to prepare for them – to review past meetings, familiarize oneself with what is to be discussed, determine strategies or lines of argument to be employed, and so on. This often entails the rehearsing of an agreed 'story' with other members of staff in order to ensure a confident, seamless 'performance' on the day. This is seen as particularly necessary in the context of the perceived 'audit culture' (Strathern, 2000) of post-incorporation FE:

> A useful pre-meeting. For a set-piece meeting like this (with the LSC [Learning Skills Council]), it's important to be prepared. I feel I know where we are now and we all know what to say. We did this with Ofsted (and got grade 1 for leadership and management – MIW). (Steven – Principal)

The preparation undertaken for a particular meeting is a function of the 'work' the meeting is intended to do. While the ostensible reason for holding a meeting may be, for example, to make a decision on a particular issue, the 'sub-text' may be about gaining consensus for a decision already made; surfacing issues or areas of dissent which may make the decision unworkable; recording individual areas of responsibility within the overall decision, and so on. In each case, the 'work' the meeting is intended to do, and the 'leadership work' required to bring this about is markedly different, even though the surface characteristics of talking, listening, negotiating, deciding and agreeing may be common to all. The range of 'leadership work' alternatives implicit in the various purposes meetings can accomplish, is suggested by the following, although not all principals make this 'sub-text' as explicit to other meeting participants:

> ... the way we operate ... is that if – you know, I want to retain the right to take decisions on some things, some matters. Therefore in terms of the agenda of our Executive we have the sort of classic decision consideration information, and I try to flag up whether I've already got, made the decision by saying – if I say something's for consideration, then that probably means I might reserve the right to not go with the consensus. If it's for decision, that generally means I'll – you know, I will abide by whatever the consensus is and we try very hard for that sort of consensus. (Andy – Principal)

The following extended example from the study data is illustrative of the more subtle sub-texts which the principal as leader may wish to pursue. It also illustrates that, even when not leading the meeting – here, it is the vice-principal, Paul, who is ostensibly in charge of proceedings – the attendance of the principal, as principal, has implications and responsibilities attaching to it. In this instance, it becomes incumbent upon him to step in to resolve a rancorous and deteriorating exchange between two of his senior managers and to refocus the meeting on achieving practical outcomes for the college. As already noted, the skills required to do this are the 'vulgar competences' (Garfinkel, 1967) of talking, listening, negotiating, etc., combined with the exercise of judgement as to when and how to intervene in the situation as it unfolds. Interestingly, in discussing this meeting afterwards with Steven, the principal, he took the view that his intervention should have been at the stage of checking Paul's planning and preparation in advance of the meeting rather than that of reclaiming a difficult situation when it was already in progress. This view was based on his prior knowledge of the personalities involved!

The Senior Management Team is discussing the results of a recent staff satisfaction survey, and has been asked by Paul (the vice-principal) to work in two groups of three to take one area of dissatisfaction and try to understand it from the staff's point of view. They are now reporting back on their discussions:

Paul: So did you get, do you want to pick one of your issues – the staff to staff or – which one, did you choose or pick one?

Sue: We took the lack of recognition and valuing one.

Paul: OK, and how far did you get with it?

Sue: Well, Lorna (Curriculum Manager, and most junior, member of the SMT) told us, essentially, what she thinks the teaching staff feel.

Paul: Which is?

Sue: That it's all about powerlessness and lack of control, and our lack of understanding of that, I think. Or lack of caring about it.

Steven: What's the solution to that, though? Or what are actions we could take that might ameliorate it?

Sue: Well, you can let people teach who they want to teach, when they want to teach them and what they want to teach them, and that would make it all better.

Steven: (long pause) I think we have to have more than that. (laughter) Because that's actually a denial of professional responsibility, isn't it?

Sue: Well, what I was saying is that this is true, but all of the opposite is the nature of teaching, as a job.

Steven: Go on – you've lost me.

Sue: Because you work to a timetable that someone else writes, you teach the kids that someone else puts in front of you, at the times that someone else tells you you will, and you teach them the content that someone else has already decided in the order that someone else has decided, you know, and the speed and even these days, God help us, the methodology that someone else has decided. So there isn't a lot of autonomy, but that is true of all teachers.

Steven: Mmm.

Peter: And it is true of all employees.

Sue: Yeah.

Stuart: But I mean all, in many respects, teachers have traditionally had a lot of autonomy. Once they got inside the classes, they could do what the hell they like, really. And the fact that it's moving away from that now, it's not the way teachers have worked. For some teachers, I think it's quite a difficult issue, and has been for a long time, and what was deemed fine before because no one knew what they were doing anyway, is now up for discussions and debate and control.

Steven: Mmm.

Stuart: And you can't avoid that, can you?

Steven: That's part of the cultural change in approach to teaching, so how – what can we do to manage that cultural change that at least gets a greater level of acceptance? They may never love it, but this is actually how it is, and there isn't any point complaining about it any more. And these are bits over which you do have control – like, they do have control over their scheme of work, don't they, because each course team discusses it and agrees it.

Lorna: Each individual doesn't, though.

Steven: No, but they're part of the team. So it's – it's an issue then about they're seeing themselves as an autonomous individual, not as part of a team that's working towards a collective outcome.

Lorna: I don't think schemes of work are an issue.

Steven: Right. Well, what is then?

Lorna: Erm ...

Steven: Is it anything we can do anything about?

Dissent from the process proposed by Paul is already in evidence here as the more practical, pragmatic Sue (also a vice-principal and definitely more 'hard-nosed' in her approach) suggests a flippant response to the question of how to make staff feel more valued. The implication of her statement that you can 'let people teach who they want to teach, when they want to teach them, and what they want to teach them' seems to be that the exercise in empathy they have been asked to engage in is soft and wishy-washy and likely to result in a proposal to give them exactly what they want irrespective of the consequences for students. Steven's measured reply forces her to expand upon her meaning without being directly challenging: the result is to generate a sensible discussion of the issue. Having made a corrective intervention, Steven largely returns to the watching brief he had previously adopted (the aim of which he has already stated as being to develop them as a team by encouraging pro-activity and responsibility across the group), participating in the discussion by asking questions rather than by expressing opinions. His tone is that of an interested colleague talking with peers: a member of the group rather than its leader. The effect is to broaden the discussion to include the two, more junior, members of the team (Stuart and Lorna) who it is part of the sub-text of the meeting to 'bring forward'. Despite this 'non-leading leader' role, it is evident from the nature of Steven's questions ('Well, what is then?' and 'Is it anything we can do anything about?') that he is frustrated by the lack of direction being exercised by Paul, and the absence of any practical decisions being made. As the discussion subsequently goes off track again – this time with an acrimonious exchange between Paul and Peter (the finance director) – Steven judges it is time to step into a conspicuous leadership role:

Peter: We're talking about things that we don't have an idea how to tackle. And we're trying to anticipate problems that we cannot yet define, whereas what we do have in front of us are problems that have been defined and have been defined for three, six, eight months, and coming back to Stuart's point, if I can paraphrase what Stuart said: If we continue to dither without actually saying "this is what we're going to do", people are either going to think that we're indecisive – God forbid – or they're going to say "they don't really think that the problems are valid, or that our suggested solutions are worthwhile". We have to pick off some of these things that we can tackle, get them underway, and we've got to then move forward. And what we have to do is, we have to keep a blinkered view on what is beneficial for us as an institution, not what makes Rosemary happier, but whether or not making Rosemary happier will produce some tangible benefit for that department or for us as an institution. But we have to be decisive, and there must be half a dozen things in these two papers that we can – we can accept and adopt and say, "right, next Tuesday, or whenever the staff meeting is, we're going to do this, and it's come from our consideration of your inputs" and we'll move on. And there's – this hasn't tackled it, lots of other things. And we could have done this if we hadn't have wandered off on this patronizing charade, we could have finished this by 6 o'clock.

Lorna: But isn't the point that we can't find the half-dozen ...

Peter: So let's do it now. Oh, can we not?

Lorna: Well, I think if we could have found them six months ago, we would have done.

Peter: All right, then. All right. I commend to you the recommendations, under c, of the, of my task group report, so I have to ...

Lorna: Right.

Paul: I object to this, to your "patronizing ... "

Peter: Well, it is.

Paul: Well, I've got to say ...

Peter: We're not 18 ...

Paul: Peter, Peter, I object to your concluding comments, it was not patronizing. This is meant to be a serious attempt to get to the bottom of some difficult issues that I ...

Peter: Well, I found the approach was so.

Peter: I know you do, Peter, but you're not the most receptive to these sort of processes ...

Steven: Right, can we ...

Paul: ... and, we've all ...

Steven: Can we ...

Paul: We've avoided it for long enough, and we can't continue to avoid it.

Steven: Right, can we draw a line under that. The point's been noted, and let's move on to try and identify some solutions.

Peter: Right.

Steven: Yep? And identifying what areas that we can take action on. (pause) OK? Right then, What – we have a range of proposals, some in Paul's paper, some in Peter's paper, some from the staff satisfaction feedback, and we can either attempt to chunk these up, or we attempt to just identify whether they are issues that we're – or they are actions that we are willing to pick up and run with, or need to look at. And I think we may be having a two-stage, some things we need to park, and some things that we need to say yes, we can move ahead. Paul?

In this second extract, Steven's perceived authority as principal of the college enables him to take over the running of the meeting, draw a line under the disagreement between his two senior managers and assert his own agenda in terms of the need to move ahead and reach some practical conclusions. At the same time, he does this without taking sides (by acknowledging some potential solutions from the papers written by both the protagonists) and without completely over-riding Paul. Thus, his reference to the vice-principal at the end of the extract ('Paul?') provides recognition that it is still Paul's meeting, and that he needs to give the OK to the way forward which Steven has proposed. What needs to be 'parked' is the issue of how the meeting degenerated in the way it did: this is something which he later discusses with Paul and Peter individually, by asking each of them how they could have avoided the situation or handled it better. This intervention by Steven is typical of the 'workarounds' and 'fixes' discussed above in the context of articulation work. What is being worked around here is the very different characters and management styles of two members of the team, with the 'fix' being a face-saving public approach to bringing the meeting to a close followed by private coaching discussions with those involved. The extract is also indicative of the possible 'work' the principal may have been attempting to do with his senior managers, over and above that contained in the explicit agenda for the meeting. This may have included expressing confidence in his vice-principal by asking him to lead the meeting; providing a (missed?) opportunity for coaching him for leadership; gaining buy-in to solutions to the issue under discussion which he already had in mind, as well as the aims of developing his senior managers as a pro-active team; and bringing forward the more junior members already mentioned.

Bureaucracy as Leadership Work

While administrative tasks are a recognized part of almost any managerial role, the burden of bureaucracy in educational leadership was greatly increased by incorporation, which 'forced college principals to satisfy external performance indicators' and produced a regulatory environment in which 'the temptation is to inform and validate policy by the use of quantitative data' (Jephcote et al, 1996, drawing on Elliot and Crossley, 1994). The perceived ratcheting-up of the audit burden and the sense of 'audit culture' (Strathern, 2000) this generated were met by an increase in the 'gambits of compliance' (Bittner, 1965) – being seen to comply with external requirements while at the same time using the system to meet internal goals – employed at college level in dealing with their government paymasters. The prevalence of an 'audit culture', involving considerable time and effort – by the leadership and staff alike – being devoted to making the work of the college accountable rather than to the delivery of 'first order', student-focused outcomes, is clear in the fieldwork observations made during the study. The work involved is routine, meticulous and unglamorous – mundane in every sense of the word – but its implications for every aspect of the college's well-being (funding, levels of provision, career prospects for staff, to name but a few) make its accomplishment a key role of the college leadership. The following sequence of field note extracts, relating to Lambton's bid for Premium Funding,[1] illustrates both the construction and performance element of the audit process, and the time-consuming nature of the underlying work practices.

Field note extract 1: SMT meeting reviews funding and planning paper prepared for the LSC – no clear guidelines as to what they want, so huge variety in what each area has provided. Steven (Principal) briefs people on how to use the draft documents at tomorrow's meeting with the LSC: use it as a prompt but don't hand it out. Need to know more about what they want in order to prepare a document for them. Steven coaches people in how to approach the meeting and how to handle questions, so they are all "telling the same story".

Field note extract 2: Peter (Director of Finance) gives other members of the SMT a clear walk-through of the financial data, and their implications for meeting LSC funding criteria. Steven: "If it's ten more IT students we need another teacher, if it's ten more modern languages then it's straight profit."

Field note extract 3: Steven works through the numbers, checking them on a calculator – likes to be one step ahead in terms of clarity – then rehearses the argument in terms of implications for funding programme ... as people leave Steven says, "A useful meeting. For a set piece like this, it's important to be prepared. I feel I know where we are now and we all know what to say. We did this with Ofsted."

Thus, the documents produced to meet an external audit requirement, and the accounts which underpin them, represent 'gambits of compliance' (Bittner, 1965) in respect of the perceived rules of conduct imposed by external agencies, such that the process through which decisions are made can be seen as 'extending to the rule the respect of compliance, while finding in the rule the means for doing whatever needs to be done.' (Bittner, 1965:273) Steven and his colleagues know what provision they want to make for students within the college, and use the audit framework imposed by their funding body as a vehicle for justifying the required resourcing. In order to maximize their chances of obtaining the funding they are seeking, the entire senior management team engages in a series of rehearsals – coached by Steven – for the forthcoming meeting. Similarly, Steven familiarizes himself with the relevant figures; how they have been derived; what their implications are for different elements of curriculum provision, and so on. Getting the funding is not about impassioned, visionary appeals, but about solid preparation for the contingencies of the meeting with the LSC.

Also in evidence here is the role of documents as artefacts or embodiments of leadership: they remain as a residue of the leadership work that has gone into their construction and agreement. In so saying, more is being claimed than that they provide a necessary audit trail against which accountabilities can be measured and praise or blame apportioned. Although paper records do satisfy this requirement, they are also an integral feature of the work itself. The processing of documents acts as a medium through which organizational actions are embedded, and the actioning of that which a document records serves as part of the transformation process through which one set of organizational actions initiates others. This is true both of the routine manner in which document formats shape the work that is performed through their use, and – as in the above example – where the construction of a major artefact can set in train a significant sequence of events, such as the initiation of new projects and the allocation of the additional responsibilities which thus arise on receipt of Premium Funding. The processes that follow from the construction and use of such paper artefacts are, as Rouncefield (2002) notes:

> ... one of the ways in which the interdependencies within a division of labour are achieved. Records are not, therefore, detached commentaries on activities but integral features of them, possessing a procedural implicativeness for the actions of organizationally relevant others because they represent organizational events and, in this way, are tied to the production and performance of organizational events. (Rouncefield, 2002:197)

Thus the 'work' of documents can be seen as processual and facilitative, acting as a prompt in the matter of 'knowing how to go on' (Wittgenstein, 1958). This is in addition to their recognized role as a repository of organizational memory and a medium through which the requirement for an audit trail can best be satisfied.

Leadership as 'Emotional Labour'

In this section we are interested in documenting some observations of the mundane work of 'emotional labour' or 'emotion work' (Hochschild, 1983) performed by leaders as part of their own everyday work. By this we mean the greetings, the smiles, the 'well done's', as well as the occasional indications of anger or disappointment, and so on that college principals regularly use to convey their opinions, their thanks and their expectations to their staff, their students and others. The idea of 'emotional labour' comes from Hochschild who, in her seminal work *The Managed Heart* (1983), draws attention to the increasing requirement for workers to manage their emotions to express only those deemed appropriate to any given situation. The fixed smile and friendly, helpful manner of airline cabin crew – even in the face of the most difficult, unappreciative passenger – is presented as the epitome of 'the social actor's ability to work on emotion in order to present a socially desirable performance and capitalism's appropriation of that skill' (Bolton and Boyd, 2003:291). Hochschild's work has inspired a range of studies, many of which critique a cynical interpretation of the kind of emotion work – 'service with a smile' – that is supposedly present in everyday work (see Bolton and Boyd, 2003). Looking specifically at education, for example, Price (2001) suggests that teachers' emotional labour is rarely a cynical act but involves drawing on 'very ordinary, universal capacities for relating to others as deserving of recognition, empathy and respect' (Price, 2001:179). Similarly Ogbonna and Harris' (2004) study of lecturers identifies emotional labour as a fundamental part of the strong professional expectations they had of themselves.

These decidedly more complex treatments of the topic have resonance with the character of emotional labour as it emerged in our study of the role of educational leaders. We do not suggest that principals are cynically acting their part. Clearly, the leadership work of a college principal or head of department requires the adaptability of a skilled emotional manager, and appears to be underpinned by values and beliefs that see such work as valuable. The congruence of displayed emotions (i.e. emotional labour) with felt emotions seems typical of the principals shadowed in the present study. So for example, when asked whether leadership was a performance, one principal responded:

> It's an effort of will – one which I find I'm naturally able to make. I couldn't live a myth. I could not sustain a performance which fundamentally is not me. And I've come to recognize that I can [make that natural effort], but not everybody can. And of course, I have my bad days and if I have a bad day, that's nobody else's fault. I can choose how I respond. (Patricia – Principal)

Thus, even where educational leaders are actively managing their emotions, there is an underpinning sense of authenticity (Erickson, 1995) in what they are presenting: emotions may be moderated – or even accentuated – in line with the expectations of others or the demands of the situation, but overall are congruent with the beliefs and values which are genuinely felt. As another principal said:

> It seems to me that the investment in the emotional involvement of staff

is important, because if we care about our students ... I'm expecting my teaching staff to invest in the same way with their students. And it's something we work hard at in our college, so it would be difficult, I think, not to invest emotionally or engage with the staff like that who you want to, you know, engage with students and care about students. (Maggie – Principal)

That it is still a labour, however – an active piece of management from which the principal can, on occasion, require a respite – is indicated by the following acknowledgement from Patricia. After saying that her professional performance as a happy, supportive, positive principal is an effort of will which she finds easy to make because it is congruent with her natural persona, she goes on to say:

The only place where I am ever miserable is within my immediate office, with the people who work immediately to me. Because if I walk down the corridor looking unhappy and that person hasn't seen me for three months, they will then regard me as inconsistent. So you have to also bear in mind the frequency and the context in which people see you, what their expectations are, and of course, if I'm going to maintain my sanity, I have to have the option of completely losing it! (Patricia – Principal)

The need to appear emotionally consistent with staff is so taken-for-granted here as to not even appear to Patricia herself as something she has to work to achieve. In contrast, however, the need for a bolt-hole where she can 'lose it' – show the emotions she is really feeling – suggests an almost constant emotional labouring in the maintenance of her professional, consistent image beyond her office door. This combination of value congruence and emotional labour, often in the pursuit of a mutually perceived professional image, appears to be a new and interesting aspect of the emotional labour construct as it occurs within the professions and other environments where the 'pure' commercialization of emotion may not apply. Arguably however, in professional and public sector situations (O'Brien, 1994) the employment of emotion work may take the form of a routine mechanism of social control for the achievement of socio-cultural and/or wider political ends. By mediating what information is conveyed in leader–staff interactions, it serves to create a particular relationship between the parties involved – be it one of trust, authority, fear or support – which operates to further particular aims and objectives within the organization or beyond. This idea of 'control through communication' (Yates, 1989) is echoed in the various communication genres (Yates and Orlikowski, 1992) – for example, the news letters, staff briefings, satisfaction surveys, and appraisal reports referred to elsewhere in this book – each loaded with emotional as well as factual content, through which the leadership shapes the information it chooses to share.

Emotional Labour and 'Feeling Valued'

'Feeling valued' is one of the possible outcomes of the everyday emotional labour of leaders – though other outcomes are easy to imagine. The notion of 'feeling valued' (White and McKenzie-Davey, 2003) captures an individualized, positive, emotional response to the praise or recognition of others – in this case, those viewed as organizational leaders – which is not just about job satisfaction (e.g. Iaffaldano and Muchinsky, 1985), or job commitment (e.g. Millward and Hopkins, 1998). Instead, it is seen as arising from a moment-by-moment, real-time expression of value for some ability or quality considered to be important, and to reside in a sense of fairness or appropriateness of such expressions. As such, it can incorporate a melange of emotions (pleasure, embarrassment, satisfaction, pride) and observable behaviours.

The role of leaders, college principals, in making employees feel valued is a topic that has seldom been seriously addressed by researchers. What appears to be involved (White and Mackenzie-Davey, 2003) is a cluster of personal and organizational factors including employees' perceptions of fairness, recognition and feedback (Kluger and DeNisi, 1996), as well as inspirational leadership (Conger and Kanungo, 1994) and feelings of inclusion and participation (Shadur, Kienzle and Rodwell, 1999). Of course this is a difficult research area: it is difficult to directly access people 'doing valuing' or 'doing being valued'. Some behaviours, perhaps indicative of feeling valued may be 'grossly observable' – a smile of pleasure, a returning of thanks – others may not. If someone is disappointed by a lack of recognition, but strives to appear professional, their feeling of not being valued may go unobserved. Similarly, if someone works harder after receiving a compliment on their performance over the past year, an observer may be tempted to say the one was a cause of the other, but the ethnographer is not entitled to do so – other reasons may include enjoyment of the particular task being performed, desire to finish it before going on holiday, a fast approaching deadline, and so on.

Instead of pursuing 'feeling valued' in this (potentially unproductive) way, we attempted to discover how members, principals and staff, construct and reproduce notions of what it is to show value or feel valued through paying attention to their accounts of instances when it did (or did not) occur. There are obviously potential pitfalls in any attempt to gather verbal data on mental (or emotional) topics or processes (see Nisbett and Wilson, 1977). Clearly it is possible that, in talking about valuing practices by their perceived leaders, teachers and support staff are, in fact, 'telling the code' (Wieder, 1974): rehearsing and reconstructing a mutually understood pattern of what is expected in that situation by members of it, and using it as a sense-making device for new events.

As we followed FE principals carrying out their daily work, we paid some attention to the valuing practices of leaders – the day-to-day actions and words through which they seek to demonstrate the value they ascribe to the work of their staff. In part, this is because it offers an indication of the extent to which such leadership work – and especially emotional labour – can be seen as being effective, i.e. to what extent staff felt valued by practices designed to achieve that end. However, at no point in our observations did a principal actually say, 'today I'm going to do valuing people': instead, it happened routinely, as a mundane component of other interactions and tasks. Valuing and feeling valued occurred as an unproblematic social accomplishment of everyday conduct, based on some shared understandings of what constitutes praise, when criticism might be perceived as constructive, what behaviours deserve to be rewarded, and so on. The recognizability of such practices, as they are mutually understood in their situated usage, has been a taken-for-granted resource in previous studies of leadership at work: here, they are treated as a topic in their own right through the explication of some of the abundant examples. Accordingly, we document the considerable time and effort devoted to valuing practices by college principals, and the manner in which notions of feeling valued are socially constructed within the college setting.

Our observations suggest that valuing practices take a variety of forms. Attending a staff retirement party, giving detailed, quality feedback on a teaching observation report, saying 'good morning' to staff while walking down the corridor: all the principals observed, consciously undertook a number of activities designed to make public their appreciation of work, to present the 'human face' of leadership to their staff. It was also clear that this work of valuing staff was seen as an important part of the leadership role, and a necessary set of skills for the effective college principal. Recognizing and understanding what makes individual members of staff feel valued, when staff need praise or when constructive criticism will be more effective, were clearly important in accomplishing the work of leadership, effectively constituting part of the 'knowledge work', part of the 'organizational acumen' of principals.

One aspect of valuing staff seemed to be spending time with them, being accessible to them, and recognizing their interests rather than merely seeing them as resources to fulfil tasks. In the following extract, the principal adapts to these 'human' or social needs of a number of staff, making himself available to them and showing an interest in their non-work-related activities:

> Field note extract: Steven (Principal) leaves his office to go "walkabout" round the college. A recent staff survey said senior management were too distant: trying to address this by being seen about the college regularly. Steven says "hello" to a member of staff in the corridor, and comments on England's performance at cricket over the weekend: knows the member of staff is a keen fan. Goes out to the main gate to talk to security staff: there was trouble at the college bus stop the previous evening and wants to check the staff are OK. Then goes to the staff room for a cup of coffee and a chat with whoever's there: making himself visible to anyone who wants to talk to him.

Constructive criticism can be as much a valuing practice as praise and recognition for a job well done. Taking time to talk these issues through in a way that is neither patronizing nor artificially encouraging is seen as an important means of valuing a staff member's current contribution, encouraging future development and maintaining motivation. In the next fieldwork extract the principal had taken time to prepare, both by gathering all the relevant information and by thinking through the most appropriate approach to take with the individual concerned in order to set a constructive, forward-looking tone:

> Field note extract: Helen (Curriculum Manager) has recently been unsuccessful in gaining promotion to the position of Director for Widening Participation, and has asked Steven (Principal) for feedback as to why she was not selected. Steven wants to make sure the meeting is positive and developmental, as he doesn't want her to feel under-valued and leave her current job. He talks Helen through the grade sheet completed by those who assessed her application against pre-set criteria for the role, giving equal weight to the strengths and weaknesses

she demonstrated: e.g. clear depth of knowledge in her own area, but didn't demonstrate thinking or ability in the wider areas she would need to step up to if she got the job. Steven encourages Helen to draw her own conclusions about where she needs to develop in order to be more successful next time (Helen: "So it's about the leadership, not the management." Steven: "Yes, that's right.") and suggests training opportunities and project work which might help her gain the skills and experience she needs. Conversation is honest and open, gives clear reasons for the decision made without being apologetic or patronizing, and focuses on the practical steps required for future development. Helen looks happier as the meeting progresses and talks more confidently about what she intends to do going forward.

These extracts suggest emotional labour and 'valuing practices' from the point of view of the principal. Whether staff regard these activities in the same fashion is debateable, for their meaning *as* valuing practices requires intersubjective negotiation with the staff towards whom they are directed: only if they are recognized and mutually understood and oriented to, as such, do they become instances of valuing practices rather than simply passing on information, or worse, being sarcastic, making fun, etc. Staff can also feel valued by a recognition of the difficulties of their job, or their personal commitment in dealing with them, irrespective of the outcomes achieved. In the data gathered for this study, it was more often the absence of this recognition than its presence, which was felt, with consequent expressions of the negative effects on motivation and commitment. For example, after listing a number of personal difficulties that had led her to go from full-time to part-time, one teacher said:

Now I worked – this sounds real sour grapes – but I worked really hard to hand over, and I handed over spick, span and perfect – and this is a team I built up, I started it, it's the biggest one in the college – and it's such a little thing, but on my last day nobody, nobody, not one person said thank you.... All it needed was just somebody to say, "thanks, we know it was hard" ... and nobody. So I just ... (shrugs). (Julie – Teacher)

Given the shared understanding which clearly exists over what constitutes valuing/being valued, it is interesting that senior management and staff can appear to have very different perceptions as to whether it is actually happening. In particular, whether the setting is constructed as one in which staff are trusted by management, appears to be an important factor in the extent to which valuing practices by leaders are successfully 'brought off'.

Conclusion: Leadership as Mundane Work

Through the explication and analysis of some of the mundane features of leadership work, the study suggests that 'leadership' as a phenomenon, quality, or ability can be argued to be virtually indistinguishable from other kinds of administrative and managerial work. Indeed, as Alvesson and Sveningsson (2003b) have observed, when one actually looks at what leaders do, 'leadership' as a concept almost seems to disappear. Admittedly, this is the inevitable result of almost any deconstructive exercise, and one could simply argue that it is not that 'leadership' itself is a distraction, but rather that leadership work is not necessarily that special or different from other kinds of work carried out in organizations. While many of the tasks accomplished by college principals – obtaining funding for a new college building, dealing with the LSC, setting standards for staff and students – are certainly a part of doing 'good' leadership, the way in which these tasks are done is actually quite ordinary. Meetings are held; proposals are planned, written and re-written; e-mails and letters are written and telephone calls are made; committees are attended, etc. What we are at pains to point out, however, is that although this kind of leadership work is not that different or unusual from management work or administrative work (or many other forms of work), the actual way in which such work is carried out is an, as yet, under-explored part of precisely what it means to be an educational leader in the learning and skills sector.

Indeed, one of the central findings of the study is that one of many skills involved in being a college principal is the accumulation of what Bittner (1965) has termed 'organizational acumen' – the ability and entitlement to interpret rules and procedures in a way that suits a particular organizational purpose. The data yields numerous examples where college staff at all levels of the organization have developed organizational acumen to achieve high grades at annual inspections, meet internal and external performance targets, or make figures and statistics tell a variety of credible stories to stakeholders. Yet such work is rarely covered in traditional studies of organizational leadership and decision-making. Certainly one of the reasons for this oversight in organizational research is due to the sensitivity that surrounds such efforts, but it is also, perhaps, because few studies of everyday practice exist, that can observe and record these practices in action. In this study, however, we see the mundane work that constitutes 'good leadership' stripped of its leadership trappings. Good leaders, the data suggests, are competent and skilled in Bittner's (1965) 'gambits of compliance'. They know what stories to tell at the right times, they know what figures to produce, how and when. They are skilled in managing performances, images and interpretations. Yet such skills are not the esoteric preserve of 'leadership'. These are skills available to anyone working in an organization, and utilized by managers and staff at all levels. If there is anything special about leadership, it is simply that researchers have yet to realize the importance of the largely unexplicated and seemingly invisible 'managerial work' that is essential in the doing of educational leadership: the daily 'grunt work' which, through consistency and ubiquity, serves to make the more traditional aspects of leadership, the vision and strategy of popular leadership theory, possible and relevant.

None of the fieldwork examples presented in this chapter is a particularly dramatic instance of the exercise of leadership. Instead, our research supports the claim that leadership is an everyday phenomenon, appearing in various mundane guises. In consequence, the examples are themselves mundane and very ordinary (and far more prolific than is reported here) in their invocation of a hierarchical relationship that exists, and is known to exist, by the parties to the occasion. It is a relationship that is unproblematically accepted as 'this is the way things are', extended in time and space. Leadership is something that is locally accomplished in action and whose coherence and very recognizability as 'leadership' is only understandable in the situated 'grammar' (Wittgenstein, 1958) of its achievement. So phrases uttered by 'leaders' – such as 'get this sorted out' or 'we need to get the numbers right' – do not in themselves indicate 'leadership'. Leadership acts as an appropriate description for what is 'going on' because the words, the tone with which they are said and, most importantly, the setting, the courses of action and the relationships within which they occur, act as documentary evidences of the mundane exercise of 'leadership'. Our research approach emphasizes understanding such leadership work as 'everyday practice', as a practical and ongoing *accomplishment* as opposed to more theoretically, sociologically informed *idealizations* of such work. Leadership in education consists of complex, but ultimately mundane and ordinary practices. Such work involves formally recognized leaders such as college principals, but also senior and middle managers, teaching staff and administrators working throughout the college. It is about arriving at *shared understandings* – and various mundane interactional competences are routinely observed to play an important part in leadership activity – such as knowing how to preface, repair and produce formulations, tell stories, develop scenarios, and so on. Knowing how to build a recognizable and coherent scenario draws upon assumed sets of common-sense understandings about 'how we do this kind of work' and 'how we get into this position'. Appeals to such common-sense recognizability are at the heart of this interactional work. But, there is no special or arcane skill here. Observations of leaders involved in 'real world, real-time' work have simply documented what Garfinkel termed 'vulgar competences' (Garfinkel, 1967) – competences or resources available to just about anyone – the ability to provide a story, a justification, a reason, an excuse – and to couch it in terms recognisable and relevant to the hearer. In this important sense, leadership is 'recipient designed'.

This chapter started by considering the 'mythologization' of leadership in current theory – and the myriad of consultancy, coaching and training literature that the modern preoccupation with leadership has spawned – and where much is made of the distinction between leadership and management. Whereas leadership is associated with strength, vision, power, transformation and change, management is cast as bureaucratic, ordinary, conservative and more concerned with stability (Barker, 1997; Zaleznik, 1977). Indeed, as Sawbridge (2000) has commented in his review of leadership in Further Education, 'leaders are generally people who do the right things, whereas managers are people who do things right' (2000:2). Similarly Fullan (1993) states that leadership is about such things as mission, direction and inspiration while management involves more mundane activities such as planning, implementing and working effectively with people. Such strong distinctions between leadership and management strengthen the notion that leadership involves something more than merely 'getting things done'. As a result, descriptions of what leaders actually *do* are often reduced, or erased from the analysis, in favour of the production of models, concepts and theories that claim to explain what is *really going on* behind the mundane talk and action that characterizes much of everyday life in organizations (Gronn, 1983; Gronn and Ribbins, 1996). Yet, as Alvesson and Sveningsson (2003a) have observed, much of what passes for leadership in organizations has first to be abbreviated and translated from the ordinary and the mundane. As they argue:

… what managers ("leaders") do may not be that special, but because they are managers doing "leadership", fairly mundane acts may be given an extraordinary meaning, at least by the managers themselves. (2003a: 1436).

Chapter 5

Leadership as Presentation, Production and Performance

Introduction

This chapter considers the ways in which educational leadership can be understood in terms of the negotiative and interpretive work that goes into the production of various 'accounts' of leadership work. That is, it documents exactly how leaders understand and respond to the emerging features of an 'audit culture' (Strathern, 2000), and how they make their own work 'accountable' both in respect of the interpretation, selection and production of documents and in the performance of everyday leadership tasks. The significance of 'audit culture' as an emerging managerial philosophy, especially relevant to issues of educational leadership, resides in the need to demonstrate competence, compliance and effectiveness to a variety of audiences. As Strathern (2000) suggests, the philosophy of 'audit' or 'audit culture' – the need to demonstrate the existence of economic efficiency and good practice and not just to practice them – is migrating from its origins in the private sector to become increasingly common in public sector institutions. Within further education this increased demand for accountability takes a variety of forms – most obviously that of Ofsted inspections, but also (at the time of this research) the various forms of reporting required by the Learning and Skills Council as the sector's funding body. Further education colleges are no different from other organizations in that, for those in the sector, it is a commonplace that everyday organizational life often consists of various kinds of 'checking up on each other'. However, the formalization of this checking and monitoring through auditing represents a break with traditional forms of organizational control in education and with its long-standing emphasis on 'professionalism' and 'professional autonomy'. While arguments about professionalism remain, increasing layers of audit are being deployed to ensure quality control – that monitoring mechanisms and procedures are in place – rather than the quality of 'first order' operations (Power, 1994:19) such as teaching and learning. Thus, the audit serves as a means of indirect control over work practices through the monitoring and regulation of other systems of control. In this context, the work of leadership includes a large element of 'justification': the conspicuous presentation of the work of the college – and the outcomes generated – to a wide range of audiences in order to recruit students, obtain funding, achieve a good Ofsted report, etc. There is a strong element of performance in this work – telling a well-rehearsed story to meet the demands of a particular audience – together with a range of activities around selecting and presenting particular pieces of information from the data available in order to construct a winning case. Thus 'calculation work' (Anderson et al., 1989) in this context takes on the form of creative selection and interpretation, rather than simply 'doing the sums' based on transparently available facts and figures. In presenting the public face of the college to its various stakeholders, there also emerges a need to practise strategy as a 'perennially unfinished project' (Knights and Mueller, 2004), constantly developing and being refined in response to external contingencies. It is with these aspects of leadership work that this chapter is concerned.

Leadership as Performance

In talking about leadership as 'performance', we are not really interested in presenting leadership work as a form of acting. Obviously, in *The Presentation of Self in Everyday Life* (1959) Goffman famously presents a dramaturgical analysis of social interaction drawing attention to the relationship between everyday, 'real-world' events and theatrical performances. It would, of course, be easy to present, or rather re-present, our data along familiar Goffmanesque lines of 'front stage' and 'back stage', impressions 'given' and impressions 'given off', etc. But we are not interested in merely fleshing out Goffman's analysis with exemplars from a different setting. While such comparisons can be engaging, our interest carries a rather different analytic and practical purpose. It concerns whether such an approach, and the rich descriptive vignettes it provides, adds much to our understanding of the accomplishment of everyday encounters since such dramaturgical analogies seriously misrepresent most people's (and certainly our college principals') approach to the serious business of everyday life and the extent to which people occupy rather than merely 'play out' social roles. In addition, it is clear that Goffman's (1959) front stage/back stage distinction may well be applied to distinguish between the external audiences for which such performances are given and the behind-the-scenes locations within which preparation and rehearsal take place. Evidently too, when the performance is given, members are expected to keep to the agreed script and present the college in a positive light; any disagreements, blunders or negotiations of the 'right' version of events are contained within the more private, 'back stage' environment of the college. However, while Goffman's notion of front stage/back stage is used to distinguish between locations where actors are 'on show' and may be said to be performing and those which are private and where they can be 'natural', the ethnomethodological view of performance is somewhat different. For ethnomethodology, the notion of performance necessarily entails elements of planning, preparation and rehearsal that are absent from Goffman as well as lacking the inevitable implication of individuals 'playing at' a role.

As already mentioned, the advent of an 'audit culture' (Strathern, 2000) in further education has prompted the development of new kinds of accountability and has generated new managerial and organizational forms and technologies through which such accountabilities can be expressed. The concept of the audit, previously constrained within financial applications, has now expanded to become a ubiquitous element of daily life, with the learning and skills sector being no exception. The result is a raft of 'technologies of accountability' – systems and procedures as well as the physical technologies which support them – which 'do as much to construct definitions of quality and performance as to monitor them' (Power, 1994:33). Hence Power (1994, 1997) suggests that although organizational life often consists of 'checking up on each other', the formalization of this checking and monitoring through auditing represents a break with traditional forms of organizational control. This is strongly evident in the learning and skills sector, where the notion of 'professional autonomy' as the driving force behind quality provision, without the need for externally imposed controls, remains prevalent, often resulting in resistance to the impositions of external regulatory bodies. In addition to the source of quality audit having moved from practitioners to external bodies, what is to be measured has also changed, with the new emphasis being on the underlying 'second order' systems and mechanisms of quality rather than the 'first order' outcomes they generate. So, for example, Ofsted inspectors will review documentation relating to lesson planning and lesson observations as an indicator of the quality of teaching and learning, and check that governors' meetings are properly conducted and minuted as a measure of the quality of college governance.

The ability to be able to 'account' for their activities, to be able to present a plausible, reasoned justification – a 'good story' – also extends to staff at all levels within the college. This is particularly true during an Ofsted inspection, when inspectors will have access to teaching and other staff and will be looking for the reasons behind the figures presented by management. Increasingly, college leadership involves coaching staff in how to respond to this type of questioning, and persuading staff of the need to have evidence and explanations ready in advance of the event. In this case, the presence of inspectors in the college is constitutive of a different 'front stage' (Goffman, 1959) situation from the normal performance of a teacher in front of a class of students, although in each case a conscious performance is (to a greater or lesser extend) being made. The level and type of preparation which precedes the performance and which occurs in the 'back stage' regions of the setting, will also differ: inspections are likely to entail coaching by senior staff; rehearsal of the agreed story; asking questions; admitting errors; and getting facts straight; whereas delivering a lesson may entail the more routine preparation of referring to lesson plans and checking required resources. This new facet of organizational life was openly acknowledged by college principals, for example:

... so one of the things that we've done is do a lot of information-giving about benchmarks and it's often good news, particularly about achievement, you know, "your achievement is 20 per cent above the national average" and they all say "that's really good". But when you then ask the question, "I'm an inspector – so how have you achieved that?" And when they say "we don't know" you say "we don't know – that's not going to impress an inspector, is it?" because they're going to say, "well it's probably the students then" or "you've just got good students". And they – we've managed to soften them up into that, almost that you've got to tell a story, so make something up then. There must be a reason, you might not be able to prove it but if you can't prove, an inspector can't prove it either. So we've tried very hard to tell stories at a College level, like that's our achievement, you know, if you look at our success rate's gone up and our achievement has gone up even faster, our retention rate's down – that could be really bad news, you know, it could be that people are getting really fed up with the teaching course, but that's not our story. Our story is that two years ago we took this view that we were going to be harder on academic neglect, we've got – you know, we can demonstrate that we have actually kicked out more students than in previous years, so that affects the retention, but the students you've got left achieve overall, and our success rate's gone up even faster. So there's a very positive story, you know, "do you understand that story?" and we try and give them those types of things. (Kate – Principal)

This does not appear to be cynicism on the part of those involved, just a practical response to the demands of the job and an attempt to manage the contingencies that are thrown up by everyday work. It is a recognition that meeting the formal requirements of audit is not a clear-cut, simple matter of just providing the information being asked for. In his classic essay *The Concept of Organization,* Egon Bittner (1965) puts forward a persuasive argument for challenging traditional notions of the 'formal' and 'informal' in organizational analysis. What Bittner proposes is not so much a new theory of organization, as an outlining of a programme of inquiry in which the production of common-sense notions of 'informal' and 'formal' organization can be studied and explicated through their use 'in real scenes of action by persons whose competence to use them is socially sanctioned' (1965:270). Bittner suggests that formal structures and organizational designs are treated as 'schemes of interpretation' by competent and entitled organizational members who can manipulate these rules to suit their own agendas and that:

> ... the varieties of ways in which the scheme can be invoked for information, direction, justification, and so on, without incurring the risk of sanction, constitute the scheme's methodological use. (Bittner, 1965:272)

What Bittner is outlining here is not a guide for rule bending or subversion, but instead recognition of the complex relationship between organizational members, formal rules and structures, and practical action. He terms this the 'gambit of compliance' that characterizes 'organizational acumen':

> We propose that we must proceed from the theoretical clarification of the essential limitation of formal rules ... to the investigation of the limits of manoeuvrability within them, to the study of the skill and craftsmanship involved in their use, and to a reconsideration of the meaning of strict obedience in the context of varied and ambiguous representations of it. This recommendation is, however, not in the interest of

accumulating more materials documenting the discrepancy between the lexical meaning of the rule and events occurring under its jurisdiction, but in order to attain a grasp of the meaning of rules as common-sense constructs from the perspective of those persons who promulgate and live with them. (Bittner, 1965:273)

Within this 'field of games of representation and interpretation' (1965:273), it is the task of the skilled administrator to find ways of getting work done amidst the formal rules, procedures, and protocols that represent rational and formal organization. Thus college leaders and their staff are exercising a range of 'gambits of compliance' – constructing a story, supporting it from the available data, presenting a professional face, satisfying inspectors' enquiries, etc. – which collectively constitute the organizational acumen required to perform a successful inspection. This interweaving of the formal and the informal in order to get the work done is echoed by Dant and Francis (1998) when they suggest the necessity of seeing rational planning as a situated practice: that within organizational settings there are a variety of ways in which the formally rationalistic 'planning system' and the contingent, member-managed processes of 'planning-in-action' are intertwined and *mutually implicative*. The example of an Ofsted inspection thus provides a vehicle for understanding how such skilled administration and organizational acumen is accomplished in practice, and how decision-making in organizations such as this are all locally organized matters (Pollner, 1987): locally organized, but performed using rituals, routines and common-sense constructs contained within the wider structure of the formal meeting (in this case, the format of the inspection) and drawn upon by its participants in order to get the work done.

Calculation Work as Production

In order for the performance to be successful, it must be founded on a solid process of preparation through which coherent stories and their supporting evidence are produced and shared. This production process is not a simple matter of picking out key figures and putting them forward. Instead, it is a complex process of selection, interpretation and calculation of numbers and information to arrive at a convincing end product. Anderson et al., (1989) have commented in their study of everyday managerial work and decision-making in an entrepreneurial firm, that the practice of calculation frequently involves:

... grappling with the sheer practical difficulties of determining which figures are wanted, pulling them out, and then knowing how to manipulate them and assess their product. (Anderson et al, 1989:105–6)

Certainly, the role of the principal requires substantial 'calculation work' of this type in satisfying the new accountabilities generated, through the performance of audit, in rendering organizational information and accounts of everyday practice visible. Much of what counts as everyday leadership work within FE colleges appears to consist of producing, sharing and manipulating accounts of events, and then reproducing a number of subtly different versions for different audiences or stakeholders. These versions of events are constructed to conform to the new accountabilities of audit in that they consist of conscious displays of compliance and effectiveness (Neyland and Woolgar, 2002), and yet they can also serve as forms of organizational communication and accountability that allow other kinds of 'ordinary' work to be done within the college (Button and Sharrock, 1998; Suchman, 1993). For example, the components of a successful Ofsted inspection may be recycled as the justification for a Beacon Status/premium funding application; an indication of quality provision to entice students to apply to the college; an opportunity for the public praising of staff; as the motivational basis for exhortations to further achievement, and so on. In each case, the mode of delivery and the specific choice of content will serve to construct a version or account suited to the leadership work it is required to perform.

Here we are concerned with documenting some of the actual work that principals do in meeting the practical difficulties of determining which figures are required for which purpose and knowing how to manipulate and present them. The leadership work here consists in the selection and calculation through which activities on the ground, as understood through the management information collected concerning them, are made to visibly fit the requirements imposed upon the organization by external agencies. It is not simply a question of seeing what is 'in the figures' and then working out what should be done since 'what is in the figures' has to be worked out. In so doing, there is a need for 'managing the interplay between precision and interpretation in calculation' (Anderson et al. 1989:121) in order to produce an appropriate, and defensible, account of events. As one Principal put it:

... the data's clean, but in terms of can you use it, is it good enough to use, would you rest your life on it today? – that's more tricky ... it's so complex, in a way you have to manage that ambiguity ... I know how many students I need to achieve overall at the College ... but that's probably got no relationship to enrolments because, you know, somebody can be enrolled on eight things, or you can break the course up into four. (Andy – Principal)

This interplay, and the leadership work entailed in constructing from the data available the right numbers to tell a story which supports organizational objectives, is further illustrated by the following field note extract from Lambton Sixth Form College:

Field note extract: Principal is finalizing update paper for LSC (re: progress against strategic targets) ... "thinking on screen and playing around with content" ... Has found a way of using the numbers re: student recruitment and retention selectively to strengthen their case for premium funding. Needs to disguise the fact that they are 31 down overall. Can say that 16–18 has grown in each of the last three years and numbers here are only 13 off target. The biggest shortfall was in 19+ which is counted in a different category. Can use this to disguise their failure to meet specific targets.

Here, the Principal is observed manipulating management data to consider how best to present important information to their funding body, the Learning and Skills Council. The existence of various categories within which colleges can calculate recruitment, retention and results, and the differing funding formulae provided for different funding streams, mask the way in which reasoning is shaped by contingencies and the 'skill' that goes with recognizing, identifying and addressing such contingencies. These circumstances influence how the 'formula' is applied in specific cases, what determines the extent or limitations of its applicability, and the requirements for making any formula 'work' and, perhaps more importantly, *be seen* to work.

Similar processes and activities were observed to underpin various areas of decision-making through which the successes and failures of educational work were benchmarked and made available for calculation and comparison. For example, the following fieldwork extract is taken from an English teaching moderation meeting, in which those involved in lesson observations for English teachers meet to discuss their qualitative observation reports and allocate quantitative grades for each individual across the department:

Field note extract: Participants read each other's observation notes; reach a consensus on grades to be allocated; check evidence in reports which support grades; moderate across reports for whole department. Take learning outcomes very seriously in "scoring" performance, but also consider ability of students to start with. Sue (VP, Curriculum – previously taught English) provided in-depth, subject-specific questions to observers without a background in English to clarify distinctions between different grades.

The process undertaken by those involved in moderating observation grades can be seen to involve a number of activities designed to delineate and calibrate the attributes of successful English teaching in a visible, rational, accountable way, thus transforming the activities of people into numbers that can be measured, audited, and shared. The use of detailed, context-specific criteria from Sue, the comparison across teaching methods, course content, student groups, etc., and the moderation of 'tough' and 'easy' observers against each other, all serve to demonstrate the calculability of the resultant grades. In the course of the meeting a framework of benchmarks was constructed by the participants, against which written observations could be allocated a defensible grade. What did not result, however, was a list of rules necessary and sufficient to the allocation of a particular grade across all circumstances. Instead, the application of the framework was embedded in the shared meanings and understandings negotiated in the course of the discussions, in relation to the people and circumstances under discussion. It was through the accomplishment of this work that the resultant grades were accepted as being fair, appropriate and rationally arrived at.

An extended example – summarized from field notes – may serve to explicate the complexity and 'imprecision' of calculation work. It relates to a meeting to discuss the rejection by the Capital Committee of the LSC of a general FE college's funding proposal for a new annex building on its existing site. This came as a blow to the management of the College since they had prepared the proposal with the assistance of the local LSC office. The meeting discussed below is attended by the College management and representatives of the local and national LSC, and was arranged to find out why the proposal was rejected and what steps needed to be taken to amend the proposal for resubmission.

The subject of the meeting hinges on one problem: what level of funding the College should say it needs in order to have a new version of the proposal accepted. The problem of which figure to use in the proposal thus presents several difficulties for those attending the meeting. For one thing, there is no 'right answer', only a shared attempt to construct a plausible case. For another, the rejection of the previous proposal has resulted in a number of sensitivities within the group. The new proposal must be agreed without suggesting that the old one – or those who prepared it or gave it tacit approval – were somehow 'wrong'. The original proposal stated that the College required 35 per cent funding, with the College then making up the remaining costs. This figure was originally chosen since the local LSC had mentioned (informally) that this is the usual level of funding awarded for such projects. The College, however, would actually need nearer 50 per cent funding, but by proposing a lower figure it was hoped that the LSC would view the College as a more financially secure investment, which would secure at least 35 per cent with a view of increasing this figure over the following three years. Unfortunately this plan backfired and the Capital Committee felt that, judging from the proposal, the College was financially too healthy to need even a 35 per cent grant. Following this decision, an amended proposal was quickly produced between the College Finance Director and a representative from the local LSC to make the College appear less financially secure. This also involved changing the level of funding required from 35 per cent to 55 per cent. The meeting described below begins following yet another rejection from the Capital Committee who are suspicious of the College's actual financial situation following the two very different proposals and now require a more detailed proposal for exactly why the College needs this new higher level of funding.

The meeting is chaired by the College Principal (John), and involves his Vice-Principal and Financial Director (Brian), the representative for the local LSC (Derek) and the national LSC (Guy). Guy opens the meeting with an explanation of why the proposal was rejected. The Finance Director (Brian) appears increasingly frustrated by what is being said, and interjects as follows:

Brian: ... I've heard, obviously, what you've said Guy but I have to say I have got some concerns about your comments. Firstly, when we met some months ago we went through parameters and you gave us some "clear steers" about the situation. I then had a period of time where I spent hours and hours on these models, forwards and backwards with the local LSC, and it reached a point where I submitted these figures and I was told "yes", you know, there's nothing coming back saying that you need to keep revising it, and this was well within the deadlines you're indicating. I think it's a little bit, sort of, pushing things a wee bit to suggest that somehow these figures were not reviewed ... Now, I don't understand, given the experience and expertise that officers have in presenting these cases nationally, why it was unforeseen that this was likely to happen, because the parameters were known, the categorizations, the borrowing levels, all the rest of it, were known well in advance of that Capital Committee meeting. No one came back to *me* and said "you need to amend these figures"...

Guy: ...I think there's two things to bear in mind here, Brian: that we met well in advance of the Capital Committee, the Capital Committee met on the 20th of April, we'd met already ... on the 2nd of April so there was like a three-week time delay which normally took about a week ...

Brian: ... but to be fair we met some weeks ago, I was told the date to submit that I was given two weeks originally to submit, then it was brought back ...

Guy: ... because the numbers were ok at the time ...

Brian: Well, it was brought back to one week, so I complied with that deadline; then there was a whole period of time where I was in discussion with the local office and they informed me that they were in discussion with you and were presenting various scenarios, and I'd revised the figures on numerous occasions, and it reached a point where I was told those figures were acceptable, so I don't understand the context of what you're saying that it went to the national committee and somehow it became unacceptable ...

If meetings are the stuff of management, part of this 'stuff' involves debate, contestation and negotiation. As with other formal encounters, meetings like the one above are structured occasions in which truths are debated and facts produced, reconfigured and argued over to produce an agreed-upon and standardized version of reality, a 'way of seeing' (Goodwin, 1994). From the outset the meeting is dominated by Brian and Guy and their increasingly heated discussion over whose version of events is correct. Brian states that he is certain that over a period of months, involving several drafts of the proposal and discussions with the local office – and what he describes as 'clear steers' – the proposal should have been acceptable to the Capital Committee (the committee responsible for the distribution of funds). The fact that it was rejected is the cause of some concern among the senior management of the College, particularly as there are only a limited number of committee meetings left to which the proposal can be resubmitted. Brian is especially concerned as it is his responsibility to prepare such documents and it is his professional reputation that he feels is being threatened by Guy:

> Brian: … what Guy is saying is that somehow you weren't 100 per cent certain of the figures and you put it to the Capital Committee simply to get it on the *agenda*, well, that's not my understanding of … !

> John: … No. No. No. I think that …

> Guy: … there's no point making accusations!

The discussion at this point begins to turn into an argument and the Principal (John) steps in to attempt to calm the situation down. His attempts at this point, however, fail as Guy takes offence at the Finance Director's suggestion that the LSC had submitted an unsuitable proposal without the College's consent. It takes Derek (the local LSC representative) to attempt reconciliation and break what has become a stand-off between Guy and Brian:

> Derek: … I, I think that Guy started with the defence which then sets the, sets the tone for the meeting. We're trying to pick through the bones of what happened … we thought that there was, there was a good chance of it going through the national Capital Committee, otherwise we wouldn't have put it out there …

> John: Yep, I think that's fine … I, I think …

> Brian: But, but what …

> John: HOLD ON BRIAN, sorry a sec, I think, erm, I think really we want to draw a line under, under what's happened, but I think, I think probably Brian's quite right to feel a little bit upset by the, the earlier comment that implied that somehow we'd got it wrong, and that if you were short of time you should have told us we got it wrong so we could have put a better case. Now, as I say, as Brian's explained it's not quite like

that and yeah, I mean, we accept that there's an element of judgement and yeah, y'know, no, it's not cast iron certainty, but I think if we just draw a line under it, for whatever reason, there was a misunderstanding about what we'd get through, and I don't think that there should be any blame on Brian, as though he's somehow produced a case ...

Guy: ... there should be no blame anyway ...

John: OK, so we're in agreement then ...

As Boden (1994) states:

> ... meetings are also ritual affairs, tribal gatherings in which the faithful reaffirm solidarity and warring factions engage in battles. They are, to borrow from Dalton's classic study, "a stage for exploratory skirmishes". When in doubt, call a meeting. When one meeting isn't enough, schedule another ... (Boden, 1994:81)

This meeting began as a series of versions of how the current state of affairs was reached. These versions were structured and organized so that, for instance, Guy was invited by the Principal to tell his version of events; Brian then countered this version with his own account of why the proposal was rejected. In both instances the meeting served as an agreed-upon organizational space in which organizational realities could be discussed, debated and solidified. Even though the reasons for the proposal's rejection may have been known prior to the meeting, the formal space it afforded was an opportunity to state things 'on the record', to have views, opinions and versions of events stated and recorded in the presence of the leadership of the college and funding council. As such, the kind of talk observed in this meeting, even when it becomes heated, follows an organized structure of turn-taking through which competing versions of the situation are played out. As the field notes go on to describe, it is the job of the chair (in this case the Principal) to then attempt to resolve conflicts and disagreements by agreeing upon a version of events that allows progress to be made and the necessary work to be accomplished.

As already suggested, the three-hour funding meeting described above was largely concerned with the practices of calculation employed in the presentation of the case for funding, with the object of calculation here being 'what funding case will appear plausible to the LSC' rather than the determination of specific 'correct' numbers. To put it another way, much of this meeting was spent discussing and debating what version of events was acceptable. As the meeting progressed, this became a question of what 'story' the figures used in the proposal should actually tell. As Anderson et al. (1989) argue, figures can be and frequently are manipulated to serve a variety of organizational agendas. Figures can tell any number of stories depending upon how they are organized and presented and, as already noted, '... success depends upon managing the interplay between precision and interpretation in calculation' (1989:121). Management information, like the calculations made in this funding proposal, has to be actively worked upon in order to tell a story.[1] As a college principal, this point is understood by John who suggests a possible way forward following the disagreement between his two colleagues:

John: ... let's move forward and discuss how we go forward from here. But just to sort of finish up my, where I was before that, before we went back I mean. One of the ways of interpreting the committee's responses, that really, that were – if the re-worked figures, which we're saying now are prudent and possibly even over-prudent, I mean, were submitted again – we're at a subjective interpretation aren't we? I mean, another way of interpreting the same outcome, there are two ways of going forward I see, one is to say 35 per cent is right, go back and make the figures come up with 35 per cent, which is what we've played before ... or to say no, the figures are right and 35 per cent is not enough.

John attempts to take on several roles here. As a leader of the College and chair of the meeting he is keen that the group finds a way forward, a solution to this problem following the argument between Brian and Guy. As an experienced manager and administrator he also knows that such a solution has to be worked out today and that although the Capital Committee had rejected their original proposal of 35 per cent funding this is not an insurmountable problem. As he states, such things are open to 'subjective interpretation'. It is not that the 'correct' figure exists, it is that this group has to decide how best to present the figures *as* 'correct' to the Committee. For John, then, this is about creative accountancy and presentation rather than mathematical calculation alone. Either the College re-submits 35 per cent and makes a stronger case for coping with this smaller figure, or they apply for 55 per cent – a more useful figure for them, but a more difficult figure to justify alongside the other stories contained within the calculations of previous funding proposals. Thus the production of coherent, well-supported stories requires an immense amount of calculation work, itself entailing selection, interpretation, negotiation and the like. On some occasions – as with the previous example – the work of production is a public affair, undertaken 'on the hoof'. In others – for example, the earlier example from Lambton – the process is undertaken 'behind closed doors'. In the latter case, the product arrived at must then be shared and rehearsed with others in the college before the public performance occurs.

The Public Face of Leadership: Strategy as a Perennially Unfinished Project

In describing the mundane work of leadership – the listening, talking, running meetings, sending emails, making presentations, etc., through which college principals accomplish their work – we highlight the 'vulgar competences' (Garfinkel, 1967) – available to us all but exercised by particular people in particular settings – that constitute leadership in all its nitty-gritty detail. Within this context, strategic leadership – by which is meant the practical working out and working through of a previously determined strategy by those whose role it is to both formulate and implement it – presents itself as a 'perennially unfinished project' (Knights and Mueller, 2004:55) with a constant need for improvisation and adjustment in order to develop, refine and successfully implement any strategic plan. The result is a necessarily 'messy' view of strategic leadership, and its effortful accomplishment. We focus in particular on the 'pre-implementation' phase of the strategizing process, and suggest how the practices of clarifying, rehearsing, upholding, adapting and elaborating are integral to maintaining the spirit of the strategy in the face of unforeseen events.

As leaders, college principals need to be responsive to a range of stakeholders, while at the same time holding some sense of strategic direction or vision of 'what the college is about'. The tension between these two aims is reflected in the day-to-day 'messiness' of college leadership, as it is in organizational leadership anywhere. At its heart, everyday leadership work has a predominantly egological and practical orientation where the issues are simply – What do I do next? Who do I need to see? What is the appropriate procedure? What is the plan? How do I react to it? and so on, something that theorizing often tends to neglect, thereby producing depictions that bear little resemblance to the day-to-day lived experience of *doing leadership work* or *developing and enacting strategy*.

When we talk of leadership behaviours – such as, for example, 'delegating' or 'planning' – we need to understand exactly what *specific* behaviours we are talking about and what leadership *really looks like* in any given setting. Thus *strategy* requires rather more than merely writing a strategic plan, but instead is 'brought off' through the mundane practices of leaders. There is obviously some resonance here with Suchman's notions of plans and planning whereby 'plans are resources for situated action but do not in any strong sense determine its course' (Suchman, 1987:52). Thus, while leaders are aware of the importance of strategy, of plans and procedures, they are also cognizant of the fact that getting a plan to work is often an effortful accomplishment, with many deviations from what is 'planned' inherent in actually achieving the 'plan' itself. Plans do not 'execute themselves' nor is the relationship between the plan and the action it directs a mechanical one. Plans are *accomplished* activities and the successful accomplishment of a plan is consequently dependent on the practical understandings about what the plan specifies in *these* circumstances, using *these* resources, *these* people, and so on. Although plans may be presented as abstractions, as manuals, as statements of procedures, and so forth, the 'just what' it takes to realize them is a practical matter of 'making the plan work' through all the various and inevitable contingencies that can arise.

The tension between what is planned and what must be responded to in order to implement the plan is articulated by Knights and Mueller (2004:55) in terms of 'a continuous process of self-formation and reconstruction' in which 'numerous stakeholders make demands and serve to condition its development' (Knights and Mueller, 2004:55–56) as those involved respond to the contingencies of its pursuance. It is thus iteratively developed and elaborated from within in the light of unforeseen developments in the situation and the reactions of a range of stakeholders. It is not the external contingencies that shape the strategy, but the strategy itself which 'keeps itself whole' at the same time as establishing how unforeseen needs and claims can be incorporated into its existing goals. Thus the notion of the 'perennially unfinished project' seems to get to the heart of the minute-by-minute, processual character of action involved in the doing of strategy. In this view leaders are seen as furnishing the strategy with coherent detail in response to inquiry and upholding the spirit of the strategy in the face of unfolding opportunities and setbacks.

We illustrate these strategic aspects of leadership work through documenting some of the strategic practices outlined in data drawn from the specific example of a sixth-form college and a college of arts and technology in the same town, planning to 'co-locate'. The two Colleges already have combined curriculum planning and entry procedures, and make joint presentations to local schools to emphasize the complementary nature of their respective offerings. A Memorandum of Understanding has been drawn up between the two Colleges, setting out the aims and extent of a proposed wider collaboration and a framework for how these aims will be pursued. To improve the quality of provision and efficient use of available resources, they are planning to co-locate onto one combined campus, but are concerned that this will be viewed as a merger. Not only do both Colleges want to maintain their distinctive identities, they are also concerned that talk of a merger will generate unhelpful speculation (both within the Colleges and in the local press) about redundancies, rationalizing of the curriculum, etc. The need to conduct these activities across two organizations, with two strategic leaders, serves to amplify and make explicit the ongoing processes of improvisation and adaptation that are an essential feature of organizational strategizing. Elaborating the idea of strategy as a 'perennially unfinished project' (Knights and Mueller, 2004:55) we set out a framework of practices employed and explicate some of the key skills and practices through which leaders navigate an implementation strategy. In particular we draw attention to the inter-linked practices of clarifying, rehearsing, upholding, adapting and elaborating.

Clarifying

The need to *clarify* strategy arises from the need to share its original formulation with key stakeholders, and to respond to their perceptions of it, in particular, instances where understanding of the strategy differs from the intentions of those who formulated it. The field note extract below begins with the two Principals (Bob and Gary) working closely with each other to co-ordinate the announcement of the co-location plan and to manage any 'fallout' that follows:

> Field note extract: Agree that Bob and his team will work on a draft of the terms of reference delimiting the proposed parameters of the collaboration, timelines for aspects of the project, etc., to present for discussion at their next meeting. Gary distributed a draft of a press release to be given to the local newspaper, and they agree some changes. Bob talks Gary through what he is planning to say at the staff briefing, and the fact that he is planning to have a "surgery" afterwards when staff can come and talk to him about any issues and concerns. Aims to surface any possible issues at an early stage, so they can be addressed smoothly and in advance. Discuss tactics for answering press questions, for example, about cost, impact on the town centre, parking issues.

In the case of the college co-location strategy, the Principals of the two Colleges are in the process of drafting various announcement documents to staff, the press and other important stakeholders. All of these documents are constantly amended and updated as the subtle, unperceived nuances of the original plan are exposed to stakeholders' reactions. So, for example, a confidential briefing document has been prepared for senior staff within the two Colleges, providing model answers to anticipated questions from staff, students and other stakeholders. Bob (Principal of the sixth-form college) is working on a staff presentation for his College, covering similar ground. Based on input from his senior team in relation to staff sensitivities, he revises the wording of key elements of the presentation in a manner that retains the sense of distinctness between the two Colleges – for example, by changing the phrase 'common timetable' to 'contiguous timetabling' to underline the intention that it is co-location, not a merger, that is being contemplated.

Rehearsing

Once outlined, strategy requires refining and internalizing through the practice of being *rehearsed* by the strategic leaders. Through repetition of the key elements of the strategy, sketching out its implications, considering possible objections, etc. the College Principals prepare themselves, and the strategy, for wider disclosure. In so doing, they build confidence for later 'skirmishes' in which the fundamentals of the strategy are likely to be challenged, and generate 'ammunition' to meet these anticipated challenges. This practice of rehearsal can occur in both private preparatory meetings, where 'scripts' are prepared and anticipated questions addressed, and in meetings with stakeholders, when key points of the strategy evolve through repetition and reinforcement.

This is illustrated by the work the Principals undertake in preparation for the various internal and external meetings related to the announcement of co-location. The internal briefing document addressing likely questions by staff, mentioned earlier, is a prime example of the practice of rehearsing. Its pre-preparation serves to familiarize the key players with the responses they may be called upon to make and to give them time to internalize them such that they will sound convincing when delivered for real. The Principals undertook similar preparations prior to meetings aimed at canvassing the support of key external stakeholders to the project – in particular those who could provide land for a co-located site and the Education Authority who will need to give approval and provide some of the funding:

Field note extract, Principal's "pre-meeting": Bob and Gary discuss plans and tactics for joint meetings later in the day, e.g. with County Hall. Gary: "So what's the agenda for that one?" ... Bob: "Shall we have a script?" ... Start jotting down headings, agree key points they need to get across and issues they are keen to sidestep. E.g. need to open the door for the property consultants to work with and get information from the Council. Different approaches to different people depending upon what they already know, what their interest/concerns will be, how the Colleges want to involve them, their personal sensitivities, etc. Develop a series of contingency responses depending upon how people react to the announcement ...

The physical drafting of related documents also offers opportunities for physical rehearsal. Hence the two Principals met with each other and with senior colleagues to actually 'run through' presentations and pre-prepared Q&As.

Upholding

If a strategy is to be more than just a well-crafted document, then its spirit – the values and aims which form its core – must be *upheld* as setbacks and opportunities arise: that is, a way must be found of incorporating unanticipated events which may change the detail of what has been planned, but which keeps intact its core principles. The practice of upholding is evident in the meetings with stakeholders where Bob and Gary's retention of the core aims of the co-location strategy – to provide a better combined vocational and academic learning experience for students, at the same time as meeting local employer and community needs – enables them to be flexible in responding to issues raised while still sticking to the spirit of what they have previously agreed between themselves. They thus present a united and consistent view of their plans, even when discussing aspects of the project which weren't agreed in advance. So for example, when a representative of the Borough Council proposes a particular location from its own landholdings as being potentially suitable for the new campus ('we've got 20 acres where we were planning to bury the dead which you might have!'), Bob and Gary can respond to this unexpected but potentially positive offer in terms of agreed priorities for students – e.g. access and parking issues, catchment areas, nearness to local employers – even though they have not considered the specifics in relation to the site on offer.

Adapting

In contrast to a simple *upholding*, a strategy may need to be *adapted* in order to keep its progress on track. The need to adjust the specific activities related to the strategy without losing sight of the underpinning goals gives rise to the practice of adapting: of making specific plans or actions 'fit for purpose' in response to unanticipated events or information. So, for example, the following extract, from the Principal's meeting with the editor of the local newspaper, is illustrative of the constant need to adapt the planned strategy in the light of unforeseen events in order to ensure that the strategy itself is implemented.

Field note extract, meeting with local newspaper editor: Brief the editor about what is happening, with Gary taking the lead and Bob seamlessly developing the themes he raises. Editor says they should delay the staff briefing until late Wednesday afternoon (paper comes out on Thursday morning) otherwise it will leak out to the nearby regional paper as a merger story (they have a track-record of "scare-mongering"). Bob and Gary agree to postpone the announcement to staff. Editor also suggests asking readers for their views on possible locations for the new campus. After they have left the meeting, Bob and Gary agree to send the editor a list of suggested options for the new location – the paper will seek public opinion anyway, so better that the Colleges manage the process by providing them with sites that are actually potential options. On his return to College, Bob meets with his senior managers to discuss other announcements he could make at the forthcoming staff meeting, rather than cancel it (which he feels would look suspicious and thus create speculation anyway). They cobble together a number of recent events that collectively make a plausible agenda.

Thus the rescheduling of the announcement to sixth-form college staff to prevent the unhelpful leaking of information to the county newspaper prior to the approved press release and local newspaper coverage required the College Principal to adapt existing plans by finding other items to talk to staff about rather than raise suspicion by cancelling the meeting entirely.

Elaborating

Finally, strategy is, almost inevitably, *elaborated* – furnished with more detail and developed into practically implementable actions – as the process continues. This idea of elaboration is reflected in Boal and Schultz's (2007) notion of organizational storytelling, such that not just in the telling of stories but in their retelling, stories enable members to make sense of events, build on past stories and construct new ones, each time filling in more detail. The extracts presented above show this beginning to happen in the case of the co-location strategy as a potential site emerges, consultants are brought in to start mapping out the implications with the relevant stakeholders, staff questions are addressed within the College, and so on. The pre-prepared answers to anticipated staff questions talked of the need to prepare a transport plan for the new site, and work already underway on preparing a bid for capital funding and an anticipated timescale for the project. And in speaking to the slides prepared for the staff presentation, Bill elaborated on the 'advantages of collaboration' by talking about 'a better deal for students; new buildings with better facilities; wider choice of and access to vocational training alongside existing academic opportunities; improved progression routes; and the potential for a more sustainable funding structure'.

In the course of these and subsequent meetings and discussions, the plans for co-location thus evolve and develop: at no point can the strategy be said to be complete or fixed, yet the aims which it embodies are always there as a potential 'finish line'. The route towards this finish line, rather than being linear or causal, is a constant sequence of adjustments and adaptations through which those responsible for its development and implementation tack their way along the course. On this view, the strategy is upheld in spirit in the face of potential challenges or setbacks, and clothed in detail on the basis of unfolding opportunities and new information. In contrast to much of the literature on strategy and strategic planning, this view recognizes the processual character of action as it is understood within ethnomethodology, and the consequent need for strategy to be accomplished on an ongoing basis.

Conclusion

The development of an audit culture in further education has resulted not only in the need to be seen to be performing in the sense of making one's activities accountable to Ofsted and the LSC, but also in the need for performance of another kind. Leadership in the sector is increasingly concerned with presenting the work of the college, its aims and image, to a wide range of stakeholders in a way that is polished and plausible. At one end of the scale, this results in what Bittner (1965) has described as 'gambits of compliance' – being seen to pay attention to the many rules and regulations with which one is expected to comply while actually using them to meet one's own aims and objectives: a sort of 'strategic lip-service' to the process and phenomenon of audit. At the other end, it is the 'management of meaning' (Smircich and Morgan, 1982:257), whereby 'leadership actions attempt to shape and interpret situations to guide organizational members (and those outside the organization) into a common interpretation of reality' (Smircich and Morgan, 1982:261). Through the selection, interpretation and presentation that is 'calculation work', combined with the subtle nuancing of the presentation of the same information between one audience and another, the study data shows educational leaders guiding stakeholders as to how to think about the issues faced by their institution. The 'right' figure for a funding proposal or the 'right' strategy for collaboration becomes a work of influence such that:

> Leadership works by influencing the relationship between figure and ground, and hence the meaning and definition of the context as a whole. (Smircich and Morgan, 1982:261)

While this claim sounds rather grandiose, and seems to follow the trend of much research in marking leadership out as something special, it takes only a brief reflection on the tools through which such influence and management of meaning are created to return us to the notion of leadership as mundane work outlined in the preceding chapter.

Chapter 6

Technologies of Leadership: The Medium and the Message

Most organizations are littered with technologies of various kinds: they appear to be essential to everyday organizational life and our observations revealed that colleges are no different in this respect. There are, however, very few studies that consider the ways in which these technologies are implicated in leadership work. This chapter is, therefore, concerned with the topic of leadership and its relationship with technology. It considers the role of 'technologies of leadership', that is, the technologies that regularly assist leaders, college principals in this case, as they go about their daily work. We document some of the complexities and difficulties involved in the provision of management information, and the utilization of the information furnished by these 'leadership technologies' in support of decision-making, managing and motivating. In our discussion we draw attention to the different forms of work that leaders achieve through the technologies they use and the different ways that technologies are woven together and into the work of being a leader. The suggestion we make here is that, much like other forms of routine, oft-neglected and under-emphasized aspects of leadership work, routine expertise in and exploitation of these technologies can be understood as part of the work of being 'a good leader'.

Given the hype surrounding new technology and the heralded transformations it will bring it is, perhaps, surprising that the focus of this chapter is what we refer to as 'mundane technologies' (Dourish et al., 2010) – e-mail (e.g. Microsoft® Outlook), word-processing applications (e.g. Microsoft® Word), spreadsheets (e.g. OpenOffice.org's Impress) and presentation (e.g. Apple's Numbers) software. By mundane technologies we mean technologies and applications that are commonplace in FE colleges, that just about everybody uses, precisely the kinds of technologies that have become the fabric of the workplace through 'their capacity to be unnoticed, to quietly mediate, that is reproduce, what have become the commonalities of everyday life' (Hillman and Gibbs, 1998). These are not novel technologies but are:

> ... technologies which are now fully integrated into, and are an unremarkable part of, everyday life. To study mundane technologies is thus to explore how they mediate and reflect everyday life, how they serve in the reproduction of local technosocial configurations. (Michael, 2003:129)

In this case the 'mediation and reflection of everyday life' and the 'technosocial configurations' are those concerned in the everyday task of leadership in an FE college. In attending to how these kinds of technologies are positioned in different streams of work and placed in the workplace we examine exactly how information is disseminated and activity is coordinated and controlled or 'articulated'. Thus this chapter extends the notion of 'control through communication' (Yates, 1989) to consider how technology is routinely implicated in 'team management' as an aspect of both the 'emotional labour' (Hochschild, 1983) and 'emotional intelligence' (Goleman, 1998) of leaders.

While the technology we are concerned with is everyday, mundane, simple even, this is not a simple story and we particularly want to avoid any simple, or simplistic, conclusions about the benefits, or failures, of technology. For we are not proposing any simple technicist type argument here but instead prefer the argument of Sacks (1972) that technology, far from transforming the world, is placed in a world that already has whatever order it has and becomes just another mechanism by which people's (leader's) already existing 'niceness and nastiness' (or leadership) is displayed:

> That's a funny kind of thing, in which each new object becomes the occasion for seeing again what we can see anywhere; seeing people's nastiness or goodness or all the rest, when they do this initially technical job of talking over the phone. The technical apparatus is, then, being made at home with the rest of our world. And it's a thing that's routinely being done, and it's the source for the failures of technocratic dreams that if only we introduced some fantastic new communication machine the world will be transformed. Where what happens is that the object is made at home in the world that has whatever organization it already has. (Sacks, 1972:548–9)

Thus we are not entranced by technology but merely note its constant and indeed ubiquitous use. Consequently, we present neither a utopian nor a dystopian vision of the relationship between technology and leadership, aware, as Kling and Dunlop (1993) write, that:

> Authors write about changes in technology and social life with a range of analytical and rhetorical strategies. They bombard us with their glowing vision of technical wonders able to rapidly manipulate large amounts of information with little effort – to enhance control, to create insight, to search for information, and facilitate cooperative work between people. Others concentrate on a darker social vision in which computerization only serves to amplify human misery ... (Kling and Dunlop, 1993:2)

Our aim then is not to contribute to what appears an increasingly futile, and rarely empirically informed, debate. Nevertheless, as Zuboff (1988) suggests in *In the Age of the Smart Machine*, we recognize that '[n]ew choices are laid open by these technologies, and these choices are being confronted in the daily lives of men and women across the landscape of modern organizations'. She describes a series of possible futures involving technology in organizations varying from utopian to anti-utopian (Kling, 1996); how 'intelligent' information systems, depending on how they are implemented, can either deskill or support critical judgement, impose hierarchical authority or map authority onto knowledge and responsibility, support surveillance or support new ways of information sharing and social interaction. These futures depend not only on the policy choices leaders make within their organizations but also on how they choose to use and exploit them and encourage their team members to exploit them. A huge change in the landscape since Zuboff's book is not only the characterization of new technologies (from 'smart machines' to 'information appliances' to 'pervasive systems' etc.) but also the sheer ubiquity of information technologies in people's (working) lives, social technologies in particular. Organizations have also, and to varying degrees of success, tried exerting control over employees' use of these technologies via both organizational policies (e.g. e-mail use policies) and technical solutions (e.g. site blocking). However, as already noted, in the pursuit of understanding novel technologies that will transform the workplace for leaders and leadership work, it is easy to forget that any new technologies 'sit' embedded in an ecology of 'old' technologies – paper, notice boards, filing cabinets, (real) desktops, shelves – and more recent technological intrusions – telephones, photocopiers and fax machines. This list does not even consider the newer technologies that have crept into the workplace in the last twenty years: e-mail, Web applications, 'office' applications and, more recently, various forms of messaging (e.g. Instant, SMS, MMS) and Web 2.0 applications (e.g. blogs, wikis, RSS feeds).

Such technologies are also transforming the boundaries between work and 'outside' life and thus leadership work now potentially extends to the car (Laurier, 2004), the café and the home to name but a few. Thus they support the management and, in Nippert-Eng's (1996) terms, sculpt the boundaries between work and 'outside' that are not unchanging but permeable and 'fluid' (Kakihara and Sørenson, 2004): boundaries that are part of a leader's life. Such boundaries inhabit both the workplace and the 'after the workplace'. Patricia, the Principal described in chapter 4 noted such a 'boundary' existing between 'the corridor' and her office: 'The only place where I am ever miserable is within my immediate office, with the people who work immediately to me.' She also noted the importance of maintaining a particular demeanour to staff members on 'the other side' of the back office-school corridor boundary. These boundaries, like those between home and work, require acknowledgement and, in some cases, negotiation. The management of these boundaries is made yet more difficult with the 'creep' of these technologies from the workplace into other areas of life, sustaining the 'greedy' organization (Nippert-Eng, 2003) and, indeed, leader. These kinds of tensions are evident in Marjory's comments (described in more detail in the next chapter) concerning her and her Vice-Principal's work difficulties with being a leader: 'We both attempted to juggle high profile jobs with family commitments with babies.'

It is not without irony that we highlight leaders' fallibilities and difficulties through a discussion of technology. However, this is a background concern in this chapter, a concern that will be taken up and discussed in more detail in the next. What we wish to concentrate on here are the day-to-day practices and methods through which technology is built into the working lives of those who use them. This is, as already noted, a description of technology that seems strangely lacking (Button, 1993) from the analysis of studies claiming to be concerned with 'the social construction of technology' – the everyday usage of ICT in the accomplishment of work is curiously absent from most studies of organizational settings. Our analysis is concerned both with actual technologies and with the skills of educational leaders and their staff in configuring and utilising information in order to get work done. In the context of educational leadership, these 'nuts and bolts' include e-mail, electronic diaries, MIS (Management Information Systems), spreadsheets, and Powerpoint. It is how these seemingly mundane technologies are integrated into, and come to shape, everyday leadership work that we seek to document and explicate.

The starting point for this chapter is then the everyday, common-place, observation that modern organizations, including colleges, are experiencing enormous growth in the deployment of information and communications technologies. Research suggests the extensive use of IT serves to 'reconfigure the organization' through its application in data analysis and processing, expert systems, communication and decision support (Zuboff, 1988; Scott Morton, 1991). Given the potentially trans-formative capacity of IT for organizations, and the challenge in using information systems to organise, store and present information in a timely and efficient manner – most notably for effective decision-making, something commonly associated with 'leadership' – technology is already, and heavily, embroiled in 'leadership work'. In speaking of 'technologies of leadership' the suggestion is not that the technology does the leading, but that it is implicated as an everyday feature of how leadership work gets done by leaders. However, while various workplace studies have provided immense detail on how technology impinges on and contributes to particular kinds of work, particular jobs or occupations, few have specifically considered the effect of information and communication technologies on 'leadership work'. So, for example, and famously, while we have an abundance of information on how air traffic control work is done (Bentley et al, 1992); how medical work is done (Hartswood et al., 2003), how steel rolling is done (Clarke et al., 2003) and so on, and on the use of particular technologies in these particular occupations, we have rather less, if any, on how leadership work 'gets done' in almost any occupation and the everyday, and increasing, role of technology in this particular kind of work. In terms of 'leadership', the majority of research relating to technology seems to have simply focused elsewhere: on the management of technology (e.g. Bowonder, 1998; Couillard and Lapierre, 2003), on leading the development of new technology (e.g. Jensen, 2003) and the achievement and maintenance of market leadership in technology (e.g. Abetti, 1997), but not, unfortunately, on how technology is routinely used as an aid to everyday, mundane, leadership work. Similarly in the field of education, the focus has tended to be on technology as a teaching tool (e.g. Cohen and Rustad, 1998; Strudler and Wetzel, 1999) or as a subject to be taught (e.g. Stein, McRobbie and Ginns, 2000; McCormick, 2004), rather than as a tool of leadership.

'Audit Culture', Technology and Everyday Leadership Work

In documenting leadership work with and through technology we are talking about the everyday work of leaders, their various social interactions and their use of a range of pretty mundane technologies, but whose successful adaption and routine accomplishment often turns out to be remarkably important for the organization. However, and keeping Sacks' (1972) comments in mind about the lack of any inherent transformative power in technology, when it comes to leadership, technology on its own rarely offers any simple, or universal solutions. Indeed the turn to technology could sometimes create problems of information overload. For example, college principals participating in our study told us:

> ... we have too much detailed information on our MIS – we don't always pick out the important bits

> ... all you do with stats is identify more stats you want to look at

> ... the quality of discussion has declined to figures and numbers – no vision

Thus technology can appear a coercive force for the collection of data with no clearly identified purpose, gathered simply because it is now possible (or fashionable, or compulsory) to do so, or as a facilitator of 'joined-up thinking' and streamlined work practices across the organization – and sometimes, often even, it is both. In detailing these practices then, what becomes clear is that the affordances of these different technologies and the new ways of presenting and working with data that the technology seemingly offers, is critical to leadership work.

As already mentioned, one of the central framing concepts for this study was the well documented development of a highly visible 'audit culture' within organizations as outlined by Power (1994) and Strathern (2000). In a time of 'audit culture' leaders face a range of problems and opportunities in their everyday use of information systems concerning the collection, utilization, integration and dissemination of data. Obviously, while we focus here on education, we believe that many of the ideas and arguments we develop here are more widely applicable as a consequence of both the widespread deployment of technology and the wide portability of the notion of 'audit'. As Power argues:

The great attraction of the audit idea is its portability across diverse contexts: public sector efficiency, corporate governance, environmental management systems and so on. The word symbolises a cluster of values: independent validation, efficiency, rationality, visibility almost irrespective of the mechanics of the practice and, in the final analysis, the promise of control. (Power, 1994: 12)

'Audit culture' brings with it, and enables, an accompanying managerial philosophy: in the case of educational leadership in FE the philosophy that currently dominates is the need to demonstrate competence, compliance and effectiveness to a variety of audiences. This involves the use of figures drawn from, displayed and created by information systems and mundane technologies. In this context, and as already explored in the previous chapter, instead of ensuring the quality of 'first order' operations or outcomes, audits serve to ensure the quality of 'second order' control systems by operating as a means of indirect control over work practices through the monitoring and regulation of other systems of control. So, for example, a post-Ofsted college newsletter proclaimed:

Ofsted inspectors identified: outstanding leadership and management; overall, students achieving GCE grades higher than those predicted by their GCSE results; very good specialist resources; thorough monitoring of student progress; excellent advice and guidance; excellent attendance and punctuality; highly effective promotion of a multicultural ethos; and safe and secure environment.

Significantly only one of these identified achievements relates to 'first order' outcomes – i.e. student results – supporting the contention that audit is about the *control of control* – being seen to have audit or monitoring measures in place, as with Foucault's notion of the 'conduct of conduct' (Burchell et al., 1991), rendering practices, actions and behaviours visible and accountable. Being *seen* to be in control is as important as actually having control. This suggests some interesting corollaries for technology. Firstly, the use of certain technologies, with their particular capabilities and limitations, can be seen to determine the format of what is required to be made visible and what is accepted as evidence. Thus lesson observation forms and formats are computer generated, funding criteria are linked to the categories of learner (14–19, 19+, adult, full-time, part-time) for which data can be gathered, and visible proxies (e.g. schemes of work and lesson plans) are substituted for qualitative assessments of the standard and relevance of curriculum provision. A corollary of this state of affairs is that, in their position as 'auditees' (Power, 1997), the users of technology can be seen as valuing what can be measured rather than measuring what should be valued: thus in constructing the evidence which supports the requirements of audit, through 'the "non-compliance-compliance" and creative strategies of submitting to audit' (Power, 1994:37) they are in danger of encumbering the organization, and themselves, with 'structures of auditability embodying performance measures which increasingly do not correspond to the first order reality of practitioners' work' (Power, 1994:37). As Power suggests, this emphasis on 'performed' audit, requires that auditors within organizations and institutions become particularly skilled at making the world verifiable and calculable within the matrices of the given audit process.

In their paper on 'leadership challenges' in FE colleges, Collinson and Collinson (2005) outline the importance of performance targets and their relation to funding mechanisms in the sector: 'There is so much time devoted to the data collection that drives funding. The number of staff needed to service data collection is unbelievable'. In particular, their respondents, college principals like ours, routinely and regularly highlighted what they saw as excessive, and excessively detailed, monitoring and contradictory funding mechanisms with the suggestion that they were now performing so many auditing activities that the practice had become counter-productive. As one principal noted:

> The Learning and Skills Council are much more performance-related but they keep changing the goalposts. We have postcode funding and a ferocious audit regime with no tolerance …

For example, one of their FE colleges was subject to five different audits:

> Financial Statements Audit (Annual audit of the accuracy and fairness of the contents of the financial statements. The opinion is expressed to the Corporation Board).

> Regularity Audit (Annual opinion on the regularity and probity of the expenditure that the college makes. The opinion is expressed to the Corporation Board and to the LSC).

> Internal Audit (60-day programme of audit assignments that are performed by an independent third party to give the Board assurance

that financial controls are working effectively. The Board approve annually the areas to be audited).

PFA Audit (Provider Financial Assurance arm of the LSC are part of the inspection process that look at the governance and financial management aspects. Not annual but in line with inspection cycle).

ILR Audit (Individualized Learner Record audit is an annual audit of the accuracy of the learner record system, returns and claims for funding made to the LSC. Auditors are employed by LSC and opinion is to LSC).

A second framing concept for our interest in technology derives from Yates' (1989) work on 'control through communication' that reflects on how technologies of various kinds are generally introduced, used and developed in accord with a range of organizational, managerial and local priorities and policies. As Joanne Yates first recognized, new kinds of accountability generate new managerial and organizational forms and technologies through which they can be expressed. Thus her historical analysis describes how changing organizational demands for technologies, for complex and formal communication systems, interact with the development of new managerial philosophies to produce particular deployments of technology for coordination and control, creating a complex, multi-layered relationship between developing technologies, organizational requirements and evolving managerial philosophies. As Yates (1989) documents with reference to the late nineteenth century, memos, files, standard forms, etc. evolved to solve problems of 'distributed coordination', as organizations became larger and the problems of management and control correspondingly increased. So, for example, the vertical filing cabinet allowed easy storage and ready access to far more information than had been possible before, thereby allowing organizations to spread across distance without the burden of having to increase the number of 'bureaucratic' centres. A similar kind of analysis might be applied to technologies such as e-mail, instant messaging or Excel spreadsheets. An understanding of 'technologies of leadership' must therefore include an appreciation of new managerial philosophies and the role of the new accountabilities generated through the performance of audit in rendering organizational information and accounts of everyday practice visible, as well as an appreciation of the technologies that make audit, and its accompanying paraphernalia such as 'audit trail', possible.

As noted in earlier chapters, much of what counts as everyday leadership work within UK FE colleges appears to consist of producing, sharing and manipulating accounts of events, producing a number of subtly different versions for different audiences and for demonstrating compliance and other internal organizational goals. As this recycling process suggests, organizational life within FE colleges in the United Kingdom is increasingly characterized by a need to construct accounts and make oneself, other members of staff and the college accountable to a variety of internal and external audiences. Such accountability work, we argue, necessarily draws upon a wide range of techniques, systems and technologies to ensure its practical accomplishment as leadership work.

In focusing on the complexities involved in the mundane use of ICT in the provision of management information, the production and use of that information in everyday leadership work, and the associated use of technology in support of decision-making, managing and communication, we document the actual, everyday, work that principals do in meeting the sheer practical difficulties of using the various technologies for calculation work and decision-making. Such work involves determining which figures are required for which purpose and, in particular, knowing how to manipulate and present them. The leadership work here consists in various aspects of selection and calculation through which activities on the ground, as documented and presented through the management information system, are made to visibly fit the requirements imposed upon the organization by external agencies, such as Ofsted or the LSC. As noted in Chapter 5, one principal remarked:

> ... the data's clean, but in terms of can you use it, is it good enough to use, would you rest your life on it today? – that's more tricky ... it's so complex, in a way you have to manage that ambiguity ... I know how many students I need to achieve overall at the college ... but that's probably got no relationship to enrolments because, you know, somebody can be enrolled on eight things, or you can break the course up into four.

That we are not just talking about 'any old numbers', or being able to extract the 'right' numbers from the data available has already been observed in the previous chapter. More specifically in this context, the numbers are not often simply there to be retrieved but have to be arrived at through using the technology.

As discussed earlier, this interplay – the selection of the appropriate source, the consideration of what (part of the) data to present, and who the data is being presented to, and consequently exactly how it is best presented, and so on – and the leadership work entailed in constructing the data available to tell a story that supports particular organizational objectives, is further illustrated by the following field note extract from another college. In this example, already considered from a different perspective in Chapter 5, the Principal is observed manipulating management data on an Excel spreadsheet in order to consider how best to present important information to the funding body, the Learning and Skills Council.

> Field note extract: Steven works through the numbers, checking them on a calculator – likes to be one step ahead in terms of clarity – then rehearses the argument in terms of implications for funding programme.

> Field note extract: 'Principal is finalizing update paper for LSC (re: progress against strategic targets) ... "thinking on screen and playing around with content"... Has found a way of using the numbers re: student recruitment and retention selectively to strengthen their case for premium funding. Needs to disguise the fact that they are 31 down overall. Can say that 16–18 has grown in each of the last three years and numbers here are only 13 off target. The biggest shortfall was in 19+ which is counted in a different category. Can use this to disguise their failure to meet specific targets.

The raw data, student numbers, student names, course titles, educational programmes etc., all exist in different formats such as class registers, the various college databases and so on. But even when gathered together and collated, the Principal's problem is not so easily resolved. Making the various funding formulae which apply to different student categories 'work' requires deciding which particular sets of data are required and knowing exactly how they can be manipulated in order to make the final figures 'show something'. Leadership decisions then, despite the proliferation of technology, are the products of complex, socially organized accounting work and, as such, are 'accountable'. Decisions are effectively 'displays' of the methods used to produce them – and in these circumstances the college principal must keep in mind exactly what others – especially those that might make judgements about him/her – might make of his or her interpretation of the information. This inevitably involves 'calculation work' (Anderson et al., 1989) and some 'fudging' of the figures to secure the best possible outcome for the institution. This example from the diary kept by a department head, concerning timetabling of staff, involved 'calculation work' as he went about what he termed 'fixing' the hours of one of his staff. The calculation work was needed to ensure he kept 'within the rules' – college rules concerning how many hours staff were supposed to be timetabled for – while ensuring he achieved the desired result that the lecturer should be compensated in some way for the fact that he taught very large classes. (It coincidentally illustrates one of the ways at least in which 'classes' are not the same):

> Diary Extract: Jim – fix hours ... Spoke to him last year about 'fixing' timetable so that he was a 'few' hours under to compensate for teaching large classes, increased marking, etc. We can fix it so that Jim teaches a timetable 15 hours light. Which means there is nothing available to put him up to the complete 756 hours (contracted contact hours). Jim really does not want to teach overtime anyway ... There is no way that I can openly simply give (him) fewer hours to teach ... What I did with Jim was give a PT lecturer 25 per cent of one of (his) classes ... this meant he is now 15 hours under. Near enough I think!

Seen in this way, the work of leaders when they engage in decision-making and analysis of management information involves a continuous (and clearly often very ingenious and skilful) struggle with the technology and the data. While the process relies on information being delivered through technology, information is not so much 'uncovered' or 'given' as continuously reconstructed. In the case above, the data (contact hours) are constructed to be close enough to the recommended figure 756 to allow the lecturer some time off to compensate for his high class sizes and consequent heavy marking load, and 'close enough' to ensure that the head of department is not expected to find more teaching hours for the lecturer. In this sense technology and applications are not there merely for the storage and retrieval of data. The technology, when in capable hands, facilitates its use for organizational ends as part of the process of performing and demonstrating leadership. The leaders in our study appear to view the construction of such accounts, and the (manipulative) role they play in the application of the management information available, as an integral part of the leadership work required to achieve organizational goals. Managerial experience, 'learning to be a leader' in effect, appears to foster more elegant and effective means of utilizing the variety of techniques that could be employed to disguise the 'true' nature of an account alongside a healthy sense of scepticism about the accuracy, or veracity of the end results.

Technology and 'Control through Communication'

As already mentioned, a second aspect of the 'technologies of leadership' considered in this chapter is how information is disseminated and activity coordinated and controlled, drawing on what Yates (1989) terms 'control through communication'. To a lesser extent, it is also about how technology and technical artefacts become relevant and used in response to changing managerial philosophies and priorities. This latter, historical, aspect of Yates' work can be seen in the duality between the growth of the audit culture in FE and the availability of technology to service it: as Yates would argue, it was not the availability of technology that led to its adoption, but its initial and continuing perception as the solution to a problem, namely that of satisfying the information requirements of a demanding external funding body and a new framework of corporate governance. This particular perception (that technology is a solution to management's need for information, for figures, for audit) has not weakened over time – quite the reverse – and alongside this, as we have already suggested, has been the use of technology to address the need to show various forms of 'accountability', to provide evidence that management and leadership are responding to a range of demands. The use of mundane technologies – e-mail, intranet systems, PowerPoint, etc. – for sharing and distributing information, exchanging ideas and honing accounts of events has contributed to the commonplace recognition of everyday work as being socially accomplished. Fieldwork for this study showed principals and their senior management teams using the medium of technology to make their activities visible to each other (and to staff in general) and to receive and incorporate the contributions of others within the group in the construction of accounts and the accomplishment of shared activities. Thus the technologies appeared as artefacts of 'distributed coordination' (Rouncefield, 2002), i.e. of the 'various ways in which the coordination of people and tasks is accomplished as a routine feature of "real-world, real-time" work.' (Rouncefield, 2002:291) In this context, the following field note extract relates to a PowerPoint presentation for a staff briefing, which had been drafted by the Principal and circulated to his two Vice-Principals for the incorporation of their sections:

> Field note extract: Principal asks VPs to come into his office to review this evening's presentation on screen. VP1 corrects the grammar and spelling and questions the content, based on the earlier version she had printed out and annotated. Much humour between the three

of them when the Principal loses the formatting, and when VP1's suggested amendments result in her assuming a bigger role in the actual presentation. VPs leave Principal to do the final tweaks, sort out slide transitions, and copy to memory stick for transportation to the briefing.

As this example illustrates, there is an integrated weaving of social inter-action and technological mechanisms through which the three people involved in preparing the presentation make visible and accountable their contributions in order to produce a coherent whole. Neither the people involved nor the tasks they are performing can be taken in isolation. Instead, they must be understood as part of an organized and coordinated whole, such that each has an awareness of the work and intentions of the others, and it is only through their coordinated interdependency that the required work actually gets done. What this brief example illustrates is how, with the rise of an emerging managerial philosophy of efficiency, system, and process (Brown and Duguid, 2002; Power, 1997), forms of internal communication need to serve as mechanisms for managerial coordination and control and new communication genres (Yates and Orlikowski, 1992) like PowerPoint presentations, clichéd though they may now appear to be, have developed as a product of organizational needs and available technologies.

As Yates and Orlikowski (1992) suggest, theories of organizational communication (particularly those involving electronic communication) require a more sophisticated understanding of the role of new technol-ogies in the production and dissemination of information since such organizational communication is embedded in social processes. As such, technologies of organizational communication shape and are shaped by organizational structures and processes. In order to understand this dialectical relationship between structures, social processes and commu-nication, they argue for a more considered understanding of both the form and substance of organizational communication. Accordingly, forms of organizational communication can also be organized into specific and recognizable 'genres' such as letters, memoranda, meetings, agendas, proposals, etc. In this sense, leadership technologies – even those as seemingly mundane as the monthly college newsletter – must be under-stood as used by principals and senior managers within colleges not only to account for, but also to promote and disseminate, specific leadership visions and objectives. Such technological accomplishments represent and draw upon specific 'genres' of communication that evolve over time as new technologies are employed to generate, process and disseminate information in new and innovative ways across organizational domains. The examples below are both recognizable as belonging to the 'college bulletin' communication genre, produced using a desktop publishing package, while simultaneously being indicative of important differences in the leadership work the documents are intended to do:

Extract 1: Our Quality Team met in December and produced an action plan to build upon our existing high standards. By any benchmark, our college has state-of-the-art facilities and excellent accommodation. Its support for students is outstanding. Nevertheless, we realize we need to work hard to maintain the high standards and to respond to emerging problems and "hotspots".

Extract 2: Lollipop ladies Lillian and Leslie have been busy brushing up their computer skills at the local Learning Centre. Between seeing children safely across the road, the crossing patrol ladies have been visiting the centre on — street. The ladies visit the centre twice a week between 11 a.m. and 1 p.m. which fits around their job. They have already completed some qualifications.

The first example reflects the use of internal bulletins to instil values through text, both reinforcing those assumed to exist and exhorting staff to further improvement. The second demonstrates the chatty, approachable style of external newsletter produced by an open access college seeking to adapt its written style to that of its target audience. At the same time, both are recognizable, in terms of form (general address of the mass-distributed communication facilitated by modern reprographics) and content (information being disseminated about the college), as the same communication genre, while specifically targeted language and content show the elaboration of the genre to support or advance equally specific organizational goals.

Technology, Leadership and Emotional Labour

The 'chatty' tone evident in the second example above points to another issue in the use of technology by college leaders. In this section we want to briefly consider the use of technology in what might be regarded as 'the soft skills of management' of various kinds – a term that embraces a range of activities including praise and encouragement as well as disciplining and censure. This involves the use of technology as part of the affective component of organizational life – making people feel valued, encouraging people to work harder or change – and draws on a growing literature on 'emotional labour' (Hochschild, 1983), aspects of which we have already mentioned in an earlier chapter. Again, we wish to draw on Hochschild's (1983) seminal work, *The Managed Heart*, in relation to the commercialization of emotion work in the service sector, and on the more complex and sophisticated understandings (e.g. Bolton and Boyd, 2003) of emotion work which followed. Here we are interested in the role of technology in this process.

We have already seen that much of the work of leadership evidently involves communication of one form or another, and that the managed display of emotions is an integral part of the many forms of interaction this entails. Emotional labour, and the 'valuing practices' that go alongside it, has been shown to be inherently communicative and embedded in the day-to-day work of leadership. As such, they are just an everyday feature of the work of a leader for whom, in Garfinkel's telling phrase, there is no 'time out'. In large organizations much of this everyday work is performed via e-mail, and below are some very different examples obtained through access to the e-mail archive of a recently appointed college head of department of how 'emotional labour' is instantiated in this technological medium. As he noted in his diary:

I started on January 5th and meandered into a mire of budget deficits, fraudulent attempts to dress up performance for a "practice" Ofsted inspection, a troupe of sulking lecturing staff, and a student retention nightmare. I began to feel like the meat in a sandwich, slapped between a slice of principalship and a slice of festering lecturer discontent. Ofsted inspected the College in December 2001 and another inspection is not due until 2005. However, in order to prepare for this inspection we are having a practice inspection. Of course, nobody is adequately prepared and anxiety has set in. We know what is expected but staff continue to indulge in "arguing with the ref". Inspectors are not going to change their views on the importance of lesson plans or schemes of work, and management efforts to help staff prepare are construed as yet more burdens indiscriminately and unnecessarily placed on already frighten-ingly overburdened lecturers. Many lecturing staff in the faculty have an unrealistic view of my power to transform their conditions. Having been promoted from within I feel that considerable expectations have been placed upon me by the lecturing staff: I was one of them; I should understand their difficulties; I should be on their side. My inability to do anything about some of these problems has sometimes been interpreted as my desertion of their cause and my absorption into a management position.

As a newly appointed head of department he is faced with a number of classic management issues – issues in which he is supposed not just to 'manage' but to show various leadership qualities as well, such as ensuring the morale of his teaching team. In the first e-mail the newly appointed head of department is attempting to reassure his staff – clearly concerned at the prospect of an imminent Ofsted inspection – while at the same time appear compliant to the demands of a college practice inspection by being able to show that he has a 'teaching observation' schedule in order to show that teaching is regularly audited through observation.

> Attached is a Post Inspection teaching observation timetable. Do not panic, do not even think about it. It's my way of assuring the inspectors that we have a plan. When they go away let's think again, as in, let's negotiate. (HOD e-mail)

In this next e-mail the head of department (Aaron) is attempting to deal with some of the everyday problems of staffing in a college on multiple sites – in this case one of the lecturers (Boris) has vehemently complained about examination invigilation duties, setting off a series of e-mails where Aaron begins by trying to get Boris to calm down, to which Boris eventually responds:

> OK, sorry Aaron. The spikiness of my e-mail was not intentional. No excuses here but some reasons for my e-mail: I'm under a lot of personal stress at the moment (both personal and professional) and the discovery last thing on Friday afternoon that I'm double booked was the last straw.

And, finally, this e-mail where the head of department (Aaron) attempts to reassure Boris and conclude the correspondence (the e-mail also, of course, provides a convenient 'audit trail' if the issue should arise again):

> Boris, OK let's make peace, we normally get along without strife. Sorry to learn that you are under pressure, I'd be surprised if there was anything I could do to help but if there is let me know. I'll fix Tuesday A-level cover. Invigilation ... is becoming increasingly difficult because of the number

of students and the size of the rooms, this puts pressure on us all. As you know, I'm not slow to express displeasure and I have already complained about this situation. Perhaps next year things will improve. Aaron.

But 'emotional labour' is not merely about control, and e-mail can also be used to express other, perhaps more humorous and clearly authentic aspects of the leader's personality – as in the following, bantering, e-mail exchange between the newly appointed head of department and some of his lecturing colleagues, obviously astonished at his promotion:

Aaron, I've just told Sally that you are the new Sarah Jones and she's still recovering from the shock. She thinks you have now become really establishment but I've explained that it's all part of your plan for the re-establishment of patriarchy ... .

To which Aaron replies:

Debra, Thanks, but Sally is right of course. I'm now completely establishment and normally I would not deem it appropriate to respond to e-mails from junior staff. However since I am currently working on a new uniform for the older female members of staff (a sort of tart and nazi combination) I thought I should at least advise you to enjoy yourself while you can and if possible get in shape, the new uniforms are designed to accentuate femininity. Regards to Sally and yourself. Aaron.

We would not want to make too much of this trivial exchange. But we have already suggested that much of the emotional labour of leaders consists of exactly these kinds of trivial interaction. Through this e-mail exchange, this new head of department attempts to assure his colleagues that he hasn't changed, he hasn't suddenly become 'one of them' in the well-known divide between 'them and us'. And the e-mail allows him to target this message – to direct it only at these two without calling a meeting or asking them to see him, and to effectively place his position on record, so that these lecturers can point to the e-mail and say 'look, Aaron is just the same'.

Conclusion: Technologies of Leadership?

The examples above illustrate the ease with which these mundane technologies have become 'at home' in organizational life – to the extent that many can now scarcely envisage everyday organizational life without them. Clearly too, the various leaders in our studies were adequately, even effortlessly, utilizing the available technologies. They have taken the technologies and in Sacks' (1972) telling phrase, made them 'at home in a world that has whatever organization it has'. The final extract below further illustrates the kinds of concerns we have addressed in this chapter.

> Ambridge field note extract: Penny (the Principal) tries to find out who is attending the meeting and whether it needs to be cancelled (it has already been cancelled once). Phones Ted (her Vice-Principal and a key player in the meeting) who claims he doesn't know anything about it and isn't coming. Penny says he was copied in on the e-mail and should know about it. He asserts that the post-inspection action plan takes priority. Penny: "I understand that, but where I'm coming from is the lack of communication with me."

This extract plainly illustrates how particular technologies are embedded into the workplace and are a taken-for-granted part of working life and particular streams of work – the Principal shifts from a face-to-face meeting to a phone conversation to a comment on e-mail. It also shows how certain technologies are more immediate, less subject to avoidance and more confrontational than others. Finally it shows that some technologies and awareness of them – in this case e-mail – bring with them certain visibility to others and, with that visibility, certain accountabilities – 'he was copied in on the e-mail and should know about it' (the meeting). The extract, taken with the others we have considered in this chapter, although not especially surprising or unusual in terms of everyday workplace technology or technology use, also illuminates some key social affordances of leadership technologies. This fits with the thrust of this book, suggesting that leadership in education consists of complex, but ultimately mundane and ordinary, practices, supported by mundane and ordinary technologies. In suggesting such technologies are 'mundane', the focus moves from the technology itself to the interactions and relationships it engenders and sustains. What is evident is the different kinds of leadership work (e.g. disseminating information, managing subordinates, etc.) that stretch across and through a whole gamut of technologies involving multiple audiences. Thus, leadership can be seen as shared work, reliant upon an ensemble of participants and, crucially for our purposes, including the utilization and manipulation of an array of technologies and systems that support and enable the practical everyday accomplishment of educational leadership. The suggestion is then that a leader requires some familiarity with using these technologies and some mastery of orchestrating these technologies to secure an appropriate, desired, outcome. In this chapter we have shown the various ways in which certain technologies have particular emotional affordances (such as supporting the expression of empathy or humour) and informational affordances (such as dispensing authoritative description or local news) that leaders can exploit as part of their everyday leadership work. We have seen how authority is exercised, albeit subtly, using the most ordinary of technologies and that, according to their (im)material form, ephemerality or permanence, such technologies make leaders and the led accountable and responsible in different ways. Taking this argument further, *particular* features of these technologies and the communication they support (e.g. asynchrony) can shape action and interaction and decisions and the way decisions are made. The extracts also illustrate the importance of considering the temporal features of often quite ordinary technologies as well as how they are placed in people's everyday working lives. In considering this, we start to see how such technologies support the layering and interspersing of work. So, as evident in the extract above, while e-mail can support information provision perhaps avoiding the messiness of consensus seeking via a telephone conversation or a face-to-face meeting, it does not replace essential group and individual face-to-face meetings. What might be discussed at these meetings may well have already been the subject of e-mail or telephone conversations but, as already pointed out in Chapter 4, these preparations for meetings are part of everyday leadership work. In examining what we have termed 'technologies of leadership', the ethnographic approach to leadership we have taken treats leadership as a practical accomplishment, and necessarily accesses the 'fine-grained empirical detail' and the necessary 'gritty observations about the social worlds in which computer systems are used' (Kling, 1996). Traditionally leadership and technology have remained separate fields of study and yet our discussion of 'technologies of leadership' clearly illustrates the ways in which leadership and technology are inextricably linked in the doing of everyday leadership work, and how specific technologies can and increasingly must play a central role in its practical accomplishment. More specifically for colleges as organizations, drawing upon Yates and Orlikowski's notion of 'genres of organizational communication' (1992), this chapter has suggested that the emergence of new technologies within the learning and skills sector is related to, and paralleled by, the development of new organizational forms, new account-abilities and new managerial philosophies.

Chapter 7

Leadership: Success and Failure

Introduction

Sociology, like all modern social sciences, concentrates most of its energy on success, that is, on the achievement of certain historically received outcomes, as pursued by social actors, from within projects that are themselves defined, in part, in terms of those outcomes. (Malpas and Wickham, 1995:37)

In a media-driven age that thrives on anything which boosts ratings one could easily argue that failure is at least as 'high profile' as success, and this is no less true of academic interest than of that of the general public. Whether one agrees with Malpas and Wickham or not, what is clear is that the words 'success' and 'failure' are constantly bandied about in the education sector at the present time. With regard to further education, the sector is said to be in crisis, with many colleges 'failing' commercially as well as in terms of the quality of provision (Goddard-Patel and Whitehead, 2000). Indeed, in the post-incorporation environment of the learning and skills sector – operating in a quasi-market economy where each college must compete for both funding and students – this financial context for failure is perhaps more prevalent than that of failed Ofsted inspections or poor academic results. In Goddard-Patel and Whitehead's (2000) review of very publicly failing colleges and the implications for education policy, seven of the ten colleges discussed were deemed to be failing on the basis of severe financial deficits or irregularities. Governance issues and discrepancies in management information (for example, concerning student numbers) were the other significant reasons for this label being applied. More routinely, Ofsted measures success and failure based on an assessment of the quality of teaching and learning, learner achievement, curriculum suitability, availability of learner guidance and support, adequacy of learning resources, adequacy of assessment and monitoring systems, and – central to the theme of this book – the quality of leadership and management (www.ofsted.gov.uk/howwework). Whichever criteria are applied, to be labelled a failing college has enormous implications in terms of the level of audit to which one is subjected, the availability of funding through whichever mechanism is currently in political vogue (the Learning and Skills Council at the time of the study), the ability to recruit students and staff, and the prestige (or lack of it) of the college leadership.

The linkage between effective leadership and organizational success is also being constantly thrust at those working within the sector (and, indeed, at leaders everywhere), with the trend towards notions of distributed leadership (e.g. Gronn, 2002) making this the responsibility of all rather than a select few. Somewhat circularly, effective educational leadership is often defined as that which generates success, i.e. on the basis of academic achievement or commercial competency, rather than as a set of practices in its own right. Such is the emphasis on outcomes as a measure of what constitutes effective leadership – or leadership *per se* – that Grint (2005) took 'leadership as results' as one of four core classifications through which he sought to make sense of the burgeoning volume of leadership research. Indeed as Blair (2002) comments, while such methods of determining effectiveness – she refers specifically to the coupling of academic achievement with effective school leadership – are subject to much criticism, it is still generally adopted, with other possible measures such as the creation of a school community or provision for under-achievers being discussed but rarely adopted in practice.

Much of the literature on educational performance has taken a quantitative approach to its assessment, and has usually attempted to show some sort of relationship – correlation or causality – with educational leadership. This has been achieved via the 'packaging up' of measures of success and the leadership attributes (or skills, or behaviours) needed to achieve them: that is, there is a normative association of particular leadership styles or behaviours with desired performance outcomes. So, for example, Cheng (1994:300) sites Sergiovanni's (1984) 'five leadership forces model' (comprising technical, human, educational, symbolic and cultural leadership) to explain how principal leadership is related to excellent school performance, and conceptualizes school performance as:

> ... a multi-level phenomenon that should be described by multi-level indicators including organization-level indicators, teacher-level indicators, and student-level indicators. (Cheng, 1994:301)

These, in turn, are broken down into structural, attitudinal and affective measures and constructed into an analytical tool which is administered across a large sample of teachers and students to produce a swathe of correlations and relationships between aspects of leadership and the various indicators.

In a similar vein, Leitner (1994) uses Hallinger's (1983) framework of instructional leadership (comprising the dimensions of defining the school's mission, managing the instructional programme, and promoting a positive school climate) as a basis for assessing the principal's impact on student learning measures using standardized test scores. His interest is in the mechanisms through which principals impact on student outcomes, as mediated by their impact on teacher behaviour. The result is a framework of linkages (cultural, structural and interpersonal) which, in turn, break down into specific mechanisms. For example, the structural linkage mechanisms are stated (after Daft, 1983) as being supervision and evaluation, rules and procedures, plans and schedules, and vertical information systems.

We acknowledge that such frameworks may have some merit in the environment of compulsory education, where there is considerable clarity concerning what constitutes success: notwithstanding the greater emphasis the teaching profession would like to see on such outcomes of their work as 'value added', there is a generally accepted focus on academic achievement as the main aim of primary and secondary education. Even here, we would argue that the resultant frameworks and relationships that are identified do little to explicate how the work actually gets done: how success – by whatever measure – is actually generated. In the post-compulsory sector, we would suggest that the picture is further complicated by the broader range of success criteria that may be applied, based on the wide range of stakeholders involved. So, for example, local employers may want a college to produce people with craft skills and professional qualifications; our parents (as OAPs) want their local colleges to provide affordable, accessible leisure courses; parents of 16+ year-olds may want a range of vocational curriculum options for their less academic children; adults may want flexible learning for basic skills and retraining. At the same time, colleges are required to be commercially as well as academically or vocationally successful. This calls for what Blythin et al. (1997) have called a more nuanced appreciation of success and failure to be developed, through an ethnographic, 'illuminative' evaluation of what success looks like and what leaders do to bring it about. In line with our previous thesis of the value of ethnomethodologically-informed studies of work, we hold that it is what members of the setting – and in particular, college principals – see as success or failure that is important here, and that explicates what it means to succeed or fail.

Such a 'nuanced appreciation' may embrace a number of questions in relation to leadership and leadership work. For example, is the proposed linkage between effective leadership and college success observable and, if so, what does such leadership look like? Given the earlier discussions of the impact of 'audit cultures' (Strathern, 2000) on FE, and the 'gambits of compliance' (Bittner, 1965) adopted by college leaders, what meaning do the terms 'success' and 'failure' have for college principals? If they are seen as comprehending more than balance sheets and Ofsted grades, can one be a successful leader in a failing college (or vice versa)? The mainstream leadership literature has much to say in terms of the criteria commonly applied in determining success and failure, but less to offer concerning what 'effective' or successful leadership looks like and how we might recognize it when we see it. In an attempt to fill that gap, in this chapter we compare data from a 'failing' college and a successful one in an exploration of the 'gross observability' of such terms and their manifestations in day-to-day leadership work. The definitions of success and failure here are those constructed and played out by members of the setting – college principals, teachers, Ofsted inspectors, and so on. We pay fine-grained attention to their accounts of 'successful' leadership and the activities through which this is accomplished, with no attempt to distil some generalized formula for what constitutes successful leadership in any abstracted sense or (as far as possible) to overlay our findings with our own preconceived ideas. We also offer data from one self-confessed 'failed' principal, by way of explicating the complexity of how such failure may be accounted for by those who bear (or claim) the title. While this latter aspect of the chapter explores the attributions of failure made by the principal in question, it is the *work* of attributing which is of interest here, rather than an examination of the specific attributions made. Thus, in contrast to attribution theory (Heider, 1944; Jones and Davis, 1965; Kelley, 1967), with its focus on dispositional versus situational causes, our focus here is on the ways in which members make sense of (i.e. the 'ethno-methods' they use) their perceived failure to accomplish the task of leadership.

Accounting for Failure – a Principal's Perspective

While the notion of a failing college tends to be seen as encompassing a range of academic and financial outcomes, success or failure for a college principal can be understood (and felt) in much more localized, personal terms. In the situation outlined below, Marjory viewed herself as having failed despite the fact that her College consistently produced good results, both for students and in terms of Ofsted inspections. For her, the notion of failure was about the poor relationship which existed between herself and her Vice-Principal, Sam, and the potential for detrimental effects to result for the rest of her senior management team and for the College as a whole. Interestingly, it is evident from her recounting of events that Sam was struggling with the Vice-Principal role – it appears from an interview conducted with Dorothy, the Assistant Principal who was at the College at the time, that Marjory could easily have instigated dismissal proceedings against him on the grounds of either incompetence or (mental) ill-health – yet she continues to see the failing as being her own rather than Sam's. The interview extracts which follow illustrate the warring notions of sound professional judgement on the one hand and an apparent lack of self-belief on the other which were both the source of Marjory's ineffective handling of the situation, and her own assessment of why and how she failed. In speaking of the situation to us (some time after it was somewhat dramatically resolved), she maintained that her failing was that of not supporting Sam enough. In recalling her assessment of his performance then, it appears just as likely that her failing was in not holding him accountable for the responsibilities he had as a Vice-Principal. As noted earlier, while we aim to avoid the 'expert' overlay of theory on the understandings of members of the setting in adopting an ethnomethodologically-informed stance, the self will inevitably intrude. It is a weakness of the principal ethnographer in this instance (MIW) that my own notions of 'good' and 'bad' leadership, of what constitutes 'success' and 'failure' in this context, can tend to seep out. My own experience of being a leader, and my own style of leadership, are not totally expunged either from my reading of the data or my writing of the text, notwithstanding the moderating influence of my fellow authors. It is, I suspect, obvious that I tend towards a belief that her failure was in not holding him accountable rather than in being insufficiently supportive – something which the reader should bear in mind when making their own interpretations of the text. Caveats notwithstanding, the account of the situation given by Dorothy, her Assistant Principal at the time, gives more prominence to this aspect of the situation than does Marjory's own version of events, not least because it impacted on Dorothy herself:

... he didn't ... carry the work, the load. You know, and that ... yes, yes, it would irritate me, erm, because in the end I was under him, in terms of I was the Assistant Principal, and yes, I was paid less, but I was, perhaps, seemed to be doing more. (Dorothy – Assistant Principal)

Although Sam was her Vice-Principal for over ten years, Marjory neither fully dispelled her initial misgivings about him, nor did she fully address them. The result was an uneasy relationship in which she felt the need to support him, rather than being able to share with him the burden of college leadership. As the situation plays itself out to a dramatic and very public departure by Sam, his defensiveness and instability appear to paralyse her as a leader. The conflicting feelings engendered by the situation, and the potential for failure, are evident from Marjory's initial explanation of the situation, early in the interview:

> I think fundamentally, I didn't believe he had the calibre to do it, although I think I was possibly wrong in that. Erm, I think also, as a person, he had a lot of insecurities. There were personal issues, outside the College for both of us, as well. In that we both had very young children, erm ... We both attempted to juggle high profile jobs with family commitments with babies. Erm, and, erm ... I mean, I'm not using that as an excuse or anything, but I always think that when people are ... have ... when people are stressed, or within their jobs there are problems, my experience suggests that they're not the only problems ... that they may have other problems that are around the stress factor. And I think from personal experience that's probably true, that when you're trying to juggle two things, if one area goes wrong, then it's quite difficult to keep the other balanced ... And ... so that was happening between us too. Erm, and, erm, Sam's style was ... erm, he ... underneath it ... he was very, very vulnerable, and his background and his home background and everything, erm, which is why I chose him. He'd not succeeded in schools, he'd gone through the FE route – his whole background left him very vulnerable in lots and lots of ways. But that vulnerability came out in a very assertive sureness of when he was right. Erm, and I found that quite difficult to cope with, when people are very self-assured. I mean, I'm probably like that anyway ... erm, and so we ... just the relationship was very, very difficult indeed. (Marjory – Principal)

Despite a rational assessment of Sam's capabilities and limitations – she later talks about his inability to use ICT effectively, his failure to complete staff assessments and the impact of his moods on staff working with him – Marjory clearly feels the need to make excuses for him and to take the blame on herself. She speaks from the perspective of one individual feeling responsible for the wellbeing of another, rather than as a principal responsible for the delivery of quality provision to her students. This 'big picture' perspective on events seldom enters her account of the situation. The following extract reiterates this very personal view of their relationship, to the total exclusion of her status and responsibilities as a Principal:

> But I got some feedback [after he had left the College and attended a job interview elsewhere], which indicated that my reading of the intellectual capability was correct. Erm, because obviously I had to provide a reference to that job, and it was fine, there was no problem with that. Erm, but through various channels, somebody had asked – somebody else that I know – about Sam, and said at the interview, intellectually, he just wasn't really there. So I sort of know from that channel that it's not me being totally prejudiced, because I've questioned myself interminably. Was I just massively unfair to him? Was I just undermining his confidence all the time? Was it because of me, why he'd not perform? Erm, but I know, for example, that it got to the stage where, if something was wrong or he'd done something wrong or he wasn't able to do something, rather than face me at all or – and I'm not a nasty person, you know – but rather than, I suppose, he would see it as being undermined again, he would go to other people and try and get help from other people. (Marjory – Principal)

These doubts were persisting for Marjory after Sam had walked out of college in the middle of a very public event and not come back. She had numerous instances of unprofessional conduct on his part – for example refusing to participate in meetings, saying outrageous and inappropriate things while representing the College, and making one department within the College a 'no-go area' for her by an attitude of extreme possessiveness towards it – but still saw the situation in personal terms. A final extract from the interview locates the specific relationship she had with Sam in Marjory's wider view of herself as a leader:

> Erm, we've got a very good College, I mean really good, and when you operate at that level you try to put minute details right. I was an English teacher, so I'm used to working out which commas and full stops are in the wrong place, and I'm afraid that comes through. So what I do is, instead of praising people, and saying to the whole world that you've done that, I sort of make an assumption – which is wrong – that they know that I think that this is OK, but if they did that bit, it would be ... they could just ... I don't do the praise bit enough. So that's ... that's ... and I know that and people tell me that, (laughs) and I'm very bad at

it. So I'm sure that as a failing Principal, my failure is that I don't praise enough. The other thing I'm not good at is, I'm not an up-front, charismatic Principal. I'm just not good at that. Erm, I'm not good at leading meetings, I'm not good at leading from the front in that sense. I've got to work with people one-to-one and try and get them on side, and I suspect that by doing that, that might create the sense that I'm trying to work with people and Sam might have felt that that was against him. I don't think it was, but there was definitely, towards the end, this feeling of erm, some teams that were either ... you were either for Sam or for me, do you see what I mean? (Marjory – Principal)

The above extracts show how Marjory constructs the notion of 'success' and 'failure' in the context of leadership through a series of 'language games' (Wittgenstein, 1958), where this phrase is understood to refer to the use of language against a shared background context which Wittgenstein referred to as a 'form of life'. In talking about 'leading from the front', having the 'intellectual capacity', not participating in meetings, behaving 'inappropriately while representing the College', or 'not praising enough', she is setting out a network of practices which together constitute a recognizable notion of what is to be understood as leadership in the context of an FE college. The language she uses – and shares with colleagues working in the same setting – situates them in 'a social world of practices, the structure of which is grounded, not merely in concepts, but in ways of acting and responding that essentially involve the *use* of language' (McGinn, 1997:52 original emphasis). It is through such language games and the situated practices they entail that sense is made of events in which members participate and the meaning of words such as 'success' and 'failure' in relation to leadership are explicated and made accountable. Similarly, in referring to 'insecurities', 'personal issues', and 'family commitments' with the caveat that she is 'not using this as an excuse', Marjory delineates the professional boundaries which (for her) operate around leadership and preclude the intrusion of practices which belong to other 'forms of life': in locating 'insecurities' and 'personal issues' in another language game – that of personal rather than professional life – she demonstrates her competency in the practice of leadership, at the same time elaborating what constitutes competence for others. As Jordon (1989, cited in Lave and Wenger, 1991:105) argues, 'learning to become a legitimate participant in a community [of practice] involves learning how to talk (and be silent) in the manner of full participants.' Through the production and reproduction of language games and the telling of 'war stories' (Orr, 1990) about past successes and failures, members learn what constitutes success, failure, leadership, and so on, within the 'community of practice' (Lave and Wenger, 1991). As Lave and Wenger make clear, such knowledge, once acquired, resides in the situated ability to perform the required practices and to recognize their performance by others, rather than in internalized, mental representations or individual understanding. Thus the existence of a community of practice can be equated with Wittgenstein's notion of a form of life, both relying on shared understandings of situated actions.

From the above extracts, we can see that for Marjory, failure is a very personal thing – personal to her in that she feels it very deeply and personal in its effects on others. She sees her failure in terms of largely interpersonal behaviours – not praising enough, undermining a colleague's confidence – rather than in structural or strategic terms. Likewise, the effect on others (and specifically her Vice-Principal) is seen as personal – increasing vulnerability, not being able to face her – rather than in relation to the tasks or responsibilities of the role. In the shared context of the college, the failure also appears to have been very visible: to have been recognizable within the language game of what constitutes leadership. Certainly it was visible to colleagues at the time. For example, Dorothy, the Assistant Principal, considered confronting them both with the need to resolve the situation for the good of the College: when interviewed, she spoke in detail of Sam's shortcomings in relation to the role he held, but also saw Marjory's shortcoming in how she dealt with the situation:

> He would probably have been challenged by just grasping some of the ... what was going on, you know ... intellectually. Having said that, in other ways, he would be more on the ball with staff – you know, sort of, on the personal relationships side ... I mean, Marjory was a classic for a damning comment that she doesn't realize will really, you know, because again, she'd be thinking of the negative and 'that needed doing and that wasn't done' and not the building people up. You know, the praise and what-have-we. Then I come into the situation and I can see both sides, as it were. There was no way I was going to go in ... the only thing I've thought since is ... what if I'd gone and said, "look, you two ...": it's a bit like telling Mum and Dad to get their act together. So I never did (laughs). (Dorothy – Assistant Principal)

Some form of failure in leadership was clearly observable in the above accounts: both Marjory and Dorothy give instances of a relationship between senior colleagues that was less than effective. In both accounts,

Sam appears as a Vice-Principal who was struggling to fulfil the responsibilities of his role, and Marjory as a Principal who was unable to resolve the difficulties of the situation. The potential for adverse impacts on other members of the team is also apparent in both accounts. Yet by Ofsted's 'account', and by that of the academic achievements of students, the College in which these events took place was successful. Other accounts may add further nuances to the perceptions of success and failure which this one situation could yield, and we would, of course, invoke the ethnomethodological practice of 'bracketing' to preclude the privileging of one version over another or the suggestion that one version is in some way 'right' or 'true'. Instead, it is the process of constructing versions – rather than the versions themselves – that is of interest to us: the behaviours and practices are 'there for all to see', but their meanings and the manner in which members orient to them are locally constructed accomplishments of the setting.

Successful and Failing Colleges – What Do They Look Like and What Do They Tell Us About Effective Leadership?

As already outlined, much of the data for this study has come from Lambton Sixth Form College – using the criteria of high student achievement and good grades from Ofsted, a successful college. The day-to-day leadership work of Steven, the College's Principal, many detailed examples of which have already been given in preceding chapters, can be taken as an example of effective leadership both in terms of external measures and a personal (though self-critical) sense of self-efficacy. Broadly speaking, his leadership can be characterized as relying on a strongly values-based message, consistently implemented in his everyday leadership practices, from the setting of strategy to the picking up of litter around the College. We can also see from the data that Steven is supported by a strong and committed senior management team, who work effectively together and have a clear vision of the role of the College in the local community. The result is clarity in terms of the College's aims and objectives, and shared ownership and responsibility from the senior team. Another college which participated in the study was 'Ambridge', a large and 'failing' FE college. The following composite description of Ambridge is drawn from fieldwork observations, the reports of external advisors, and the admissions of Penny, the College Principal.

After two poor Ofsted inspections, Ambridge is improving slowly, but still has a long way to go. Construction and Health & Social Care were both graded

4 (unsatisfactory) at the most recent inspection, and retention and results were disappointing across the board. Staff morale is low, and there appears to be no shared vision for the future. The College is housed in aging, dilapidated buildings, and is perpetually short of space. This results in valuable management time being lost to fire-fighting on maintenance and accommodation issues. After three years as Principal, Penny feels she is running out of time to turn things around. In particular, she feels she needs to address the poor quality of accommodation the College currently provides, the fact that the College vision – to the extent that it goes beyond surviving their next inspection – is 'laminated, not lived', and the lack of coherent leadership currently being provided by the senior management team.

The last two of these problems can be said to arise directly as a result of poor leadership, firstly by Penny's predecessor (ousted from his post for financial mismanagement) and now (arguably) by Penny herself. Although the College does have a vision statement, it appears in documents in the same format as it has for years, and fails to relate to the College's future, or to inspire and direct current effort. Staff are focused on 'today's problem' rather than on 'tomorrow's goals' and have no clear or meaningful framework within which to direct their efforts or make day-to-day decisions. Also absent are the policies and procedures required to underpin the vision and translate it into day-to-day practices for both management and staff. An external advisory team identified weaknesses in systems and procedures for staffing, timetabling, quality assurance and improvement, performance monitoring, and decision-making, with consequent negative impact on the quality of teaching and learning. Policies and procedures in these areas were either found not to exist currently, or not to be widely disseminated, such that management and staff have to 're-invent the wheel' every time an issue arises or a decision requires to be made. In terms of coherent leadership, the College senior management team are currently working as individuals, rather than as a team. They frequently introduce contradictory initiatives, or fail to cooperate and communicate effectively with each other. Individual members of the team regularly 'pass the buck' for things they should have been responsible for and don't seem to take personal ownership of issues that need resolving. This is proving costly in terms of wasted time and resources, and is creating a poor working atmosphere within the team. The Vice-Principal frequently undermines Penny in front of colleagues or simply 'goes his own way' without consulting her. This results in divided loyalties within the SMT and confusion among the staff. Penny frequently ends up bailing them out or acting as arbiter when situations get out of control.

The following field note extracts provide a comparison of the leadership practices observed in each of the Colleges. They comprise vignettes of the Principal in each case working with their leadership team, on a range of issues, as well as a sense of the climate which results. By juxtaposing what constitutes 'leadership work' in the two very different Colleges, we hope to offer some insights into how the leadership of each contributes to its success or failure. This said, we would place the now familiar caveat around any conclusions drawn from the comparison: they are, of necessity, situated insights. They relate to one leader's practices in the setting in which they find themselves. The leader is not 'causing' the success or failure, nor should their behaviours be imbued with any normative overtones for other, apparently similar, settings. We would not wish to undervalue them on that account however: while not claiming 'generalizability' for our findings in a positivist sense, we do see them as having typicality and recognizability. And on this basis, we would expect readers to be able to orient to them as having resonance with their own experience and understanding of what it means to lead or to work as an effective leadership team. And as already noted, we don't need to see a hundred instances of something to know whether it is ordinary or exceptional: the reactions of members of the setting will tell us that immediately. In relation to success and failure, our own reactions to the present explication of everyday leadership work in this context can still be seen as adding to our understanding of a sector in which such notions are a constant driver.

The first extracts deal with issues of communication and the existence (or not) of shared management priorities:

Ambridge field note extract: Penny asks John (Assistant Principal for Teaching and Learning) if he is going to the "blue sky" strategizing meeting with their ICT consultants later in the day, concerning the development of a new MIS for the College. He says he hasn't received any information about the purpose of the meeting, so decided not to go. Penny doesn't assert herself in terms of the importance of the right people attending the meeting, and John retains the initiative and authority he had established earlier in the meeting. Penny: "I appreciate you've made an executive decision, but next time could you talk it through with me, because we could end up looking a bit silly if I don't know who's attending the meeting." After he has left, Penny tries to find out who is attending the meeting and whether it needs to be cancelled (it has already been cancelled once). Phones Ted (her Vice-Principal and a key player in the meeting) who claims he doesn't know anything about it and isn't coming. Penny says he was copied in on the e-mail and should know about it. He asserts that the post-inspection action plan takes priority. Penny: "I understand that, but where I'm coming from is the lack of communication with me."

A number of things are evident from this extract, the failure of Penny to assert her priorities with her team being, perhaps, even more striking than the poor communication between members of the senior management team and the absence of a shared understanding of management priorities. She takes an almost apologetic tone with her senior managers, and appears defensive in her attempt to justify her own position. When the meeting does finally take place, John takes the lead in terms of liaising with the ICT systems consultants and ideas put forward by Penny appear to be as much for consideration by her colleagues as by the consultants. There is no sense of a 'shared script' or agreed vision that they are bringing to the meeting. The result is a statement from one of the consultants that: 'What I don't understand is who's driving this within the College.' In contrast, the following extract from Lambton is an example of members of the senior management team working effectively together, on the basis of clear lines of communication and a shared understanding of what needs doing and why. As in this instance, their discussions tend to be open and frank, with Steven often appearing as the 'first among equals': facilitating rather than directing proceedings to ensure that an agreed conclusion is reached:

Lambton field note extract: The SMT are meeting to discuss the budget. Peter (Director of Finance) hands out revised versions of the review of the current position which he and Steven have prepared. Steven reminds everyone that the meeting needs to understand and respond to the final funding allocation announced by the LSC and consider the implications for next year's budget. Sue (Vice-Principal – Curriculum) probes and questions the review document to make sure she understands the numbers: uses her strong sense of what's happening on the ground to sense check what she is reading. Steven asks Sue for her view as to whether or not they should cut part-time, adult provision. Sue thinks hard before responding, answers on the basis of the practical risks of not making target numbers. Peter asks what the deadline is for making a decision. Sue responds by setting out the tolerances they have in terms of marketing evening classes and adjusting teachers' timetables, and the types of additional work they as a team could do to get better quality, firmer data during that time. Group discusses the knock-on effects in terms of issuing staff contracts, losing students to the local FE college, etc. Decide they need to make a decision by the following week's SMT meeting, and agree the parameters of the decision itself. Steven summarizes the latter: 'If we believe we can make 1,815 full-time students, then we cut the part-time provision.'

This discussion illustrates the clear priorities to which members of the SMT are working in terms of quality provision within a prudent financial framework, and the strong ownership they exhibit in respect of their individual areas of expertise. They come to the meeting knowing what it needs to achieve, and being prepared to contribute in a well-thought-out and meaningful way. Although Steven nominally leads the meeting, it is clear that they are all 'on track', such that his leadership can be very light touch: having opened up the discussion he largely limits himself to summarizing what has been agreed to ensure clarity.

The next extracts relate to the leadership work that goes into managing the College governors – keeping them informed, shaping their responses to important College issues – undertaken thorough preparation for the big 'set piece' meetings at which the senior management team are held to account by the Corporation. This preparation reflects the fact that, although the governors are 'insiders' to the College in many respects, they are also an audience to which the College needs to present itself in a coherent and professional way. Both Penny and Steven have a good working relationship with their chair of governors, and their boards consist largely of capable, proactive governors, but the way in which they approach this aspect of their work is significantly different:

Ambridge field note extract: Penny's secretary brings in some final drafts of papers for Friday's meeting of the Corporation, which will need to go out today. Penny comments that it will be a miracle if they all go out on time. Neil – the Clerk to the Corporation – pops in to discuss an issue which needs to be sorted out at Friday's meeting: Malcolm, the Chair of Governors, seems to have a different understanding of what the meeting needs to achieve from that which he and Penny have. Penny doesn't seem to have been proactive in briefing/managing the governors on this issue. Neil: 'I think we could do with a bit more clarity on this.'

As already indicated, on the whole Penny has a good relationship with her Chair of Governors, but the above example is an indication of her tendency to under-prepare for what could be considered external meetings and big set pieces. As with the ICT meeting, there is no sense of a 'shared script', of issues having been aired and viewpoints aligned in advance, or of the various contingencies of the situation having been considered and managed. In the above example, it is Neil who has identified the discrepant views as a concern, and is prompting Penny to talk the issue through with Malcolm in advance of the formal meeting on Friday. The following extract from Lambton, shows the very different approach taken by Steven:

Lambton field note extract: Steven is meeting with Frank (Chair of Governors) in advance of the full Corporation meeting, to talk through the issues on the agenda (papers have already been circulated to governors, having been discussed and approved by the SMT). Begin by discussing local issues of relevance to the College – appointment of a new Head at local secondary school where Steven is on the board of governors, potential for local MP to become a governor of the College, implications of the poor 14–19 area review just published and the role the College should play in leading future strategy in this area. Then talk through topics to be addressed at the Corporation meeting – LSC funding, summer building project, report of the internal auditors. Frank is meticulous and diligent in checking his understanding of the issues, the implications for the College, and the role governors should play. Before the meeting, Steven described him as a challenging, though positive, force in the management of the College: his questions are not intended to embarrass them or catch them out. They hold pre-meetings so that Frank can raise any issues he has and Steven can prepare to answer them in advance: also so that Steven can brief him on any background to the topics he should know about in advance. Where they disagree on issues, they discuss their views openly and with conviction, then agree what line they will take at the meeting.

This extract shows the two sides of Steven's relationship with his Chair of Governors – working with him to ensure there are no surprises at the formal meeting of the Corporation, but also recognizing the position of accountability he holds in relation to Frank and the consequent need for thorough preparation in advance of any formal encounter. Although they clearly get on well together – for example, they discuss cricket and the local political gossip as well as the business of the meeting – their relationship retains an element of 'performance' to it as a recognition of the roles they are each called upon to play. This is emphasized in the Corporation meeting itself, when Steven addresses Frank as 'Mr Chairman', and defers to him procedurally as the leader of the meeting. Also evident from this extract are the clear procedures which exist in respect of governance issues: which issues have to be approved by which sub-committees, when papers have to be circulated, what internal approvals they require before being sent to governors, etc. All the 'machinery' of governance appears to be well established, understood by everyone concerned, and to roll on smoothly as a matter of course.

The next vignette from Ambridge is, perhaps, the most telling in terms of why the College might be regarded as failing: worse, even, than the lack of planning and preparation it displays is the lack of teamwork within the SMT, the undermining of the Principal by her Vice-Principal, and her failure to remedy the situation in some fashion – by asserting her authority, bringing her Vice-Principal in line, uniting them under a shared vision or whatever:

Ambridge field note extract: Senior team come for a pre-meeting before meeting with the LSC Regional Director, to reassure him that the College is capable and resourced to deal with the planned new build as well as the improvements required in teaching and learning following the recent inspection. Penny wants to talk about their strategy for running the meeting. Ted (Vice-Principal) and John (Assistant Principal for Teaching and Learning) hold side conversations and make 'laddish' jokes between themselves, not really paying attention. Penny is called out of the room to take a phone call, and the others immediately settle into a serious conversation about questions the LSC might raise and how they might address them. Penny returns and hands out copies of a recent report on their project management skills by an external consultant. Ted immediately makes a joke about his previous copy of the report having rude comments about governors on it. When Penny tries to focus their attention on the need for planning and preparation, Ted doesn't take her seriously: "We're good at winging it, Penny!"

This extract shows the manner in which Penny allows herself to be undermined by her Vice-Principal in front of other senior colleagues and does nothing – either in the meeting or subsequently – to assert her authority or challenge his unprofessional behaviour. In other observations, Ted repeatedly prefaced comments with Penny's name in an attempt to patronize her, used the ethnographer's presence as an excuse for not addressing the issues she raised (and refused the ethnographer's attempt to leave to facilitate the discussion), placed his own priorities over and above hers, and presented himself as 'the real leader of the College' in public meetings. In many respects, she colluded in his assumption of leadership by making herself 'invisible'. In the absence of a strong lead from her, it was easy for him to step in and fill the gap. So, for example, in the subsequent meeting with the LSC, it was Ted who gave his judgement on the fairness of the inspection, the strengths and weakness of the College in terms of their project management abilities, and the likelihood of the new build project distracting attention from the need to improve teaching and learning. Penny acted in a supporting role by providing the more 'nuts and bolts' information concerning project planning, in a reversal of the strategy-versus-implementation roles it would have been usual for a principal and their vice-principal to adopt. In contrast, Steven's authority with his team is too palpable to require voicing. At the same time, they clearly operate as a group of committed professionals united by shared values and beliefs. There is an underlying consistency of priorities and purpose evident in the whole body of data gathered within the college which clearly emanates from the SMT. Colleagues are not afraid to disagree with each other, but do so in a spirit of professional respect and for the good of the college. Also, such disagreements happen 'behind closed doors' – i.e. in the pre-meetings which take place within college – and not when they are presenting the College to an external audience. So, for example, at one SMT meeting they engaged in heated discussions in relation to the findings of a staff satisfaction survey (already referred to in an earlier chapter), showing themselves willing to voice professional disagreement amongst themselves. In contrast, the subsequent implementation of agreed practices in response to areas of staff dissatisfaction, and the 'united front' the SMT showed when the outcomes were fed back to a meeting of staff – the whole SMT attended the meeting, sat together at the front of the hall, and fielded questions based on the agreed responses – indicated the high degree of coherent leadership which Steven was able to command from his team.

The following extract from Lambton addresses the other aspect of 'leadership work' which appears to be absent from Penny's approach: that of holding her managers accountable for the professionalism and performance that may reasonably be required of them. It relates to Steven's practice of having regular, formal meetings with his Vice-Principals, at which progress on agreed areas of responsibility are discussed and minuted:

Lambton field note extract: Steven prepares for his regular, fortnightly meeting with Paul (Vice-Principal). Writes a list of topics to be discussed in a record book he keeps of meetings with his SMT. Looks through recent records to remind himself of what is outstanding and what Paul has committed to do by when. He is late in delivering three things, all of which are important – this is not good enough and Steven takes him to task over them when he arrives. Agrees, and makes a note of, revised completion dates. Discuss some information re. student retention which Paul was supposed to find for the report being prepared for the LSC. Paul claims it doesn't exist: Steven produces a copy of the relevant document and points out that Paul is on the circulation list. Asks him why he wasn't aware of it and what he is going to do about the high level of drop-outs at AS level. After the meeting, Steven prepares for a similar meeting with Sue (Vice-Principal – Curriculum) – less preparation required as he knows Sue will have done all of the things on her list. Says she is tough, decisive and highly respected within the college, whereas Paul is well-liked but not as accountable.

Once again, the mechanisms in place, and the strong undercurrent of Steven's absolute conviction and consistency in everything he does, ensure the routine-ness of holding his team accountable to agreed performance targets. The need to enforce this way of working with Paul appears to be the exception rather than the rule, with other members of the SMT falling in line to take responsibility of their own accord. Even Paul is willing in principle and understands the responsibility he is expected to take, and only fails to comply through a lack of organization and poor time-management. When interviewed on this issue, Steven was clear that he sees himself as neither a charismatic leader nor an authoritarian one: people don't follow him by virtue of the strength of his character or his will. Instead it is the mundane, painstaking consistency of the detail of what he does that gets the work done, and prompts others to do their work likewise.

On the theme of mundane work, the vast quantity of data generated as part of the audit culture within which college principals operate mean that it is only too true that 'the devil is in the detail'. The ability to grasp great quantities of information, and dissect it for its implications for the college, is an important aspect of leadership work in this setting. Once again, it is work that is handled very differently in the two Colleges:

Ambridge field note extract: Louise (Head of Personnel) comes in to see

Penny to update her on various staffing and recruitment issues. Hasn't managed to tie up the different bits of information she has received from different people. Penny doesn't seem to have a handle on this either:

Louise: "What's this then? Is it a sessional conversion?"

Penny: "I don't know. I suppose it must be."

Louise: "It's as clear as mud, isn't it? There are so many stories."

Penny: "Confusing, isn't it?"

Louise: "I don't know what these posts are. They're not on the system."

Penny doesn't challenge her on this.

This extract shows Penny neither grasping the information she is being shown herself, nor holding her Head of Personnel accountable for understanding it! Neither party seems to take responsibility for the accuracy of the data, or for understanding its implications for the College. As the meeting progresses, Louise blames John, the Assistant Principal for Teaching and Learning, and his department for the impossibility of reconciling the numbers (they are inaccurate in what they provide and uncooperative when she goes to them with questions) and looks to Penny to step in and resolve the situation. Penny tells her to leave it with her, and she will take a more detailed look and see if she can sort it out. The meeting thus concludes with nothing resolved either in terms of the accuracy of the information being discussed or the ownership of its production. In contrast, extracts relating to Steven conducting similar meetings show him undertaking considerable preparatory work to ensure he understands the issues, checking his managers understanding of what they are presenting to him and, where necessary, working through the figures in detail himself. He both demands to understand the data himself and expects those responsible for producing it to have an in-depth understanding of it too. So for example:

Lambton field note extract: Steven, Paul and Peter are meeting to finalize the numbers they will present to the LSC for their premium funding bid. Steven starts the meeting by identifying an error he has spotted in the student numbers which have already been sent to the LSC, leading to an error in the financial calculations which have been made subsequently. Paul looks at it and realizes he had picked up the wrong number. Steven emphasizes the need to get the numbers right, and tells Paul the right number to insert. They then get into the nitty-gritty of the numbers – getting a detailed understanding of what they are saying. Steven works through the numbers with a calculator and questions Paul and Peter about where they have come from and why they are as they are. Steven is one step ahead in terms of clarity of thinking: rehearses the argument in terms of the implications for funding. Peter gives a clear run through of what the financial data is saying. Steven: "We want it on record that we are a poor, under-funded sixth form in need of premium funding! And we want a clear indication we're going to get it when we meet the LSC!"

Conclusion – Recognizing the 'Grossly Observable'

So what can we say about success and failure in educational leadership based on the study data? If we accept the criteria for organizational success and failure which are imposed upon the learning and skills sector – and on the whole, those in the sector do accept such criteria, even if they complain that they are 'too exam focussed', 'too academic', and so on – then we are left with some interesting, and potentially contradictory conclusions. The very different leadership styles evidenced by the extracts from Lambton and Ambridge would tend to support the proposed linkage between effective leadership and organizational success. We would all look at Steven and see a more 'effective' leader than when we look at Penny. The leadership practices related above – the consistency, the attention to detail, the planning and preparation, the accountability demanded of colleagues – while in no way dramatic, would all appear to be 'grossly observable' as contributing to effective leadership (although one could equally well argue that they constitute 'effective management' rather than 'effective leadership' – a distinction that is discussed elsewhere in this book). By the same token, Penny's lack of many of Steven's characteristics, and the very different leadership practices through which these are reflected, seem to exemplify its opposite. So score one for the quantitative researchers who would convince us of the correlation between leadership and results? Well, perhaps. But we would suggest that this is an over-simplification, in many ways. For example, the success of Steven's leadership is a situated phenomenon: it works in *this* college at *this* time, given all the other circumstances which surround its day-to-day accomplishment. Similarly, Penny's 'failure' occurred in a specific setting comprising a specific set of circumstances to which her leadership practices appear not to be an effective remedy. Combine these contingencies with the numerous amendments which could be made to the criteria used to judge success and failure, and reductionist conclusions concerning effective leadership and organizational success seem (thankfully) less secure. What we are left with is the 'grossly observable': the situated practices and activities and their outcomes in very localized settings. At this level, these phenomena continue to 'make sense' to us all in the 'real-time, real-world' order of our daily lives such that, in general, we can perhaps recognize, and agree on, 'effective leadership' when we see it.

Marjory's situation is, perhaps, less clear. By the same measures applied above, her College must be deemed successful: student outcomes have been consistently high and Ofsted inspection results good. Yet failings were evident – to her, at least – in her performance as a leader. The difficult relationship she had with her Vice-Principal had more in common with the SMT at Ambridge than with that at Lambton. Certainly, her 'failure' as a leader, though characterized slightly differently by her Assistant Principal, was clearly evident to her and was recognizable to others within the language game which constituted the 'form of life' operating within the College. So why did this deficiency apparently have no adverse impact on organizational performance? And how do the differing accounts of failure presented in this instance sit with the notion of the 'grossly observable'? Fortunately, it is beyond the scope (and methodology) of this chapter to address the first of these questions, although we might suggest a number of possibilities – the strength of other members of the team in covering for his weakness; their willingness to do this for an otherwise effective Principal, or the mediating effect of widely shared policies and systems within the College to name but three. It does, once again, however, raise interesting issues concerning the limited explanatory power of quantitative research into such complex relationships: the reductionist tendencies of this type of 'explanation' are surely in danger of obscuring as much as they reveal. The second point – that of gross observability – has already been touched upon, in terms of the localized sense making of members which surrounds the grossly observable practices and activities of the setting. We would suggest that one thing does emerge clearly from this chapter's explication of leadership in the contexts of success and failure, however: as in previous chapters, leadership work – whether effective or not – emerges as the triumph of the mundane over the dramatic.

Chapter 8

Conclusion: Reflections and Cautionary Tales

Much has been made in recent years of the value of 'good' leadership in the post-compulsory sector by government and the research community. Good leadership, we are told, is necessary for improving the quality of teaching and learning and for increasing the effectiveness and competitiveness of our educational institutions. Yet, surprisingly, little is known about what it is that educational leaders actually do. To paraphrase Gronn (1982:24), 'the question still remains: what do [educational leaders] *do* at their desks, *do* with their talk, *do* in the corridor, *do* on tours, and *do* with their writing?'. Models and theories of leadership in education tend to overlook (and more often erase) the seemingly mundane, ordinary and everyday practices of leadership work in favour of more abstract references to 'vision building', 'producing strategies', or 'transforming or engineering cultures'. And yet such accounts of leadership rarely explain how such work is (or should be) carried out in practice. For us, such questions have yet to be adequately dealt with in leadership research, and this lack of understanding of the everyday *doing* of leadership work may risk jeopardizing any attempt to prescribe appropriate methods for improving educational leadership within the sector. This is the 'gap' that we have identified and attempted to fill with this research and with this book.

The general, practical, motivation behind our research into leadership and leadership work was a very pragmatic interest in supplying material for 'leadership development' programmes of various kinds. Our intention was to provide a more nuanced understanding of leadership and leadership issues through our detailed descriptions of leadership work in practice, to demystify leadership and leadership work in a way that made leadership more accessible, recognizable and teachable and to suggest some new ways in which the problem of leadership might be addressed. In this concluding chapter we are therefore interested in looking back at our research: re-examining some of our data; presenting some 'lessons learned' – some reflections and 'cautionary tales' from our ethnographic studies of leaders as they went about their everyday work – and examining the contribution such a rich, 'situated' examination of leadership practice can make to both academic understandings of the concept of 'leadership' and to the practice of educational leaders themselves.

Cautionary Tales: the Value of 'Theory'

We want to start our 'cautionary tales' with some short stories about academic leadership theory, in particular considering whether depending on academic or theoretical analyses of leadership for guidance in the practical business of leading is fruitful, helpful or sensible. This may come as some surprise since, if you have managed to read this far in the book, the more perceptive of you will, no doubt, be more than aware of some scepticism on our part towards 'leadership' theory, and the proliferation of leadership theories that have spawned in recent years. In our research we had no expectation and no intention of coming up with a new, improved, theory of leadership by which the sector would be radically improved. In providing a nuanced explication of how a setting is rendered orderly through the intersubjective understandings of those involved, ethnomethodology eschews the ironic overlay of theoretical understandings beyond those of members themselves. To superimpose externally generated theoretical generalizations on a situation is to obscure the order and 'lay theory' that already exists. It is also to offer explanations and suggest causal relationships that may be unrecognizable to members of the setting. Nor are we alone in this regard. Lakomski (2005), for example, draws on the discrepancy between members' day-to-day experience of workplace settings and theoretical accounts of leadership and organizational functioning to suggest that the notion of leadership is obsolete. Instead, she suggests that research attention should be redirected towards the study of 'the fine-grained properties of contextualized organizational practice' in order to develop a 'bottom-up' model of how things get done in organizations. Our interest in theory has always concerned itself with the question, what work does theory do? It seems clear that it does some work and it would be overly cynical, and, importantly, not supported by our empirical data, to suggest that it operates only as a kind of rhetorical device or as a framework to explain or excuse particular leader behaviours. The college principals we followed and questioned had all attended various leadership development courses, they had all read a number of texts on leadership and consequently were able, when asked, to frame their own behaviour, tell their own stories or cautionary tales, in terms of particular, favourite, theories or concepts.

Of course, college principals have a lot of 'leadership theory' books to choose from since it has to be admitted that books and theories on leadership are ubiquitous: from the popular, 'airport lounge' book (e.g. Goleman et al, 2002; Senge, 1992; Covey, 1990) to the more 'academic' contributions found in academic journals, theories of leadership are inescapable. What passes as 'theory' in this context covers a broad range of options from a fully integrated set of propositions purporting to explain how leadership 'works', through models and frameworks of varying degrees of complexity and coherence, to lists of 'tips and tricks' for the would-be leader. The vast array of literature on leadership includes a wide range of themes and theoretical approaches, such that, as Grint notes, (2005:17) leadership remains an 'essentially contested concept'. However, theory's use in the real world, real-time activities of practitioners – in the case of this study, educational leaders – is seldom explored. Using data from the study, we considered how practitioners viewed theory and whether and how they incorporated specific theories into their everyday practices.

So, for example, one principal described himself as being 'theory led' in his leadership practice, seeing theory as a means of 'benchmarking' what his staff and managers were telling him in the absence of personal teaching experience on his part, and outlined a research-based approach to leadership issues:

> I rely on theory a lot to think things through. We try – it's partly because of my background, because I'm not a teacher. I was very conscious that I had to rely very heavily on what people were saying to me about teaching and management. But I wanted to effectively underpin that with real experience – you know, did it actually work – and constantly testing it out. So it was more that sort of role, I'd let somebody propose some things and I'd ask why, how they could demonstrate it was going to work, and evaluate it afterwards. (Andy – College Principal)

In terms of deciding which theory to apply to a given situation, the data suggests that principals 'latch onto' any theory or framework which has resonance with the current situation of the college and adopt it in a wide-ranging, 'across-the-board' manner rather than holding a stock of theories in reserve and applying different theories to different aspects of their current situation. So, again for example, texts such as James Collins' (2001) *Good to Great: Why Some Companies Make the Leap – and Others Don't* and Hughes and Potter's (2002) *Tweak to Transform: A Practical Handbook for School Leaders* were each chosen as guiding frameworks by colleges within the study. For Andy, this provided post hoc justification for an existing way of working, thus:

> ... we've had a fair amount of the "Good to Great" research that was done – looking at those that – what's the difference, between companies that are great over a long period as opposed to those that are great for short periods or not great at all. And just looking at the differences, and there was lots that came out of that about getting the right people, and then worrying about what they could do second. Not worrying overmuch about the strategic plan because if you get good people you can work that out afterwards. Being quite hard on sort of people management, particularly in the early part, so as an example of that is we're unusual, I think, in the way we do probation in that, generally speaking, around 5 per cent of all our staff fail their probation periods. And we did that before the research came out, so actually the pattern of turnover in great companies was different but the actual overall attrition rate was exactly the same. (Andy – College Principal)

Good to Great was one of two theoretical frameworks – the other related specifically to leadership practices – that recurred in the data from Andy's college, both in interview data with him and in field notes of his interactions and discussions with staff. This constant application of one theory across time and audiences was seen as a necessary source of consistency in 'getting the message across':

> And we try very hard to show how everything fits together, so if we've done work with schools at 14–16 we try very hard to show that we're not doing that just because the government says we should. We're doing that, actually, because we know we'll get better motivated 16-year-olds in the college, so it will improve things for the college as a whole. So it's coherent in the way the different bits fit together. And we – I think that's one of the things we're quite good at, is trying to do that. I don't particularly like saying the same thing over and over again, but I've learned you have to – keep doing that with governors and, to some extent, staff because you have to keep saying the "Good to Great" thing over and over again. (Andy – College Principal)

Similarly, such texts were used as the basis of a college-wide strategy for improvement, a shared goal couched in visionary terms:

> ... now I come back to "Tweak to Transform". Although it's written for schools, the thesis of it is how do school leaders manage a change process to improve quality of teaching. And a "tweak" is a small but significant adjustment, as opposed to a radical change or transformation, but if you have enough tweaks, you transform. And the better the institution, the less scope there is for transformation – you can only ever tweak. And what this book is doing is suggesting an approach and a way of making teaching and learning very obviously the predominant focus of management, and the leadership. (Steven – Principal)

Steven related how he was given the book by a member of his staff, read it, bought copies for his senior managers to read, agreed with them to adopt it as a college-wide approach, bought copies for the entire middle management team, and intends to use it to inform the staff development programme. In this way, the framework becomes a shared language for members of the college; a 'verbal shorthand' for expressing intersubjectively articulated goals and methods for achieving them. The phrase 'tweak to transform' – or just 'tweak' – was regularly used by curriculum managers in discussing changes to practice with their staff, as a justification or inspiration for what was to be done. In addition to explaining in a very few words what was driving a particular change, it also had the advantage of 'depersonalizing' the need to improve. Thus it provided a means of 'selling' the idea of change to those who might have baulked at being told their own practice wasn't up to scratch, but could buy into the idea that if everyone 'tweaked' then collectively they could 'transform'. The same characteristics of 'verbal shorthand' and 'depersonalizing' were also evident in the use of leadership models. So, for example, Andy articulated his own leadership practice in terms of the six leadership styles developed by Goleman (2000). This framework outlined six patterns of leadership behaviour (referred to as Authoritative, Democratic, Pacesetting, etc. leadership styles), each of which could be pulled from a 'toolbox' of leadership skills for use in the appropriate situation. Andy recognized that he tended in the past to fall into a particular style or way of leading, and that this might not be appropriate to his current situation. The interposing of the model between himself and his day-to-day practice enabled him to distance himself from the implication that 'choosing the wrong leadership style' might be the same as 'being a bad leader':

Well, where we are now is – I mean, my management style is not … I went on the Principal's Programme and the one thing I knew it would come out with was, I tended to be sort of mainly about Pacesetting, and that's because I've always spent three years in an organization that's started from scratch or needed to be improved and I suppose that's what I learned worked and so just kept repeating it. And I wanted to – one of the reasons I wanted to do this job for a much longer time was to do some, was to actually try and do something different rather than get something going and … so I know I've had to, I'm having to try and change from that sort of one dimensional. And I think with the staff I have now, I need to be more Democratic and Coaching. (Andy – College Principal)

As this extract demonstrates, the necessary element of simplification that is apparent in theory can provide a useful means of making sense of a complex world. By providing clear-cut 'compartments' to put thoughts, behaviours, problems, etc. into, and by using this as a means of recognizing similarities and differences, the member is able to reduce the complexity of his or her situation to a manageable level. Through naming and categorizing such activities into – in the case of theory-usage as opposed to theory-development – a pre-determined framework, a sense of order can be accomplished. So, for example, although Andy may undertake a myriad of different tasks and activities in his role as Principal, by seeing them as 'Pacesetting' or 'Democratic' he can characterize them as being similar to or different from each other and so appropriate to the different kinds of situations he encounters. This reflection on similarities and differences as a source of sense making was also applied between theoretical frameworks and college 'reality':

I mean, one of the interesting things for us in terms of the research that's just coming out – there's been a report from Hay [McBer] on schools culture – and in a way, I know I'm looking for research that backs up what we're doing, but it seemed to be very clear that the best – that schools that perform most effectively are those that have a service culture rather than a professional culture. And in a way, I think that's what we've tried to do. Interestingly, that research also said it's not what teachers want. They don't want a service culture. So those … that actually helps me understand the tensions inside the College. (Andy – College Principal)

The study thus showed theory being used as a tool of critical reflection, both personally and in relation to organizational issues. This reflection could sometimes be prompted by external inputs (such as conferences), rather than as something that was specifically sought. This said, the intention in attending such conferences was acknowledged as being to gather new ideas and inputs, as a constant source of resources with which to do the job. So, for example Steven, the principal at Lambton Sixth-Form College, attended an FE sector conference in which one of the speakers used the McKinsey 7-Ss Model to discuss his own success as a college principal. The model breaks leadership down into 3 'hard' Ss (Strategy, Structure and Systems) and 4 'soft' Ss (Staff, Style, Skills and Super-ordinate Goals, or Shared Values), and prompted Steven to review his own strengths and weaknesses:

> Principals can stifle development and change and many of the stagnating colleges are because the principals are into maintenance of the status quo ... and change is not necessarily leadership. You can have principals – manager principals – changing things often to no good effect, but that isn't necessarily leadership. It's the way in which it's done and the purpose with which it's done. (referring to the model – MIW) But what I would say is that manager principals are good at Strategy, Systems and Structure. And you can be a good principal and have a good college – and I would say this is a strength of mine, and it's certainly a strength of Sue's (Vice-Principal – Curriculum), and it is also a prerequisite where you have a failing college. So you need this (pointing to 3 hard Ss) but you want this (indicating 4 soft Ss) on top of it to get that extra level, and to get that extra level of performance out of people. And that's the ... that's the leadership bit. (Steven – Principal)

Steven went on to talk about the need for a 'mix' of the 7-Ss within any leadership team, and the restructuring and recruitment that he instigated within his own team to compensate for the fact that both he and his vice-principal are strong on the 'hard' Ss but weak on the 'soft' ones. Although these structural initiatives were already in place prior to his awareness of the theoretical framework, working with the framework has resulted in a focus on specific practices that he will need to support the changes already made. Considering the framework reflexively, he recognized that the changes he had already made had been in line with his 'hard S' way of working, and that 'soft S' practice changes would also be required.

What the examples make clear is that the practitioners' interest in theory is different from that of the academic or the researcher. Our college principals were interested in a theory's ability to suggest workable solutions to real, everyday problems; to present graspable, communicable simplifications of the complexity of everyday practice. This is not to say that their interest was only at the level of prescriptive models or airport lounge 'tips and tricks': they often brought a level of critical thought and reasoned reflection to their use of theory, and to its relationship to the real time, real world problems they faced. But the 'work' that theory did was in informing or accounting for practice, rather than in generating knowledge or understanding for its own sake. As a sense-making device, a shared language or a verbal shorthand, theory served as a method for ordering and communicating existing practice, and as another possibility for injecting ideas for new or alternative practices that might be effective.

So, for example, the Goleman (2000) framework of six leadership styles appeared to be well known in the FE sector, with a number of principals referring to it or speaking of their own leadership in terms of its taxonomy. They were clearly able to see their own leadership behaviours in terms of the 'packaged' styles defined by the framework, and frequently classified individual leadership behaviours in this way in the process of intersubjectively determining whether a given leadership intervention had been appropriate or effective. An illustration of this matching of empirical data to a framework is provided below:

Field note extract – Coercive leadership style (Intention – immediate compliance): Steven (Principal) is meeting with Paul (VP – Students and Quality) to talk through some draft papers the latter is preparing for a forthcoming governors' meeting. Paul is often late in delivering on issues he is responsible for, or poorly prepared for important meetings. Steven takes a tough line with him in pinning down what needs to be done and by when. Steven: "And we need to get the numbers right, don't we?" He then tells Paul the right figures to insert. Asks Paul when he will have the final version of the document ready. Paul: "It will be ready for the June meeting, hopefully." Steven: "No, I think we'd better not be hopeful. It *will* be ready." Steven specifies an interim date, prior to the June meeting, by which he would like to see the final version.

Field note extract – Authoritative leadership style (Intention – sharing a vision): First day of term. Principal speaks to all new students (in groups of 200) about what the College expects from them, and what they can expect the college to deliver in return. He talks about high standards of achievement; adult and inclusive learning environment; supportive but challenging staff, etc. He then mentions a few College rules, but mostly focuses on the ethos of the place: what they as a college believe and value and how students can make the most of the opportunities presented to them.

Of course, if a framework is comprehensive enough and any definitions vague enough all behaviours can be similarly 'matched'. Quite what this accomplishes, what work it does, is another matter. This outline simplifies the phenomenon to the point where it is all but lost and what remains is unrepresentative of (if not unrecognizable as) the work of leadership practitioners and fails to recognize the interweaving and overlapping of individual behaviours within each style, and hence within each situation. In this instance the researcher is fitting empirical reality to a theoretical framework, imposing the researcher's understanding of particular behaviours and their appropriate uses onto an already orderly situation: that is, one in which the practitioner employs particular practices as a result of their own, member's understanding of what will work in any given situation. Their leadership is accomplished as they go along, not in response to some pre-determined format of abstracted generalizations, or with the benefit of hindsight.

Inevitably, what results from this type of exercise, fitting theory to the data, is a gloss: a selective and simplified version of what actually happened. It is, however, a gloss that practitioners in the study were found to use. Thus Andy, an FE college principal, described himself as generally adopting a 'Pacesetting' style of leadership, and Steven, principal of Lambton Sixth-Form College described his strengths and weaknesses as a leader in terms of the 7-Ss framework. Such frameworks at least, if not their underlying explanations, do appear to have currency in the 'real world' of educational leadership. But the converse may also be said to be true: the rich, contextual detail of ethnographic data adds valuable nuances to otherwise 'bland' models and frameworks. Where such frameworks are used (as they often are) as developmental tools, it could be claimed that it is the situated descriptions that trainers use to illustrate the features of the framework as much as the underlying framework that prompts discussion, reflection, and learning. Our cautionary tale, then, concerns an over-reliance on leadership theories; an unjustified expectation that the theory will somehow, someway, tell leaders what to do, what the best course of action is in the circumstances – when the trick, of course, is being able to determine exactly what circumstance is, what the problem is, in the first place.

Cautionary Tales – Being a 'Good Leader', Leadership and Change

In this next section we describe and examine how the various leaders we followed and interviewed talked about, told stories about, their own sense of leadership and the leadership of others. For us, stories provide one means of discussing some of the stark and often less visible realities involved in doing educational leadership. What is more, the collection and sharing of such stories, stories that are not generally articulated in the everyday working life of principals and managers, may act as a positive means of inculcating a sense of professional vision amongst new generations of educational leaders. As Erickson (1996) has argued in his study of the use of storytelling in design:

> Stories provide a good first pass at what is important, from the point of view of users; they provide the designer with a glimpse of what the users terrain feels like, and thus provide a starting point for further exploration. (Erickson, 1996:3).

For us, questions concerning the nature or role of leadership in Further Education can benefit from an analysis of some of the stories that principals and senior managers tell about their experiences and encounters with leadership. As Erickson comments, such stories – although only snapshots of much more complex processes of organization – provide a good first pass at what is important from the perspective of the practitioner.

In the course of our research we built up a set of stories that suggested something about the 'professional vision' required to be a 'good' leader in the sector. As Goodwin (1994) puts it, 'professional vision' consists of:

> ... objects of knowledge that become the insignia of a professions craft: theories, artefacts, and bodies of expertise that distinguish it from other professions ... By applying such practices to phenomena in a domain of scrutiny, participants build and contest professional vision, which consists of socially organized ways of seeing and understanding events that are answerable to the distinctive interests of a particular social group. (Goodwin, 1994: 606)

Those who occupy positions of leadership in FE colleges draw upon a broad array of experiences to define what it means be a 'good' college principal, a 'good' manager and a 'good' leader. Indeed, as Loots and Ross

(2004) have stated in their own study of academic leaders in FE, principals and senior managers 'have few or no formal management qualifications and rely on experiential learning that draws heavily on their previous posts with Further Education' (2004: 19). For us, one way in which this experiential learning is expressed and passed on to others (including us researchers) is through the telling of stories. Being interested in the *socially organized ways of seeing and understanding events* we collected some of the stories that different leaders told. One of the commonest concerned what it meant to be a 'good leader':

Manager: There was a guy who used to play for Wigan called Ellery Hanley ...

Researcher: Oh yeah, I've heard of him, yeah.

Manager: ... and the Australians christened him "The Black Pearl". He went out to Australia, which is the proving ground in rugby league and he played for a ... not the top – not like the Manchester Uniteds of this world – he played for a team like Blackburn and they played really well, and that's the sign of a great player, and they really rated him. But what he said was "you've got to put your body on the line" and I've always thought, which is this thing, is that you don't ask others what you're not prepared to do for yourself. So you've got to be a worker and you set examples, so role modelling is just do it and try and be polite and pleasant, but be a human being. I think a lot of it's about that, but I think I'm a soft touch to be honest. So I think that's what prevents me from being a Principal because I don't think I'd want to be because I think that you've got to have a level of ruthlessness that I don't want to have because I've got to live with myself.

This analogy between sports stars and great leadership is a common one – particularly in popular management literatures, but it is used here to emphasize this manager's own values. Leaders have to be prepared to 'put your body on the line'. A good leader is one that demonstrates their ability through good example and struggling against adversity. There is also the feeling that lower level leadership in a college can involve a certain amount of humility – being a good human being. In contrast, being a principal is seen here as requiring a degree ruthlessness.

We also interviewed a newly appointed principal who had once worked in the same collage as the above interviewee and under the same principal.

Here the principal gives his own account of the leadership style of his previous employer:

> My previous College was very, very heavily influenced by one man [the Principal]. He had a vision for [the College] and he dragged it kicking and screaming into a new era. It really did need a root and branch look at it. It was in very poor condition, and he did that, it was his vision, his drive, and being a very charismatic leader, and so on, he did all that. But, I mean, a personal view is, I think, he's a bit of Winston Churchill character, y'know, and of course you venerate him and so on, but y'know, he's not a particularly good leader in the peace I don't think. Because I don't think he knows how to deal with that, I think constantly he's, he's looking for change rather than consolidation, and I think sometimes the College just lost its way a bit on systems and written down procedures and so on. It took its eye off the ball ...

Several of the college principals we have interviewed and observed have similarly stressed the importance of *change,* and reacting to change, in their colleges. The sector itself is very much defined by change (Kerfoot and Whitehead, 1998), but accompanying the many structural and environmental changes that have affected colleges is a sense that 'good' leadership must involve transformation; the transformation of the image of the college, the transformation of the interior and exterior of building, the transformation of organizational structure etc. Instigating and coping with such changes seem to play an important role in perceived notions of leadership in this sector. The principal quoted above, however, is a rare example of someone who rejects a call for change. He had been promoted within the last few months from deputy to principal following the former principal's transfer to another college. For this principal, his main task was to avoid undoing the good work set down by his predecessor, but also to retain a sense of stability in this college for the benefit of staff and students:

> Well, I mean, I wanted to try and keep the culture as positive as [the previous principal] did. I'm probably a bit more hands-on than he was, but there will probably be a cost to that which will probably mean I won't be out as much in the community as [name] was. Now, I'll try and vary from that but, I mean it's what I've done, I do enjoy being around the kids, I enjoy mingling and being in the College. I mean [name] did, but [name] saw a different priority for this College at that time.

While stories of success, mistakes and lessons learned are common in our data, there is obviously a sense in which such stories – particularly sagas – represent a kind of polished account. These are clearly stories that have been told a number of times and which form a kind of stock of 'storyable' experiences that principals and managers are able to call upon. One of the advantages of long-term ethnographies, however, is that they allow the researcher to spend greater amounts of time with participants, through which less polished stories can emerge. These are stories that again provide an insight into the methods used by principals and managers to build and contest their sense of professional vision as educational leaders:

> Principal A: ... part of the problem is the buck stops with the Principal, y'know, and at the end of the day, we are entirely accountable for the decisions, and all sorts of members of the management team can make decisions and can influence things but, in any case, you have to have a kind of faith in each other. Some people, for example, you know that you can bring them along and nurture and support them – all the things that a good leader should do – but you also have to come to the realization that there are some people that are not going to change.
> Principal B: ... it's like when you do something wrong, that carries far more weight than the eight things you've done right. It's how you actually manage and sort out the mitigating strategies in place when things are cocked up.

Each of the above extracts from interviews and discussions with college principals reveal a side to 'doing' leadership that is not commonly discussed within the discourses of transformation, heroic or charismatic leadership. The first comment by principal A is echoed by many principals, particularly those recently appointed, who quickly realize that the 'the buck stops with them' when it comes to decision-making and action. This personal accountability is made more troublesome when staff refuse to comply with the visions and requests of their leaders. A similar problem is voiced by principal B who feels, as many working in the sector do, that mistakes are far more visible (and memorable) than successes, and that, once again, it is often the principal that is held accountable. For other principals, however, being seen as a leader brings with it issues of confidence in ones ability to live up to the role:

> Principal C: I would have thought they would have wanted a sort of more typical Principal, but they specifically didn't want that ... so the first time

I met the course leaders I was very nervous, I thought, you know, I'll just come across as stupid. I'll ask them about the course and they'll wonder what I'm talking about.

Issues concerning accountability, blame, and fears of failure are common features of daily life for college principals. Yet such stories are rarely articulated to other managers or staff. For us, stories like these are particularly important as they provide a counter to other kinds of organizational 'sagas' and models of transformational leadership and 'cultures of excellence' currently colonizing the UK learning and skills sector. These discourses of excellence can inspire, but they can also oppress leaders who have to live the imagined ideal of educational leadership that they evoke:

> Principal D: ... the only difference between an experienced principal, for example, and an inexperienced one is you've just had more time to make more mistakes and to learn from them. The critical thing, I suppose, is to be able to know your mistake, because you don't learn anything, really, like as much until you find out. You like to try and convince yourself, on your better days, that something may have gone right, but you learn a lot more from this – from the things that go wrong. And it often is so frequently tied up with people who just aren't quite doing what you want them to do. Or aren't by a long way doing what you want them to do. The people side to this job, it seems to me, presents most of the leadership challenges that you face.

One of the more common forms of leadership story observed in our research is what Clark (1972) has referred to as the 'organization saga':

> ... accounts of achievements and events in the history of a person or group, [that] has come to mean a narrative of heroic exploits, a unique development that has deeply stirred the emotions of participants and descendents ... (Clark, 1972:178).

Many of the sagas we heard involved stories of some form of organizational change, periods of great instability either from the 'good' or 'bad' old days of the college. The following is one such saga that combines what could be described as the 'ancient' history of the college with the more recent changes in the early 90s involving a major cultural-change programme that is still being followed today. This extract is taken from a speech given five times during one day by the college principal to mark a new phase in the culture-change effort of the senior management team. Along with the retelling of the organizational saga, the audience – made up of staff and students – are reminded of the college's set of core values which must (according to the Principal) be 'lived' by all those working and studying at the college:

> When I first came to [this college] I was actually intimidated. Before I even got inside I had to push through a gang of students stood smoking near the main entrance, y'know, literally push my way through. I'm being honest here, I felt intimidated, and I remember thinking, if I feel intimidated and I'm the Principal then how are other visitors to the College going to feel? When I reached what is now the main reception area I was greeted by the sight of bodies – bodies everywhere – students standing around, lying around, chatting. It looked like what we used to call back home a "doss house". I remember thinking "what kind of place have I come to?" For me a good college is not a youth club, it's a place of learning, it can be fun as well, but people have to take responsibility for that. We have to make each other feel valued. That's why we don't have strict rules here. We don't need them so long as we have mutual respect ...

This Principal took great pride in the change that had taken place in the college since his arrival over two decades earlier. This was evident in the number of times the story of the college's transformation was recounted over the course of the ethnography. It was a story told, not just by the principal but, by the senior managers, middle management, administrative and teaching staff. It is a story that people within the college drew upon to build a sense of professional identity. As this history lecturer told one of our researchers following one version of the principal's speech:

> I think that it's quite a comfort having such explicit values. It's like having Ten Commandments that you and the students can work within, and I really think that that creates a mutual respect ... I mean, I teach history so I know something about political systems and I think that this system really does work. That's why its true what [the Principal] was just saying, we really don't need a lot of rules here because we have such explicit values ... It's now a well-oiled machine.

Yet there was a tension evident at this college between these explicit values and the role of leadership. For instance, staff throughout the college felt a sense of ownership of the culture and its values, but at the same time commented that it was the principal that 'breathes life into the systems and culture'. As another lecturer within the college commented, 'I think they're his values, but they've been refined over the years'. Similarly, other staff commented on the difficulty the college would face when the current principal retired, since the culture of the college was bound up with his work, efforts and values. The telling and re-telling of the story of the college's transformation as a saga, therefore, was both a means of empowering those working and studying throughout the Ccollege – making them both responsible and accountable – but at the same time the hero of the story remains the charismatic and transformational principal as recognized leader. As his retelling of the story above explains, it was he who came to a failing college, they are his values, yet they have to be accepted and lived by others. This organizational saga is about empowerment, responsibility and organizational citizenship, but it is also a story through which the principal can be seen to be doing leadership.

Organizational sagas, such as the one above, can be carefully staged managed and used as a means of transforming the culture of a college, but some of the sagas we have observed in other colleges are not always so empowering and positive:

> When I came, having been a Principal elsewhere, looking back on it now my behaviour was informed by that previous experience having been a Principal even though I knew that this was a different job. And the key element in the previous job as Principal was that I went into a failing college that required rapid diagnosis and action, with leadership from the top, in a fairly proactive manner …

As this Principal went on to say, the approach in his previous institution was very much that of the 'trouble-shooter' in that he had come from what was perceived as a 'failing college' and had to take swift and decisive measures to make changes for the better. He drew on his experience as a principal from his previous college to inform his approach to the management and leadership of this new institution. This kind of 'experiential learning' is a central resource from which principals and managers drew in accomplishing their work:

> … the day I arrived the College got notice that it had been granted accredited college status by the Further Education Funding Council, that it was identified in the top 10 per cent of the country. Now at

the same time the results had dipped, so I identified that – yes, this was a College that was ostensibly much better – but in fact there was a problem. And while I thought I was, in my own terms, measured in my analysis and then in my presentation – "the speech" – looking back on it, I would not necessarily do it in the same way now ...

'The speech' that this principal goes onto recount was his first general address to his staff and in his own words was a 'measured' attempt to capture the feeling of achievement and success of the recent recognition of the national position of the college, but this was tempered with a message that more work had to be done to sustain this high standard:

... so when you stand up at your first staff meeting and say, "these are the results and they're really not very good", it caused a) huge shock waves and b) resentment and tension. "Who's this bloke coming in and saying we're not very good, when we've just got accreditation?!" First part of the speech was "you've got accreditation, well done for that", second part of the speech was "this year's results were down, this show's there's a real problem." And that speech is still referred to today.

In effect, this first address to staff became another kind of organizational saga. It was referred to by staff throughout the college and set the tone for the relationship between the principal and the rest of the college for the next two years, effectively serving to define and sustain a 'them and us' culture within the college:

... the egos were incredibly tender, and so they all limped out feeling incredibly savaged and bruised by what I thought was simply a neutral analysis – and I said, you know "we're not going to blame here, we're just into analysis so let's stick to that, what we've got to do is a review and find out what has caused the problem, what are the contributory factors" – so I launched a review sort of right at the beginning. And we then spent the next six months carrying out a review as to how do we improve the quality. That was also a process that enabled me to get to know lots of people by working in focus groups and all this sort of stuff. But what I'd totally underestimated was the negative impact that this initial contact had had.

What this particular saga also demonstrates is the ability of storytelling, and particularly the robustness of the organizational saga, for providing what could be described as 'teachable moments' for college principals. This story, shared throughout the college, seemed to haunt this particular principal and served as a continual reminder of a serious mistake turned into a hard lesson learned. The very fact that this story (including events surrounding the college review that followed the fallout from 'the speech') was referred to again and again throughout the period of fieldwork, suggests that its repeatability served as a point of reference for the future actions and decision making in the college.

The purpose of retelling such stories is not merely as resources for a kind of community of practitioners, but a reminder and reinforcement of the relationship between the college leadership and the workforce. In the first example, the saga of organizational success through culture change serves to remind organizational members of the strong and visionary leadership that brought about this change and the empowerment of the workforce. In the second example, it is a constant reminder to the leadership of the college that the workforce have a certain amount of collective strength and that criticism should be handled more delicately in future. Most importantly for our purposes, this second saga also demonstrates the value of storytelling as a resource for leadership development – a kind of personal leadership benchmark against which all other decisions and actions are checked. As this principal goes on to say, the lesson learned here is that:

... the way in which you move a College that is successful forward is different, I think, to the way in which you take a failing College and turn it round.

Reflections and 'Teachable Moments'

One of the main justifications for the ethnographic approach we have adopted in our work is supposedly the old North American Indian adage that 'you should never criticize a man until you have walked a mile in his moccasins', which, at least in the old joke, is usually followed by, 'because then, when you do get to criticize him, you're a mile away ... and you've got his shoes'. And so, finally, from a safe distance away and clutching a whole pile of odd shoes, we offer some simple reflections on our work; four key and recurring reflections that we think should be incorporated into any leadership development programme.

Reflection 1: Leadership is largely mundane work and, against all expectations, charisma and heroism are rarely enough. Good leadership is the product of an attention to mundane work, management and administration.

The central theme of our research from the outset has been to challenge the popular notion of leadership as a set of embodied traits, behaviours or skills that are the esoteric preserve of a select few. Even in contemporary research, leadership is still framed as something extra-ordinary or heroic. And though we are told that such qualities can be learned, the means through which this learning can effectively take place remains ambiguous and poorly articulated in research literatures and leadership texts. It is against this backdrop that our own research into educational leadership in the UK learning and skills sector has sought to understand leadership as everyday practice; leadership as a particular job of work that can be understood and learned like any other job or work practice.

Part of our commitment to the study of everyday ordinary leadership has been to examine the supposed distinction between 'leadership' and 'management'. It is worth noting that even though most literatures – following Zaleznik's (1977) seminal article – perpetuate the notion that leadership is something more than 'mere' management, it is often overlooked that for prominent management theorist Henry Mintzberg (1975) 'leadership' was merely one component of good management. Management, according to Mintzberg, is a complex craft that requires many qualities and abilities including interpersonal skills, being a figurehead, leader, liaison, monitor, disseminator, spokesperson, entrepreneur, distur-bance handler, resource allocator and negotiator. For us, such diverse practices better represent the challenge of being a leader in the learning and skills sector that involves a range of extra-ordinary *and* mundane practices that require managers to engage in shared activities and decision making. In short, leadership work is collaborative and heavily reliant on systems and technologies that, until now, have played little part in our understanding of leadership-in-action.

By looking at the everyday practices, or ordinary/mundane leadership work that goes on in educational institutions in the sector we have highlighted the taken-for-granted work done by those seen to occupy leadership roles. However, these individuals do not necessarily see their role as that of a leader:

Janet: I'm not pretending I'm, I'm going to be exclusively a leader – although it would be nice – but walking six inches off the ground, y'know, everyday, is going to take it out of you.

Sue: I think, I think that's the issue isn't it? That, y'know, I don't think we go around describing ourselves as "leaders" because it does imply something more magnificent than the reality really is.

Such comments were commonplace in our study. Sector practitioners are uncomfortable describing themselves as leaders and their work as leadership. The reality of the work is less 'magnificent' and our research has spent some considerable time documenting and describing exactly what work in this more mundane reality might involve.

Reflection 2: It is difficult for sector practitioners to be visionary leaders if most of their time is spent 'fire-fighting' – this is applicable at all levels but seems especially relevant to those occupying leadership roles in middle management.

My particular management brief is to try and do something about improving teaching and learning within the faculty, however my ability to even get started on this task has been limited by a number of continuous distractions that I suspect are the everyday fare of middle managers. So insistent are some of these issues that whatever ability I might have to think about and understand the underlying problems, my chances to do anything about them are constrained by the everyday business of muddling through.

Above is a diary comment from a newly appointed head of department whose attempts at leadership are constantly frustrated by the everyday work involved in muddling through, in 'fire fighting' – 'everyday, time-consuming, fix this now, stuff'. As we have persistently documented in our research, sector practitioners who occupy positions of leadership in middle management are caught in this dreadful tension between wanting to be the kinds of visionary leaders promoted by leadership textbooks, development courses, and more recently by government, and the realities of getting the everyday job of management done. As this middle manager explains:

... it's this kind of minute-to-minute kind of justification in this place, you have to do ... you know, if you give up your time or if you're kind of engaging in trying to do something different and you've got this whole admin stuff loaded on you, which is like burial rather than trying to make it easier for you – you know, to improve student experience – I think that is kind of ... could be put under the term undermining, really.

Much of this involves routine work of holding meetings, sending e-mails, filling in forms, working with spreadsheets, and doing what we have called 'calculation work'. Such calculation work isn't just numerical. It is about drawing on managerial knowledge and experience (organizational acumen) to present and put forward a case, produce meaningful data and to convince others and it is time consuming and frustrating. As we have demonstrated in this book, presenting a convincing case is not just a matter of knowing the right figures, or producing 'accurate' accounts. Like so much of managerial work 'accuracy' is something that has to be socially negotiated and agreed upon, as shown earlier in the book in the recorded interchange during a meeting between a college and representatives of the Learning and Skills Council (LSC):

> Principal: ... I don't know what the committee expects of us. Are they expecting to see the same proposal with thirty-five percent grant level requested, but re-worked figures, or are they expecting to see it come back with a request for a, a higher grant? ... I think we've only got two options haven't we? Change the figures or change the grant level ...

As we suggested, this captures exactly the kinds of challenges facing leaders in this sector. Forming a plan of action means recognising that, in this particular grant proposal, figures can be calculated to tell a specific story. There are 'degrees of optimism' that can be worked within. The important skill for the principal and his managers is to determine which figures tell the most appropriate story in this context. To do this they draw on their acumen as competent managers rather than as visionary leaders.

Reflection 3: The burden of bureaucracy. Coping with regulations and audits is another barrier to becoming an effective leader. If leaders in the sector are to be more innovative and creative in their practices, they need a system of regulation and inspection that supports this need for greater flexibility and trust rather than inhibiting (or even penalizing) it.

Spending any time with sector practitioners reveals the extent to which an 'audit culture' (Strathern, 2000; Power, 1994) of inspections, audits and regulation dominate everyday work for senior managers, middle managers, teaching and support staff. For many staff frustrations with the current system of regulation centre on what could be described as a concern with 'second order' outcomes rather than the quality of teaching and learning as it is delivered. In other words, measures have now become targets for both colleges and inspectors to meet. As such, audits and inspections have ceased to be effective tools for improving work practices and standards within the sector. In some cases the way in which colleges were graded by Ofsted seemed to directly hinder attempts to create a more inclusive student centred environment. For example, Ofsted did not inspect the enrichment activities run (at some expense) by colleges to enhance the student experience. Similarly another college that specialized in providing courses and facilities for students with physical and learning difficulties felt similarly excluded by and unrecognized within the existing inspection criteria. As managers and lecturers from these institutions ask, how can they offer the services associated with good leadership if their efforts are not reflected or rewarded by the sector's governing bodies? Similarly pressures to produce transparent accounts of college activities to bodies like the Learning and Skills Council have put college managers under significant pressures which, again, hinder attempts to improve teaching and learning through effective leadership. The requirements of external accountability and the performance of audit have an inevitable impact on perceptions and workloads further down the college structure. The reasons behind the 'gambits of compliance' employed at leadership level often get lost, leaving staff with a perception of a useless administrative burden and a lack of trust.

One example cited by many practitioners was the funding council's requests for college data in a variety of formats and with seemingly little regard for how such figures will be used. Take this extract from one frustrated college senior manager:

Well, I, I've sort of challenged them [the Learning and Skills Council] on some of the things that we have to do for them, like the staff individualized record which is to be done once a year. You collect all the data on your staff and send it off. And I said to them, "what do you actually do with that when you get it? I'm interested". And they said, "well actually, we don't do anything in our office because colleges don't get these back on the deadline", y'know, "so we get half of them in, then they're coming in dribs and drabs, and we never get in a position where we've got all of the data in at the same time and so we don't actually use it". And I said, "Well, unless colleges use it themselves for sort of like monitoring, ethnicity and general, y'know, different rates of pay and things, it's actually not used for anything then, except by keeping ministers happy and telling them well, we know the statistics of staff in the sector". And, there is a sort of like, "Do you realize how long it takes colleges to actually produce this document for you? and really what you could be doing is actually making it useful for us in terms of giving us comparative data so we can see how our turnover compares with other colleges and sort of benchmark ourselves on what others are doing", but that sort of perception just wasn't there. It was like, "Oh well, y'know, it's just filling in a spreadsheet and e-mailing it off, it's not that onerous". But really, to do it rigorously, it is.

This particular practitioner had herself become annoyed with the seemingly ever-changing formatting criteria demanded for college data, and the lack of advice regarding appropriate database and spreadsheet software available. Her suggestion was a simple one: to have a nationally recognized piece of software for college data production, and that within this software a template can be developed through which all colleges can collate and send the required data.

Another college-level perception that emerges from the data was that the bureaucratic burden might be changing, but it wasn't decreasing. In some cases, it was even seen as having become worse, as a result of transitional arrangements or additional 'audiences' to whom the audit had to be performed. These perceptions at ground level suggested that the transparency called for by the then 'Bureaucracy Task Force' was yet to materialize, and that the intentions driving change were getting 'lost in translation' between the funding bodies and the providers. Linked to the idea of a changed, rather than a decreased, administrative burden was that of a lack of joined-up thinking – a perception that individual changes were implemented without thought for their implications elsewhere in the system. In reflecting back our research findings to the principals we studied, there was a common dismay at the prevalence of audit-related work in their everyday practices and a sense that this was wasted time in terms of the experience of students within their colleges.

Reflection 4: Being a leader, particularly an inspiring leader, can take an enormous emotional toll on individuals. Failure to appreciate the emotional work – the emotional labour – of holding a leadership position can undermine the effectiveness of the leader-follower relationship.

You would struggle to find much about 'emotional labour' or 'emotion work' in most of the standard treatments of leadership theory and yet our research recorded it as a persistent and difficult feature of every college leader's mundane work. This is not to suggest that colleges are emotional hothouses in which hurt feelings run rife. Rather it is to point to the simple, observed, empirical reality that the principals involved in our study consciously undertook a number of activities designed to make public their appreciation of work done or to present 'the human face' of leadership to their staff. Such valuing practices took a variety of forms; attending retirement parties, giving appropriate feedback to staff, the casual comment in the corridor, appearing cheerful and so on. A key aspect of valuing staff appeared to be about spending time with them, being accessible to them, and recognizing their interests as people rather than merely seeing them as resources to fulfil tasks. We have included numerous examples of this in the data already discussed in previous chapters. Much of this work we regarded and analyzed as a form of emotional labour based on Hochschild's (1983) discussion of the increasing requirement for organizational members to manage their emotions such that they express only those deemed appropriate even in the face of the most difficult circumstances. While Hochschild (1983) documented such work among airline cabin staff we noticed both similar and different sorts of work amongst college principals. Such emotional labour, even if clearly an exercise in will power, is not necessarily inauthentic, and the telling and sharing of such stories is a powerful tool for leadership development. Creating a non-judgemental space in which any experience of leadership can be shared provides practitioners, programme designers and researchers with an insight into the pedagogy of leadership. Telling a good story not only provides an insight into some of the unique leadership challenges within the sector, relaying such stories to others prompts practitioners to share their own stories and represents what we have called 'teachable moments', moments from the world of practice that others can engage with and learn from.

Conclusion

Our interest in leadership was initially based on looking for ways for research to contribute to the implementation of leadership development programmes. Consequently we have approached leadership as a 'design' problem rather than a theoretical problem. For us leadership is what Rittel and Webber (1973) might term a 'wicked problem' and viewing it as a practical design problem, as opposed to a theoretical concern, may have some benefit. In other words, we want to know, from the interdisciplinary perspective common to the design enterprise, what the 'requirements' for a leadership development programme might be, and how it could be designed and deployed for use in a specific organizational setting.

When leadership is regarded as a 'design' problem – rather than one associated with personality traits or cultural characteristics – our interest shifts from a concern with theory to developing a set of scenarios or 'teachable moments' that resonate with participant's experiences. In this case, these are moments captured and re-told that connect with the reality of everyday leadership work in the post-16 educational sector. These are the 'teachable moments' that we have attempted to outline in this final chapter. In this way we accommodate what is sometimes termed 'the turn to the social' in design (Grudin, 1990): the recognition of and central concern with users and understanding situations of use. This invokes a common ethos that designers need to better understand those they design for: designers need to understand the everyday accomplishment of everyday work as well as idealized representations of it. Leadership, therefore, needs to be understood first and foremost as 'work': work that is, in part, defined by its setting and not merely by idealized constructs, theories and models. The challenge is to design teaching and learning programs for leaders and managers in the post-16 education sector that somehow mesh grace-fully and meaningfully with the readily observed practices and activities of Further Education. In other words, we are seeking to look beyond developing generic management or leadership skills towards identifying and encouraging skills and abilities that are rooted in the sector.

What we have attempted in this final chapter is to present a number of 'cautionary tales' about leadership work as a first step towards this design goal. Set against the backdrop of post-incorporation FE, this book has documented some of our empirical research into the everyday *doing* of leadership in colleges from across the UK. Unlike traditional studies under-pinned by existing concepts, models and theories of leadership we have been interested in recording exactly how the phenomenon of leadership has been expressed and sustained in everyday practice. The aspect of leadership we have been interested in involved the telling of 'leadership stories', including what Julian Orr has referred to as 'war stories' (Orr, 1996; 1998) – 'cautionary tales' told and re-told to impart knowledge and experience for the benefit and development of others. Here leaders were reflecting on their own and others experiences and recounting them as cautionary tales. We have documented, analyzed and discussed some of the stories that principals and their management teams told; and considered the function of such storytelling practices in the understanding of everyday leadership work. We suggest that such stories, such cautionary tales, can play a role in the development and inculcation of forms of 'professional vision' (Goodwin, 1994) capturing what we regard as 'teachable moments'.

In this final chapter we have looked back and reflected on our empirical findings and our analysis to consider what stories, what cautionary tales, about leadership and learning to be a leader, emerge from our work: the stories we would like to tell, the stories that might inform the development of a leadership programme. We believe that the rich and detailed ethnographic data that we have uncovered in our work provides a wealth of 'teachable moments' for current and prospective leaders.

Notes

Chapter 1

[1] Occurring in the early 1990s, this was the process through which colleges became 'independent' of Local Education Authorities. It coincided with an increased emphasis on commercial and educational accountability – exercised through a raft of inspection and target related structures – which underpinned government educational policy, such that independence was often perceived as being 'given with one hand and taken away with the other'. A practical consequence of incorporation was the need for college principals to manage business issues – finance, strategy, personnel, marketing, etc. – which had previously not been part of their remit.

[2] See the National College for School Leadership's website for initiatives such as 'Leading from the Middle'.

Chapter 2

[1] Although the increased focus in recent years on the so-called 'soft' skills, such as emotional intelligence, consultative and consensus-based decision making and coaching – all of which have traditionally been viewed as more feminine attributes – does allow more room in the picture for 'great women'.

[2] See Avolio and Gardner (2005) for a cross-matching of the characteristics of authentic, servant and spiritual leadership, together with those of their transformational and charismatic forebears, and Dent, Higgins and Wharff (2005) for a review of the definitions, distinctions and embedded assumptions within the spiritual leadership literature.

[3] More usually, they will retain a role in lesson observation programmes.

Chapter 3

[1] Together with all the other names of colleges and participants in the study, this is a pseudonym.

[2] Garfinkel uses the notation 'order*' to indicate that, for ethnomethodology,

order is a locally produced and accountable phenomenon: this is in contrast to the mainstream sociological view of order as an extra-local, 'transcendental', generalizable phenomenon.

[3] Wittgenstein (1958) makes the distinction between 'rule following' and 'rule using' as a recognition of the irredeemable incompleteness of such instructions: no matter how detailed and explicit a rule is, it can never foreshadow and document every possible, specific instance of its applicability. As Wittgenstein expresses it, 'no rule dictates the terms of its own application'.

Chapter 4

[1] Additional funding from the Learning and Skills Council, received on the basis of the quality of provision in relation to certain pre-specified – though recently amended – targets and obtained via the presentation and justification of a proposal to the Council.

Chapter 5

[1] There is a growing literature on storytelling in organizations, both in terms of how they are told and the purposes they serve. While (unfortunately) Brown (2004:1421, reviewing Gabriel) suggests that 'in organization studies, an early predilection for treating stories as *in vivo* cultural artefacts that yielded insight into processes of organizing has given way to more sensitive and imaginative approaches: some of the earlier work (e.g. Boje, 1991) recognized the performance of organizational story telling as 'a key part of members' sense making' (1991:106). Earlier writings from Gabriel (2000) also recognize the sense-making aspects of storytelling, seeing the interpretation of stories as a 'core part of story-work in organizations, through which events are 'infused' with meaning or meaning is 'discovered' in facts (2000:35). This said, much of the storytelling literature – as with much of sociology generally – is concerned with different ways of theorizing stories rather than with explicating their practice by members.

References

Abetti, P. (1997), 'Convergent and divergent technological and market strategies for global leadership'. *International Journal of Technology Management*, 14, (6–8), 635–57.

Abzug, R. and Phelps, S. (1998), 'Everything old is new again: Barnard's legacy – lessons for participative leaders'. *Journal of Management Development*, 17, (3), 207–18.

Adair, J. (1973), *Action-Centred Leadership*. New York: McGraw-Hill.

Alvesson, M. (1992), 'Leadership as social integrative action: a study of a computer consultancy company'. *Organization Studies*, 13, 185–209.

Alvesson, M. and Sveningsson, S. (2003a), 'Managers doing leadership: The extra-ordinarization of the mundane'. *Human Relations*, 56, (12), 1435–59.

—— (2003b), 'The great disappearance act: difficulties in doing 'leadership': *Leadership Quarterly*, 14, 359–81.

Anderson, R. J., Hughes, J. A., and Sharrock, W. W. (1989), *Working for Profit: the Social Organization of Calculation in an Entrepreneurial Firm*. Aldershot: Avebury.

Atkinson, P. and Hammersley, M. (1998), 'Ethnography and participant observation', in N. Denzin, and Y. Lincoln, (eds) *Strategies of Qualitative Inquiry*. Thousand Oaks, CA: Sage. 110–36.

Avolio, B. J. and Gardner, W. L. (2005), 'Authentic leadership development: getting to the root of positive forms of leadership'. *The Leadership Quarterly*, 16, 315–38.

Barker, R. (1997), 'How can we train leaders if we don't know what leadership is?'. *Human Relations*. 50, 343–62.

Bass, B. M. (1985), *Leadership and Performance Beyond Expectations*. New York: Free Press.

Bass, B. M. and Avolio, B. (1994), *Improving Organizational Effectiveness Through Transformational Leadership*. California: Sage.

Bennett, N., Wise, C., Woods, P. and Harvey, J. (2003), *Distributed Leadership*. Nottingham: National College for School Leadership.

Bennis, W. G. and Nanus, B. (1985), *Leaders: the Strategies for Taking Charge*. New York: Harper & Row.

Bentley, R., Rodden, T., Sawyer, P, Sommerville, I., Hughes, J., Randall, R. and Shapiro, D. (1992), 'Ethnographically-informed Systems Design for Air Traffic Control'. *Conference on Computer-Supported Cooperative Work: Sharing Perspectives*,, New York: ACM Press, 123–29.

Bittner, E. (1965), 'The concept of organization'. *Social Research*, 32, (3), 239–55.

Blair, M. (2002), 'Effective school leadership: the multi-ethnic context'. *British Journal of Sociology of Education*, 23, (2), 179–91.

Blake, R. and Mouton, J. (1964), *The Managerial Grid*. Houston: Gulf Publishing.

Blythin, S., Hughes, J. A., Kristoffersen, S., Rodden, T. and Rouncefield, M. (1997), 'Recognizing 'success' and 'failure': evaluating groupware in a commercial context'. *Group 97*, Phoenix, Arizona, USA.

Boal, K. and Schlultz, P. (2007), 'Storytelling, time, and evolution: The role of strategic leadership in complex adaptive systems'. *The Leadership Quarterly*, 18, 411–28.

Boden, D. (1994), *The Business of Talk: Organizations in Action*. Cambridge: Polity Press.

Boje, D. M. (1991), 'The storytelling organization: A study of story performance in an office-supply firm'. *Administrative Science Quarterly*, 36, 106–26.

Bolden, R. (2004), *What is Leadership?* Exeter: University of Exeter Leadership South West Research Report.

Bolton, S. C. and Boyd, C. (2003), 'Trolley dolly or skilled emotion manager? Moving on from Hochschild's managed heart'. *Work, Employment and Society*, 17, (2), 289–308.

Bowonder, B. (1998) 'Competitive and technology management strategy: a case study of TELCO'. *International Journal of Technology Management*, 15, (6–7), 646–80.

Boyatzis, R. (1982) *The Competent Manager*. New York: John Wiley.

Braverman, H. (1974) *Labour and Monopoly Capital: the Degradation of Work in the Twentieth Century*. New York: Monthly Review Press.

Brown, A. D. (2004) Special book reviews on narratives. *Organization Studies*, 26,(9), 1421–32.

Brown, J. S. and Duguid, P. (2002), *The Social Life of Information*. Boston, MA.: Harvard Business School Press.

Bryman, A. (1992), *Charisma and Leadership in Organizations*. London: Sage.

—— (1996) 'Leadership in organizations', in S. Clegg, C. Hardy, and W. Nord (eds) *Handbook of Organizational Studies*. London: Sage.

Bryman, A., Stephens, M. and à Campo, C. (1996) 'The importance of context: qualitative research and the study of leadership'. *The Leadership Quarterly*, 7, (3), 353–70.

Buchanan, D. and Huczynski, A. (2004), *Organisational Behaviour: An Introductory Text* (5th edition). London: F T Prentice Hall.

Burchell, G., Gordon, C. and Miller, P. (1991) *The Foucault Effect: Studies in Governmentality*. London: Harvester Wheatsheaf.

Burns, J. (1978), *Leadership*. New York: Harper Row.

Bush, T. and Glover, D. (2003), *School Leadership: Concepts and Evidence*. Nottingham: National College for School Leadership.

Button, G. (1993), 'The curious case of the vanishing technology', in G. Button (ed.), *Technology in Working Order: Studies of Work, Interaction and Technology*. London: Routledge.

Button, G. and Sharrock, W. W. (1998), 'The organizational accountability of technological work'. *Social Studies of Science*, 28, (1), 73–102.

Carless, S. and Allwood, V. (1997), 'Managerial assessment centres: What is being rated?'. *Australian Psychologist*, 32, (3), 101–5.

Cheng, Y. C. (1994), 'Principal's leadership as a critical factor for school performance: evidence from multi-levels of primary schools'. *School Effectiveness and School Improvement*, 5, (3), 299–317.

Ciulla, J. B. (ed.) (2004), *Ethics, the Heart of Leadership*. (2nd edition). Westport, CT: Preager.

Clark, B. R. (1972), 'The organizational saga in higher education'. *Administrative Science Quarterly*, 17, 178–84.

Clarke, K., Hughes, J., Martin, D., Rouncefield, M., Sommerville, I., Hartswood, M., Procter, R., Slack, R. and Voss, A. (2003), 'Dependable red hot action', in P. Dourish and G. Fitzpatrick, (eds) *Proceedings of the European Conference on Computer Supported Cooperative Work*, Helsinki, September, 2003, 61–80.

Clifford, J. and Marcus, G. (eds) (1986), *Writing Culture: the Poetics and Politics of Ethnography*. Berkeley: University of California Press.

Cohen, S. and Rustad, J. (1998), 'High-tech/high-touch: high time'. *Training and Development*, 52, (12), 30–37.

Collins, J. C. (2001), *Good to Great: Why Some Companies Make the Leap – and Others Don't*. London: Random House Business Books.

Collinson, D. and Collinson, M. (2005), *Leadership Challenges*. Lancaster: Lancaster University Centre for Excellence in Leadership Working Paper Series.

Conger, J. (1989), *The Charismatic Leader: Behind the Mystique of Exceptional Leadership*. San Francisco: Jossey-Bass.

Conger, J. and Kanungo, R. (1987), 'Towards a behavioural theory of charismatic leadership in organizational settings'. *Academy of Management Review*, 12, 637–47.

Couillard, D. and Lapierre, J. (2003),'Leadership, learning and resources for the high-tech firm: an integrated view of technology management'. *International Journal of Technology Management*, 26, (7), 767–87.

Coulter, J. (1999), 'Discourse and mind'. *Human Studies*, 22, (2–4), 163–81.

Covey, S. R. (1990), *The Seven Habits of Highly Effective People: Restoring the Character Ethic*. New York: Fireside Books.

Crabtree, A. (2000), 'Talking work: language-games, organizations and computer supported cooperative work'. *Computer Supported Cooperative Work*, 9, 215–37.

Crabtree, A., Nichols, D. M., O'Brien, J., Rouncefield, M. and Twidale, M. B. (1999), 'Ethnomethodologically-informed ethnography and information system design'. *Journal of the American Society for Information Science*, 51, (7), 666–82.

Cuban, L. (1984), 'Transforming the frog into a prince: effective schools research, policy and practice at the district level'. *Harvard Educational Review*, 54, (2), 129–51.

Daft, R. (1983), *Organization Theory and Design*. St Paul: West Publishing Company.

Dant, T. and Francis, D. (1998), 'Planning in organizations: rational control or contingent activity?'. *Sociological Research Online*, 3, 2. www.socresonline.org.uk

Darrah, C. (1994), 'Skill requirement at work – rhetoric versus reality'. *Work Occupation*, 21, (1), 64–84.

Davenport, E. (2002), 'Mundane knowledge management and microlevel organizational learning: An ethological approach'. *Journal of the American Society for Information Science and Technology*, 53, (12), 1038–46.

Dent, . B., Higgins, M. E. and Wharff, D. M. (2005). 'Spirituality and leadership: An empirical review of definitions, distinctions, and embedded assumptions'. *The Leadership Quarterly*, 16, 625–53.

Dourish, P. (2001), *Where the Action is: The Foundations of Embodied Interaction*. Cambridge, MA: MIT Press.

Dourish, P., Graham, C., Randall, D. and Rouncefield, M. (2010),'Theme issue on social interaction and mundane technologies'. *Personal and Ubiquitous Computing* 14, 3.

Earl, L. and Lee, L. (1998), *The Evaluation of the Manitoba School Improvement Program*. Toronto: Walter and Duncan Gordon Charitable Foundation.

Edles, L. D. (2002), *Cultural Sociology in Practice*. Malden, Mass: Blackwell Publishers.

Edmonds, R. (1979),'Effective schools for the urban poor'. *Educational Leadership*, 37, 15–24.

Elliot, G. and Crossley, M. (1994), 'Qualitative research, educational management and the incorporation of the further education sector'. *Educational Management and Administration*, 22, (3), 188–97.

Erickson, R. J. (1995), 'The importance of authenticity for self and society'. *Symbolic Interaction*, 18, (2), 121–44.

Erickson, T. (1996), *Design as Storytelling*. Retrieved: 24/08/04 from http://www.pliant.org/personal/Tom_Erickson/Storytelling.html

FENTO (2000), *Management Standards for Further Education (draft 6)*. http://www.fento.ac.uk/manage.htm

Fiske, D. W. (1949), 'Consistency of factorial structures of personality ratings from different sources'. *Journal of Abnormal and Social Psychology*, 44, 329–44.

Fleishman, E. (1953), 'The description of supervisory behaviour'. *Personnel Psychology*, 37, 1–6.

Fraser, C. (1978), 'Small groups: structure and leadership'. In H. Tajfel and C. Fraser (eds), *Introducing Social Psychology*. Harmondsworth: Penguin Books.

Frost, D. and Harris, A. (2003), 'Teacher leadership: towards a research agenda'. *Cambridge Journal of Education*, 33, (3), 479–98.

Fry, L. W. (2005), 'Toward a paradigm of spiritual leadership'. *The Leadership Quarterly*, 16, 619–22.

Fullan, M. (1993), *Changing Forces: Probing the Depths of Educational Reform*. London: Falmer Press.

—— (2001), *The New Meaning of Educational Change* (3rd edition). New York: Teachers College Press.

Gabriel, Y. (2000), *Storytelling in Organizations: Facts, Fictions, and Fantasies*. Oxford: Oxford University Press.

Gallie, W. B. (1955–6), 'Essentially contested concepts'. *Proceedings of the Aristotelian Society*, 56, 167–98.

Garfinkel, H. (1967), *Studies in Ethnomethodology*. Englewood Cliffs, NJ. Prentice Hall.

—— (1991), 'Respecification: evidence for locally produced, naturally accountable phenomena of order, logic, reason, meaning, method, etc. in and as of the essential haecceity of immortal ordinary society (I) – an announcement of studies.' In G. Button (ed.) *Ethnomethodology and the Human Sciences*. Cambridge. Cambridge University Press.

Garfinkel, H., Lynch, M. and Livingston, E. (1981), 'The work of discovering science construed with materials from the optically discovered pulsar' *Philosophy of the Social Sciences,* 11, 131–58.

Garfinkel, H. and Weider, L. (1992), 'Evidence for locally produced, naturally accountable phenomena of order, logic, reason, meaning, method, etc.', in G. Watson and R. Seiler (eds) *Text in Context: Contributions to Ethnomethodology.* London: Sage, 175–206.

Geertz, C. (1973), *The Interpretation of Cultures: Selected Essays.* New York: Basic Books.

Gemmill, G. and Oakley, J. (1992), 'Leadership: An alienating social myth?', *Human Relations,* 45, (2), 113–

Gerson, E. M. and Star, S. L. (1986), 'Analyzing due process in the workplace'. *ACM Transactions on Office Information Systems,* 4, (3), 257–70.

Goddard-Patel, P. and Whitehead, S. (2000), 'Examining the crisis of further education: An analysis of 'failing' colleges and failing policies'. *Policy Studies,* 21, (3), 191–212.

Goffman, E. (1959), *The Presentation of Self in Everyday Life.* Garden City, NY: Doubleday.

Goleman, D. (1998), *Working with Emotional Intelligence.* London: Bloomsbury.

—— (2000), 'Leadership that gets results'. *Harvard Business Review,* 78, (2), 78–90.

Goleman, D., Boyatzis, R. and McKee, A. (2002), *The New Leaders: Transforming the Art of Leadership into the Science of Results.* London: Little, Brown.

Goodwin, C. (1994) 'Professional vision'. *American Anthropologist,* 96, (3), 606–33.

Gosling, J. and Murphy, A. (2004), *Leading Continuity.* Exeter: University of Exeter Centre for Leadership Studies.

Grint, K. (1997), *Leadership: Classical, Contemporary and Critical Approaches.* Oxford: Oxford University Press.

—— (2004), *What is Leadership? From Hydra to Hybrid.* Oxford: Oxford University Said Business School and Templeton College.

—— (2005), *Leadership: Limits and Possibilities.* Basingstoke: Palgrave Macmillan.

Gronn, P. (1982), 'Methodological Perspective: neo-taylorism in educational administration?' *Educational Administration Quarterly,* 18, (4), 17–35.

—— (1983), 'Talk as the work: the accomplishment of school administration'. *Administrative Science Quarterly,* 28, 1–21.

—— (1995), 'Greatness revisited: the current obsession with transformational leadership'. *Leading and Managing,* 1, (1), 14–27.

—— (2002), 'Distributed leadership', in K. Leithwood, P. Hallinger, K. Seashore-Lewis, G. Furman-Brown, P. Gronn, W. Mulford and K. Riley (eds) *Second International Handbook of Educational Leadership and Administration.* Dortrecht: Kluwer.

—— (2003), 'Leadership: who needs it?'. *School Leadership and Management,* 23, (3), 267–90.

Gronn, P. and Ribbins, P. (1996), 'Leaders in context: postpositivist approaches to understanding educational leadership'. *Educational Administration Quarterly,* 32, (3), 452–73.

Grudin, J. (1990), 'The computer reaches out: the historical continuity of interface design'. *Proceedings of the SIGCHI Conference on Human Factors in Computing Systems.* Seattle: Washington.

Hallinger, P. (1983), *Assessing the Instructional Management Behaviour of Principals.* (Unpublished doctoral dissertation, Stanford University).

—— (2000), 'A Review of Two Decades of Research on Principalship using the Principal Instruction Management Rating Scale'. (Paper presented at the *Annual Meeting of the American Educational Research Association*, Seattle, Washington).

—— (2003), 'Leading educational change: reflections on the practice of instructional and transformational leadership'. *Cambridge Journal of Education*, 33, (3), 329–51.

Hallinger, P. and Murphy, J. (1985), 'Assessing the instructional leadership behaviour of principals'. *Elementary School Journal*, 86, (2), 217–48.

Halpin, A. and Winer, B. (1957), 'A factorial study of the leader behaviour descriptions'. in R. Stogdill and A. Coons (eds) *Leader Behaviour: Its Description and Measurement.* Columbus. Ohio State University Bureau of Business Research.

Hammersley, M. (1985), 'Ethnography: what it is and what it offers', in S. Hegerty and P. Evans (eds) *Research and Evaluation Methods in Special Education.* Philadelphia: Nefar-Nelson. 152–63.

—— (1992), *What's Wrong with Ethnography?* London: Routledge.

Hammersley, M. and Atkinson, P. (1985), *Ethnography: Principles in Practice.* (2nd edition) London: Routledge.

Harris, A. (2005), 'Leading or misleading? Distributed leadership and school improvement'. *Journal of Curriculum Studies*, 37, (3), 255–65.

Hartswood, M. J., Procter, R., Rouchy, P., Rouncefield, M., Slack, R. and Voss, A. (2003), 'Working IT out in medical practice: IT systems design and development as co-realisation', *Methods of Information in Medicine*, 42, 392–97.

Hatcher, R. (2005), 'The distribution of leadership and power in schools'. *British Journal of Sociology of Education*, 26, (2), 253–67.

Heider, F. (1944), 'Social perception and phenomenal causality'. *Psychological Review*, 51, 358–74.

Hemphill, J. and Coons, A. (1957), 'Development of the leader behaviour description questionnaire', in R. Stogdill and A. Coons (eds) *Leader Behaviour: Its Description and Measurement.* Columbus: Ohio State University Bureau of Business Research.

Heritage, J. (1987), 'Ethnomethodology', in A. Giddens and J. Turner (eds) *Sociological Theory Today.* Stanford, CA: Stanford University Press. 224–71.

Hersey, P. and Blanchard, K. (1984), *The Management of Organizational Behaviour.* (4th edition) Englewood Cliffs, NJ: Prentice Hall.

Hillman, D. and Gibbs, D. (1998), *Century Makers: One Hundred Clever Things We Take for Granted Which Have Changed Our Lives Over the Last One Hundred Years,* London: Weidenfield and Nicolson.

Hochschild, A. (1983), *The Managed Heart: Commercialization of Human Feeling.* Berkeley, CA: University of California Press.

Hogg, M. A. (2005), 'Social identity and leadership', in D. M. Messick and R. M. Kramer (eds), *The Psychology of Leadership: New Perspectives and Research.* Mahwah, NJ: Erlbaum. 53–80.

Hopkins, D. and Jackson, D. (2003), 'Building the capacity for leading and learning', in A. Harris, C. Day, D. Hopkins, M. Hadfield, A. Hargreaves and C.

Chapman (eds) *Effective Leadership for School Improvement*. London: Routledge Farmer.

Hughes, J., O'Brien, J., Rouncefield, M., Rodden, T. and Blythin, S. (1997), 'Designing with ethnography: A presentation framework for design'. In the *Proceedings of Designing Interactive Systems*, 1997. Amsterdam: AMC Press.

Hughes, M. and Potter, D. (2002), *Tweak to Transform: A Practical Handbook for School Leaders*. London: Network Educational Press.

Iaffaldano, M. T. and Muchinsky, P. M. (1985), 'Job satisfaction and job performance: a meta-analysis'. *Psychological Bulletin*, 97, 251–73.

Jackson, D. (2000), The school improvement journey: perspectives on leadership'. *School Leadership and Management*, 20, (1), 61–78.

Jensen, R. (2003), 'Innovative leadership: First-mover advantages in new product adoption'. *Economic Theory*, 21, (1), 97–116.

Jephcote, M., Salisbury, J., Fletcher, J., Graham, I. and Mitchell, G. (1996), 'Principals' responses to incorporation: A window on their culture'. *Journal of Further and Higher Education*, 20, (2), 33–48.

Jones, E. E. and Davis, K. E. (1965), 'From acts to dispositions: The attribution process in person perception', in L. Berkowitz (ed.) *Advances in Experimental Psychology*, 2, 219–66.

Jordon, B. (1989),'Cosmopolitan obstetrics: Some insights from the training of traditional midwives'. *Social Science and Medicine*, 28, (9), 925–44.

Kakihara, M. and Sørensen, C. (2004), 'Practising mobile professional work: Tales of locational, operational, and interactional mobility'. *The Journal of Policy, Regulation and Strategy for Telecommunications*. 6, (3), 180–87.

Katz, D. and Kahn, R. (1952), 'Some recent findings in human-relations research in industry. In E. Swanson, T. Newcomb, and E. Hartley (eds) *Readings in Social Psychology*. New York: Holt, 650–65.

Katz, D., Maccoby, N. and Morse, N. (1950), *Productivity, Supervision and Morale in an Office Situation*. Ann Arbor, MI: Institute for Social Research.

Katzenbach, J. and Smith, D. (1993), *The Wisdom of Teams: Creating the High Performance Organization*. Boston, MA: Harvard Business School Press.

Kellerman, B. (2004), 'Leadership: Warts and all'. *Harvard Business Review*, November, 88–95.

Kelley, R. E. (1967), 'Attribution theory in social psychology', in D. Levine (ed.) *Nebraska Symposium on Motivation*, 15, 192–238.

Kerfoot, D. and Whitehead, S. (1998), 'Boys own stuff: masculinity and the management of further education'. *The Sociological Review*, 46, (3), 436–57.

Kerr, S. and Jermier, J. M. (1978), 'Substitutes for leadership: Their meaning and measurement'. *Organizational Behaviour and Human Performance*, 22, (3), 375–403.

Kling, R. (1996), 'Hope and horrors: Technological utopianism and anti-utopianism in narratives of computerization', in Kling, R. (ed.) *Computerization and Controversy*. San Diego: Academic Press. 40–58.

Kling, R. and Dunlop, C. (1993), 'Controversies about computerization and the character of white collar worklife'. *The Information Society*, 9, (1), 1–29.

Kluger, A. and DeNisi, A. (1996), 'The effects of feedback interventions on performance: A historical review, a meta-analysis, and a preliminary feedback intervention theory'. *Psychological Bulletin,* 119, (2), 254–84.

Knights, D. and Mueller, F. (2004), 'Strategy as a 'project': overcoming dualisms in the strategy debate'. *European Management Review,* 1, 55–61.

Knights, D. and Wilmott, H. (1992), 'Conceptualizing leadership process: A study of senior managers in a financial services company'. *Journal of Management Studies,* 29, (6), 760–82.

Kotter, J. P. (1990), *A Force for Change: How Leadership Differs from Management.* New York: Free Press.

Kouzes, J. M. and Posner, B. Z. (1993), *Credibility: How Leaders Gain and Lose It, Why People Demand It.* San Francisco: Jossey Bass.

Lakomski, G. (2005), *Managing Without Leadership: Towards a Theory of Organizational Functioning.* Melbourne: Elsevier.

Lashway, L. (2003), 'Distributed leadership'. *Research Roundup,* 19, (4). Eugene, OR: University of Oregon, Clearinghouse on Educational Policy and Management.

Laurier, E. (2004), 'Doing officework on the motorway'. *Theory, Culture and Society* 21, (4/5), 261–77.

Lave, J. and Wenger, E. (1991), *Situated Learning: Legitimate Peripheral Participation.* Cambridge: Cambridge University Press.

Leithwood, K., Jantzi, D. and Steinbach, R. (1999), *Changing Leadership for Changing Times.* Buckingham: Open University Press.

Leithwood, K. and Montgomery, D. (1982), 'The role of the elementary principal in program improvement'. *Review of Educational Research,* 52, (3), 309–39.

Leitner, D. (1994), 'Do principals affect student outcomes: An organizational perspective'. *School Effectiveness and School Improvement,* 5, (3), 219–38.

Likert, R. (1961), *New Patterns of Management.* New York: McGraw-Hill.

—— (1967), *The Human Organization: Its Management and Value.* New York: McGraw-Hill.

Loots, C. and Ross, J. (2004), 'From academic leader to chief executive: altered images?' *Journal of Further and Higher Education,* 28, (1), 19–34.

Lord, R. and Maher, K. (1991), *Leadership and Information Processing: Linking Perceptions and Performance.* Cambridge, MA: Unwin Hyman.

Lynch, M. (1993), *Scientific Practice and Ordinary Action: Ethnomethodology and Social Studies of Science.* Cambridge: Cambridge University Press.

Mahony, P. and Moos, L. (1998), 'Democracy and school leadership in England and Denmark'. *British Journal of Educational Studies,* 46, (3), 302–17.

Malpas, J. and Wickham, G. (1995), Governance and failure: on the limits of sociology. *Australia and New Zealand Journal of Sociology,* 31, (3), 37–50.

McCall, M. J. and Lombardo, M. (1983), *Off the Track: Why and How Successful Executives Get Derailed.* (Technical report no.21) Greensboro, NC: Center for Creative Leadership.

McClelland, D. (1965), 'N-achievement and entrepreneurship: A longitudinal study'. *Journal of Personality and Social Psychology,* 1, 389–92.

—— (1985), *Human Motivation.* Glenview, IL: Scott Foresman.

McCormick, R. (2004), 'Issues of learning and knowledge in technology education'. *International Journal of Technology and Design Education,* 14, (1), 21–44.

McCrae, R. and Costa, P. (1989), 'The structure of interpersonal traits: Wiggin's circumplex and the five factor model'. *Journal of Personality and Social Psychology*, 56, 586–95.

McGinn, M. (1997), *Wittgenstein and the Philosophical Investigations*. London: Routledge.

Meindl, J. R. (1995), 'The romance of leadership as a follower-centric theory: A social constructionist approach'. *The Leadership Quarterly*, 6, (3), 329–41.

Meindl, J. R. and Ehrlich, S. B. (1987), 'The romance of leadership and the evaluation of organizational performance'. *Academy of Management Journal*, 30, (1), 91–109.

Meindl, J. R., Ehrlich, S. B. and Dukerich, J. M. (1985), 'The romance of leadership'. *Administrative Science Quarterly*, 30, (1), 78–102.

Michael, M. (2003), 'Between the mundane and the exotic: time for a different sociotechnical stuff'. *Time and Society*, 12, 127–43.

Millward, L. J. and Hopkins, L. J. (1998), 'Psychological contracts, organizational and job commitment'. *Journal of Applied Social Psychology*, 28, (16), 1530–56.

Mintzberg, H. (1975), 'The manager's job: folklore and fact'. *Harvard Business Review*, 55, (4), 49–61.

Mortimer, P. (1993), 'School effectiveness and the management of effective learning and teaching'. *School Effectiveness and School Improvement*, 4, 290–310.

Mulcahy, M. D. (1998), 'Designing the user/using the design'. *Social Studies of Science*, 28, (1), 5–37.

Mulford, B. and Bishop, P. (1997), *Leadership in Organizational Learning and Student Outcomes*. Launceston, Australia: University of Tasmania.

NCSL (2001), *Leadership Programme for Serving Headteachers* (course materials) Nottingham: NCSL.

Neyland, D. and Woolgar, S. (2002), 'Accountability in action? The case of a database purchasing decision'. *British Journal of Sociology*, 53, (2), 259–74.

Nicolaidou, M. and Ainscow, M. (2005), 'Understanding failing schools: Perspectives from the inside'. *School Effectiveness and School Improvement*, 16, (3), 229–48.

Nippert-Eng, C. E. (1996), *Home and Work: Negotiating Boundaries Through Everyday Life*. Chicago: University of Chicago Press.

—— (2003), 'Drawing the line: Organisations and the boundary work of "home" and "work"'. In N. Paulsen and T. Hernes, (eds) *Managing Boundaries in Organizations: Multiple Perspectives*. New York: Palgrave Macmillan, 262–80.

Nisbett, R. E. and Wilson, T. D. (1977), 'Telling more than we can know: Verbal reports on mental processes'. *Psychological Review*, 84, (3), 231–59.

O'Brien, M. (1994), 'The managed heart revisited: health and social control'. *The Sociological Review*, 393–413.

Ofsted (accessed 22/08/05) www.ofsted.gov.uk/howwework

Ogbonna, E. and Harris, L. C. (2004), 'Work intensification and emotional labour among UK university lecturers: An exploratory study'. *Organization Studies*, 25, (7), 1185–1203.

Orr, J. E. (1990), 'Sharing knowledge, celebrating identity: War stories and community memory among service technicians', in D. S. Middleton and

D. Edwards (eds) *Collective Remembering: Memory in Society.* Beverly Hills, CA: Sage Publications.

—— (1996), *Talking About Machines: an Ethnography of a Modern Job.* Ithaca, NY: ILR Press.

—— (1998), 'Images of work.' *Science, Technology and Human Values,* 23, (4), 439–55.

Penn, R. (1990), *Class, Power and Technology: Skilled Workers in Britain and America.* Cambridge: Polity Press.

Pollner, M. (1987), *Mundane Reason.* Cambridge: Cambridge University Press.

Power, M. (1994), *The Audit Explosion.* London: Demos.

—— (1997), *The Audit Society: Rituals of Verification.* Oxford: Oxford University Press.

Price, H. (2001), 'Emotional labour in the classroom: a psychoanalytic perspective'. *Journal of Social Work Practice,* 15, (2), 161–80.

Puwar, N. (2001), 'The racialised somatic norm in the senior civil service'. *Sociology,* 35, (3), 651–70.

Randall, D., Harper, R. and Rouncefield, M. (2005), 'Fieldwork, ethnography and design: A perspective from CSCW'. *Ethnographic Praxis in Industry Conference Proceedings,* 2005, (1), 81–99.

—— (2007), *Fieldwork for Design: Theory and Practice.* Leiden: Kluwer.

Rayner, S. and Gunter, H. (2005), 'Rethinking leadership: perspectives on remodelling practice'. *Educational Review,* 57, (2), 151–61.

Reave, L. (2005), 'Spiritual values and practices related to leadership effectiveness'. *The Leadership Quarterly,* 16, 655–87.

Rittel, H. and Webber, M. (1973), 'Dilemmas in a general theory of planning'. *Policy Sciences.* 4, 155–69.

Rost, J. (1991), *Leadership in the Twenty-First Century.* Westport, CT: Preager/ Greenwood Publishing.

Rouncefield, M. F. (2002), *"Business as Usual": An Ethnography of Everyday (Bank) Work.* (Unpublished doctoral thesis, Department of Sociology, University of Lancaster).

Sacks, H. (1972), 'On analyzing of stories by children', in J. J. Gumperz and D. Hymes (eds) *Directions in Sociolinguistics.* New York: Holt, Rinehart and Winston.

Sawbridge, S. J. (2000), *Leadership in Further Education: A Review of the Literature.* Learning and Skills Development Agency.

Schutz, A. (1970), *On Phenomenology and Social Relations.* Chicago: Chicago University Press.

Scott-Morton, M. (ed.) (1991), *The Corporation in the 1990s: Information Technology and Organizational Transformation.* New York: Oxford University Press.

Senge, P. M. (1992), *The Fifth Discipline: the Art and Practice of the Learning Organization.* London: Century.

Sergiovanni, T. J. (1984),'Leadership and excellence in schooling'. *Educational Leadership,* 41, 4–13.

Shadur, M., Kienzle, R. and Rodwell, J. (1999), 'The relationship between organizational climate and employee perceptions of involvement: The importance of support'. *Group & Organization Management,* 24, (4), 479–503.

Shamir, B. (2007), 'From passive recipients to active co-producers', in B. Shamir,

R. Pillai, M. C. Bligh and M. Uhl-Bien (eds) *Follower-centred Perspectives on Leadership.* Greenwich CT: Information Age, ix–xxxix.

Shamir, B., Pillai, R., Bligh, M. C. and Uhl-Bien, M. (2007), *Follower-Centred Perspectives on Leadership: A tribute to the memory of James R Meindl.* Charlotte, NC: Information Age.

Sharrock, W. and Anderson, B. (1984), 'The Wittgenstein connection'. *Human Studies,* 7, 375–86.

—— (1986), *The Ethnomethodologists.* Chichester: Ellis Horwood Limited.

Sharrock, W. and Button, G. (1999), 'Do the right thing! Rule finitism, rule scepticism and rule following'. *Human Studies,* 22, (2–4), 193–210.

Shaw, M. (1976), *Group Dynamics* (2nd Edition) New York: McGraw-Hill.

Sievers, B. (1994), *Work, Death and Life Itself: Essays on Management and Organization.* New York: DeGruyter.

Silins, H. and Mulford, B. (2004), 'Schools as learning organizations – Effects on teacher leadership and student outcomes'. *School Effectiveness and School Improvement,* 15, (3–4), 443–66.

Sims, H. P. and Lorenzi, P. (1992), *The New Leadership Paradigm: Social learning and cognition in organizations.* Newbury Park, CA: Sage.

Slack, R. (2000), 'Reflexivity or sociological practice: A reply to May'. *Sociological Research Online,* 5, 1. www.socresonline.org.uk/5/1/slack.html

Smircich, L. and Morgan, G. (1982), 'Leadership: The management of meaning'. *The Journal of Applied Behavioral Science,* 18, (3), 257–73.

Stech, E. L. (2004), 'Psychodynamic approach', in P. G. Northouse (ed.) *Leadership Theory and Practice.* New York: Free Press.

Southworth, G. (2002), Think piece from NCSL. *Times Educational Supplement* .

Spears, L. and Lawrence, M. (eds) (2004), *Practising Servant-Leadership: Succeeding Through Trust, Bravery and Forgiveness.* San Francisco: Jossey Bass.

Stein, S., McRobbie, C. and Ginns, I. (2000),' Recognizing uniqueness in the technology key learning area: The search for meaning'. *International Journal of Technology and Design Education,* 10, (2), 105–23.

Stogdill, R. M. (1948), *Personal Factors Associated with Leadership: A Survey of the Literature.* Englewood Cliffs, NJ: Prentice Hall.

—— (1974), *The Handbook of Leadership: a Survey of Theory and Research.* New York: Free Press.

Strathern, M. (2000), *Audit Cultures: Anthropological Studies in Accountability, Ethics and the Academy.* London: Routledge.

Strudler, N. and Wetzel, K. (1999), 'Lessons from exemplary colleges of education: Factors affecting technology integration in preservice programmes'. *Educational Technology Research and Development,* 47, (4), 63–82.

Suchman, L. (1987), *Plans and Situated Action: The Problem of Human-Machine Communication.* Cambridge. Cambridge University Press.

—— (1993), 'Technologies of accountability: of lizards and aeroplanes', in G. Button (ed.), *Technology in Working Order: Studies of Work, Interaction and Technology.* London: Routledge.

Tannenbaum, R. and Schmidt, W. (1958), 'How to choose a leadership pattern: should a leader be democratic or autocratic – or something in between?' *Harvard Business Review,* 37, March–April, 95–102.

Tichy, N. M. and Devanna, M. A. (1986), *The Transformational Leader.* New York: Wiley.

Tierney, W. G. (1989), 'Symbolism and presidential perceptions of leadership'. *Review of Higher Education,* 12, 153–66.

Timperley, H. S. (2005), 'Distributed leadership: developing theory from practice'. *Journal of Curriculum Studies,* 37, (4), 395–420.

Tourish, D. and Vatcha, N. (2005), 'Charismatic leadership and corporate cultism as Enron: The elimination of dissent, the promotion of conformity and organizational collapse'. *Leadership,* 1, (4), 455–80.

Travers, M. (2001), *Qualitative Research Through Case Studies.* London: Sage.

Troman, G. (2000), 'Teacher stress in the low-trust society'. *British Journal of Sociology of Education,* 21, (3), 331–53.

Van Knippenberg, D. and Hogg, M. A. (2003), 'A social identity model of leadership effectiveness in organisations'. *Research in Organizational Behavior,* 25, 243–95.

Wainwright, H. (2003), *Reclaim the State.* London: Verso.

Weber, M. (1948), 'The sociology of charismatic authority', in H. H. Gerth and C. W. Mills (eds) *From Max Weber: Essays in Sociology.* London:. Routledge and Kegan Paul.

—— (1968), *Economy and Society.* New York. Bedminster.

White, M. I. and Mackenzie-Davey, K. (2003), 'Feeling valued at work? A qualitative study of corporate training consultants'. *Career Development International,* 8, (5), 228–34.

Wieder, D. L. (1974), *Language and Social Reality.* The Hague: Mouton.

Wittgenstein, L. (1958), *Philosophical Investigations.* (2nd Edition). Oxford: Basil Blackwell Publisher Ltd.

Wright, N. (2001), 'Leadership, 'bastard' leadership and managerialism: confronting twin paradoxes in the Blair education project'. *Educational Management and Administration,* 29, (3), 275–90.

Yates, J. (1989), *Control Through Communication: the Rise of System in American Management.* Baltimore: John Hopkins University Press.

Yates, J. and Orlikowski, W. J. (1992), 'Genres of organizational communication: A structural approach to studying communication and media'. *Academy of Management Review,* 17, (2), 299–326.

Yukl, G. (2002), *Leadership in Organizations* (5th Edn) Upper Saddle River, NJ: Prentice Hall.

Zaleznik, A. (1977), 'Managers and leaders: Are they different?' *Harvard Business Review.* May–June, 67–8.

Zimmerman, D. H. and Pollner, M. (1973), 'The everyday world as phenomenon'. In J. D. Douglas (ed.) *Understanding Everyday Life: Towards the Reconstruction of Sociological Knowledge.* New York: Routledge and Kegan Paul.

Zuboff, S. (1988), *In the Age of the Smart Machine.* Oxford: Heinemann.

Index

Lightning Source UK Ltd.
Milton Keynes UK
UKOW040633250113

205316UK00001B/15/P